THE LORD'S VOICE CRIES TO THE CITY ...
MICAH 6:9

IRIS NASREEN

Carpenter's Son Publishing

The Lord's Voice Cries to the City: Micah 6:9

©2014 by Iris Nasreen

Published by Carpenter's Son Publishing, Franklin, Tennessee

Published in association with Larry Carpenter of Christian Book Services, LLC
www.christianbookservices.com

Interior Design by Suzanne Lawing

Editing by Robert Irvin

Printed in the United States of America

978-1-940262-15-4

Take note that the name satan and related names are not capitalized.
We choose not to acknowledge him, even to the point of violating grammatical rules.

This book is supported extensively with Bible Scriptures from the KJV/New King James version to make my message clearer, understandable, and convincing for readers. Emphasis within Scripture is related with the counsel of the Holy Spirit.

How do we hear the LORD's voice?

1 Kings 19:11, 12

*And he said, Go forth, and stand upon the mount before the LORD. And, behold, the LORD passed by, and a **great and strong wind** rent the mountains, and brake in pieces the rocks before the LORD; but the LORD was not in the wind: and after the wind an **earthquake;** but the LORD was not in the earthquake: And after the earthquake a **fire;** but the LORD was not in the fire: and after the fire **a still small voice.***

Great and strong winds, earthquakes and fires *indicate that the **LORD** is passing by us.*
*But the **LORD** is calling all mankind with a **still, small voice** to embrace them in **HIS protection as a Father to a son.***

Are we willing to hear the voice of the LORD?

Note: Scripture sections placed in bold, italics, or underline—or some combination—are placed in those fonts for my emphasis. — I.N.

ACKNOWLEDGMENTS

My deepest recognition is to the Lord Jesus Christ for making me His maidservant to deliver His urgent message to the world in the Last Days. I thank You for the supernatural empowerment of the Holy Spirit to assemble manuscript of this book from the start to the finish. I praise You for giving me the privilege of sharing Your Word and this testimony - about Your love, judgments, and the End Times prophetic revelations. I deeply appreciate You for giving me an experience of joy indescribable in serving You. I honor You for uplifting me, protecting me and my family in all the battles that satan caused against us, while working on my call to write this book.

My husband Romel, my son Silas, and my daughter Myra – I appreciate your inexhaustible patience and tolerance of unlimited hour of separation from me. I loved your understanding to recognize the importance to my obedience to God's will over and above your needs. Thank you for your sacrifices and sufferings…I would have not been able to finish this job without you.

Rachel Grant, for your offer to help me to edit this book. You were a God sent support, and I would have not done it without you. I still remember the sufferings you endured for the sake of this work that the satan directed towards you – in order to stop the publication of this life changing message of God. I don't have words to appreciate your partnership.

Jessica Leone, you are like a daughter to me. Thank you to help me edit this book. I still remember how God connected you to partner in His work. It still amazes me. You being a young girl without any knowledge of satan's ways to fight against God's will – you still persevered and stood by my side to the best of your ability, instead of unbearable sufferings in the form of the death of your cats, hospitalization of your grandmother, and many other incessant major crises---until I had to let you go before the final work of this project.

Donna P., I appreciate your child like faith that believes the witness of the Lord without doubt. I have seen your gradual transformation into a new creation in Christ during my personal working relationship with you at a bank for the last ten years. I bombarded you and other coworkers with my incessant prophetic dreams. I have seen the fear when all the revelations given in my dreams came to pass. This gift of prophecy has not only helped you to believe in the Lord; but your faith has helped me to stand up strong to obey my call of God. I thank you for your child like faith.

Pastor Randy, Ron and Church members, I honor your love, communion and interceding prayers during the work of this book, that lifted me up in my worst trials. Thank you for the encouragement and support in all times of our family's needs. I am blessed to be a part of a faithful Bride of Christ.

MATTHEW 18:3
And said, Verily I say unto you, Except ye be converted, and become as little children, ye shall not enter into the kingdom of heaven.

ENDORSEMENTS

*My soul rejoices my Lord who has endorsed me
to declare His glory to the ends of the earth.*

This end time warning message from the LORD through this humble, obedient, dedicated and prayerful servant has brought great spiritual revival to many across the globe.

Christians who are asleep, persecuted, discouraged, confused or fearful of end time occurrences can receive comfort and assurance from this book. For skeptics who do not believe the reality and certainty of God's judgement, fulfillment of the prophesies contained in it will shock them.

It is my prayer that whosoever reads these messages will respond appropriately by turning away from sin and accepting the free salvation in Christ Jesus. This is the only way to avert His wrath. This is exactly what the book is saying.

—*Dr. Akolo Namo, Lafia, Nigeria*

***

This book "THE LORD'S VOICE CRIES TO THE CITY...Micah 6:9; is a tragic illustration of God's heart for our nation, America - as we plan our days without seeking God as top priority in our lives. The survival of our nation depends on our walk with an Almighty God whose cry is for our nation to experience the abundant life and salvation. May God be with thee. This book is a must read to avoid God's wrath and to see the deliverance of our cities in America. I have read many books before, but never a book like this. It feels like Holy Spirit breathing on you at the reading of it.

—*Janet Elisa Workman*

***

The Lord's Voice Cries to the City...Micah 6:9 begins with the sentence: Listen to what the Lord says: so there is an urge from God for the people to listen to a serious affair, to give attention to the person He has given the mouthpiece to deliver to the nations.

May the Spirit uses this prophetic message in this book to set free all inhabitants of the Earth.

Be bless Iris

May God releases to you in 2014, All promises belonging to you

—*Nancy Pauli, Netherlands Antilles*

***

It's an urgent call to human kind to repent and seek the Lord wholeheartedly. This prophecies which she speaks from the very mouth of the Lord, WILL pass imminently. If you want to prepare for what's coming up next, you must read this message. Your life _____on earth__ depends on your listening.

—*Carolina, USA*

CONTENTS

FOREWORD 11

CHAPTER 1: About Me 17

CHAPTER 2: Prophetic Warnings
                       for Upcoming Natural Disasters 33

CHAPTER 3: End Times Tribulation 65

CHAPTER 4: God's Final Verdict 77

CHAPTER 5: Jeremiah 24's Relevance in the End Times 89

CHAPTER 6: The Year 2012 97

CHAPTER 7: The Year 2023 111

CHAPTER 8: Rapture Is at Hand 125

CHAPTER 9: Revelation of War 137

CHAPTER 10: God's Hand Over Israel 145

CHAPTER 11: Who . . . Why . . . and When Does God Judge? 163

CHAPTER 12: Emotions of God 179

CHAPTER 13: Why Take God for Granted? 215

CHAPTER 14: Disparity Between the
                       Godly and the Worldly 243

CHAPTER 15: Jesus Is Our Only Rescue 255

FOREWORD

I was really surprised for the unexpected and unplanned purpose of my life "*to serve the Lord*," when the Lord Jesus Christ revealed Himself in a dream to appoint me His servant in 1997. Since that year of receiving God's calling for His purpose in my life, I always wondered what line of service the Lord desired for me. During all these years, God has taken over my life and transformed me from a physical being into a spiritual being in such a way that my heart, mind, and flesh are completely separated from the world and its temptations; for example, a diamond has no more importance then a rock to me.

This marvelous outpouring of the Lord's love has taught me how to worship Him in spirit and truth, and also to live a complete, sacrificial life for His people with a love of God that now abides in me. The Lord revealed my calling for His Kingdom and for His purpose in 2007 with a vision that shook my inner being. I was confused; how can an insignificant person like me convey His message to the whole world? In my perplexity to figure out how to witness globally, *God spoke to me at 3 am of February 10th, 2008 with a voice saying, "Ezekiel Chapter 12, verse 24".* This verse reads: ***"For no more shall there be any false vision or flattering divination within the house of Israel."*** This incident shook me because I did not even know if there was a book named Ezekiel in the Bible. Not only does this book exists, but the chapter 12 verse 24 reference is a clear sign from the Lord God Almighty that all the visions He is showing me are true and must be taken seriously. They need to be declared to the world efficiently and effectively. It was enough to awaken me from my laziness. I started communicating with the world via Internet ministry and began to serve the Lord to reach the whole world with all the force within my own capacity, from year 2008 onward.

In September 2011, God put it in my heart to write a book to share His messages to the world. God chose to use one of my worst talents; writing a book will be the worst of all, because my writing skill is my most feeble quality. Writing a book, for me, is like asking a ten-year-old child to fly a plane and transport passengers safely to another continent. In my personal walk with the Lord I have learned how to step out in faith, which helped me overcome the fear of failures. In my obedience to the Lord I have learned to be dependent, completely, upon Him for everything because I am totally incapacitated when it comes to comprehension of His Word, The Bible. The only support I have is the counsel of the Holy Spirit—with the obedience to His will with an open heart, mind, eyes, and ears. This book in your hand was written by the inspiration of the Holy Spirit, because within my own capability, I cannot do this job. I would greatly thank God that He sent helpers Jessica Leone and Rachel Grant for their help to edit this book.

I am not a theologian, not one to understand the depths of the Bible prophecies. I just know that Lord has called His servants to speak according to the instruction of the Holy Spirit—and I am doing so. I am called to share the revelations that the Heavenly Father gives me through His son, the Lord Jesus Christ, with the inspiration of the Holy Spirit. I might not comprehend it completely, but I trust the Lord and believe all that He declares is the only virgin truth. God's servants understand that all learning and knowledge come only from Him, supernaturally, as the Lord Jesus Christ instructed His disciples how to speak, in Matthew 10:19, 20. He said, "But when they deliver you up, ***do not worry about how or what you should speak. For it will be given to you in that hour what you should speak; for it is not you who speak, but the Spirit of your Father who speaks in you.***"

The Lord's messages that I am sharing with you are like the wind. I don't know where they come from or where they go; but I know that the source of this wind is the Lord God Almighty, whom I trust. In John 3:8, the Lord said, ***"The wind blows where it wishes, and you hear the sound of it, but cannot tell where it comes from and where it goes. So is everyone who is born of the Spirit."***

I also know that I only need to obey the Lord's calling and declare His messages in complete obedience with faith, purity, and honesty as I trust the LORD, for only He knows His purpose for all humanity. His word, witnesses, and testimonies will reach the multitudes and save them from upcoming judgments. God's works are like parables that fulfill their purposes as only He intends to accomplish.

ISAIAH 55:11
So shall My word be that goes forth from My mouth;
It shall not return to Me void,
But it shall accomplish what I please,
And it shall prosper in the thing for which I sent it.

The writing of this book has been an intriguing, challenging, and sometimes excruciatingly painful experience that has helped my spiritual maturity in my walk of obedience to God's will and purpose. The first inspiring moment in writing of this book —September 2, 2011— while cooking in my kitchen, I asked, "Lord, you told me to write a book. Tell me what would be the title of this book?" That very moment the Holy Spirit led me to the Bible to Micah 6:9: *"The LORD's voice cries to the city . . . "* The title of this book and the messages in it are from the Lord our God Almighty, whom I hear because His sheep hear His voice.

I began to write this book as the Lord desired, with an enthusiasm out of His love in my heart, and a faithful trust that the Lord Himself will finish this project in His own wisdom, strength, and power. I began this mysterious journey of obedience like a racer who begins a final race with a full force. On my journey to this race I dealt with many hurdles and troubles from satan. My breaking point began on December 9, 2011, when God gave me a warning about the forces of darkness that are ready to destroy me like a house completely lifted from the ground in a deadly storm. The Holy Spirit said to me in that dream, "This will exactly happen to me (like a house completely ripped apart after a deadly storm) if I am away from Jesus for a single day." From that day I did cling to my Lord Jesus more aggressively, as I began to experience the worst challenges from satan, in many forms, such as financial breakdown, sickness, diseases, mental anxiety, and stress and family conflicts.

My daughter would have been dead if the Lord Jesus Christ had not been my shield. I would have had a nervous breakdown if Lord had not comforted me. Each and every day would begin with a new challenge. I began this race for fulfillment of my Lord's will with full force, but now I am so tired, injured, and sore that it is like crawling to reach the finish line of this race. I didn't care that I did not sleep well for last nine months, as I only had a few early morning hours till I had to leave for work to write this book. I decided that I would not quit this project, even though satan would bring a new surprise of troubles each day in such a way that I got physically and emotionally exhausted continuing to work on this book. I kept dragging myself in the strength of my LORD, because the love of His people in my heart is stronger than the fear of the enemy's attacks. I honored the prayers of my church, friends, and family that kept me spiritually nourished. I have never fasted as tenaciously in my life as I did to complete this manuscript—a three times forty-day fast, a ten-day fast, a three-day fast, and a final fast that I began on June 10, 2012, that was to end when this book is published.

I would only praise our Lord God for giving us the privilege to hear His witnesses and testimonies every day all over the world. The Word of God that reaches us through His servants is more precious than all the riches of the world, because it is an eternal life. It is my humble prayer that this book will also contribute to saving lives, bringing people to the feet of the Lord Jesus Christ in humility and repentance. To give mankind a hope and a way to life eternal, away from the tribulations of the world and into the love, peace, and joy of His Kingdom. It is my desire that the world can understand the depth of the love of God for them. I also wish for mankind to acknowledge the fear of the Lord, because it truly is the beginning of wisdom, as we read in Job 28:28: *"And to man He said, 'Behold, the fear of the Lord, that is wisdom, And to depart from evil is understanding."*

We all are living in the Last Days, when mankind will witness the fulfillment of the prophecies of the Bible speedily. Is there any escape from them? Of course, there is none, except to accept the Creator of the universe as the Lord of our lives and to walk in the righteousness of His will in a love relationship with Him. Acts 2:17-21 is the practical fulfillments that we are all witnessing. The Word of the Lord is already going out to every corner of the earth, and it will increase with the tremendous outpouring of the Holy Spirit on all flesh that this generation has not seen before. Now we have entered into the age when the great signs and wonders will be witnessed from the hands of His manservants, maidservants, sons and daughters, young men and old men in the power of the Holy Spirit in prophecies, dreams and visions, miracles of healing and restoration, rising of the dead, and also many breath-taking witnesses that will arise to declare that the Lord is the only one YAHWEH to heal our diseases and sickness, our wounds of the souls and pains of our hearts.

ACTS 2:17-21

And it shall come to pass in the last days, says God,
That I will pour out of My Spirit on all flesh;
Your sons and your daughters shall prophesy,
Your young men shall see visions,
Your old men shall dream dreams.
And on My menservants and on My maidservants
I will pour out My Spirit in those days;
And they shall prophesy.
I will show wonders in heaven above
And signs in the earth beneath:
Blood and fire and vapor of smoke.
The sun shall be turned into darkness,
And the moon into blood,
Before the coming of the great and awesome day of the LORD.
And it shall come to pass
That whoever calls on the name of the LORD
Shall be saved.

Acts 2:19-21 is the voice of the Lord declaring His works of wonders at the End of the Age in Heaven above, and on earth beneath in blood, fire, and vapor of smoke. What we have witnessed so far is only scratching the surface. The Lord has begun to root out the dominion of satan from the earth—where he empowers over the lives of innocent humanity—in such a manner that the sun shall be turned into darkness and the moon into blood. The Lord our shepherd will come soon on His great and awesome day with the good news for all those who repent from their sins *"that whoever calls on the name of the Lord Shall be saved."*

I have shared everything that the Holy Spirit has revealed to me so far: but for future God-given predictions and prophecies, visit the web-page: www.gods-messenger.webs.com.

I will ask all of you to read this book and witness it with your friends and family, as the time is at hand. With the love of the Lord in our hearts, we want to see our loved ones saved. It has always been my prayer that my obedient service to the Lord will not save hundreds, nor thousands . . . but millions of souls. Amen.

CHAPTER 1

ABOUT ME

My name is Iris Nasreen Albert. I was born in the eastern part of the world. I belong to a simple and godly family of both parents and four siblings. Our upbringing was in a middle- class Christian home where my spiritual guide was my mother. My father was a perfect head of the house and we all looked to him as a pillar of support and guidance. I was a middle child between two older sisters and two younger brothers. My family has always been a blessing from above in my life, both before and after marriage. Now I have a caring and loving husband, son, and a daughter. We live in Pennsylvania.

When I think back on my life, I remember that my childhood in the '70s was filled with joy. I don't remember crying a lot, except when I was teased by my younger brother or if I missed a school assignment. I was always a very positive person and always stayed away from gossiping friends, aunts, or neighbors. Playing with friends all day and getting yelled at by our housekeeper for not taking an afternoon nap was really fun. In the '80s I was a teenager in school and then in college; I was full of ambition—positive and purposeful ambition at that—to become an accountant. I got married in 1991 and migrated to the United States of

America in 1994. Today I have a full-time job as a banker as well as a homemaker. Truly, my hands are full.

My spiritual connection with the Lord was always in my soul even when I did not understand it. I still remember that in my junior years I would look toward heaven and say, many times, "I love you, God." If I look back in my past, I can recall that nothing materialistic would impress me—not things like big houses, expensive cars, rich attire, gold and diamonds, or having an impressive life status. I remember that I would always smile at people around me who would be miserable running after those things. Later, at maturity, I recognized that they were the "normal" majority in our culture; I was the different person, not knowing why I was that way. I am still the same; in fact, this feeling intensified, because now I feel like an alien in this world, like I am a heavenly being living temporarily on this earth void of the desires of this world, and passionately in love with the Lord God Almighty.

My First Dream Portrayed God's Purpose in My Life

In the year 1997 God blessed me with an incredible dream that revealed my purpose on earth. Though I did not understand the exact assignment for my life indicated in this dream by the Lord Jesus Christ, it shook me completely, as I knew it was directing me to something very important. Please join me to explore God's plan for my life that was explained in this dream.

In the **first part of my dream** I saw water, black as the darkest night, rushing against a grand, beautifully crafted ship made of wood and gold carvings for decorations. (Allow me to move the telling of the next part of this dream into present tense, as though you are experiencing it, along with me, for the first time.) People are standing outside the middle royal chamber at the deck railing of this ship. At the bow end of the ship, two men in the likeness of royal Roman soldiers stood to throw everyone—standing in two rows waiting for their punishment—overboard, to be engulfed in the black water of death and desolation.

People outside the Throne Room of the Lord Jesus Christ represent those servants who cause His people to stumble due to their corrupted hearts. I saw the practical implications of Mark 9:42, when Jesus warned the unfaithful and disobedient of their offenses of misconduct that make others fall and reject God.

MARK 9:42
Jesus Warns of Offenses
"But whoever causes one of these little ones who believe in Me to stumble, it would be better for him if a millstone were hung around his neck, and he were thrown into the sea."

In the center of the ship there was an enormous room. **Yeshua Ha'Mashiach—the Lord Jesus Christ—**sat upon a throne of immense light and pureness. I was standing among this group of people before the Lord Jesus Christ who is His appointed servants called to serve Him. These servants will suffer for sake of their call, in the likeness of peeling of skin off the flesh. . This group of people in the center of this majestic ship was standing very humbly in two rows, on both sides of the room, before their Savior, sitting in the center on His throne. The Lord Jesus Christ looked like a perfect King of kings and the Lord of lords in a royal golden chair. I will never forget the sense of humility—complete humility—I felt before His throne. I was standing, but my knees were as weak as if I were going to fall, and kneel down before Him. I felt urged to ask for forgiveness. After granting His mercy and forgiveness, God revealed my calling on earth in the next part of a dream.

The people standing in the interior room of the ship before the throne of the Lord Jesus Christ represent those who are His faithful and obedient servants bonded in His relationship and protection.

In the **second part of this dream**, I found myself standing in sparkling clean spring water before two saints who stood in white robes. I saw the rocks and colorful tropical fish swimming in crystal clear water, like the reflection in a mirror. This water flowing around my ankle was giving me a sense of refreshment and purity.

Then the Lord's messengers in white robes told me to go and join the laborers who were already busy repairing the house of the Lord. This house of the Lord looked like a huge temple in ruins at the top of the mountain. I saw the laborers carrying a container filled with soil from the bottom to the top of the mountain. They used this to repair the ruins. They were carrying all that weight on the top of their heads, and the robes they were wearing were filthy with soil. Their labor was filled with excruciatingly hard work that required extreme physical and emotional suffering.

These two messengers of God witnessed the washing of my feet and designated me the Most High's servant as they ordered me to go and join His laborers in repairing the ruins of the Temple of God. *The Lord God Almighty appointed me His servant in 1997, as this dream clearly enlightened His purpose in my life.*

After seeing this dream I came to know that this experience was of great significance. I knew in my heart that there was something that God had called me to do, but did not know how and what would I do for Him. How would I contribute to the building of His temple?

Without my knowing, the Lord took control of my life to prepare me spiritually for a mysterious job; he made me pass me through tough life situations, just like threshing of wheat. I never knew what I should do to fulfill God's calling for His purpose until the Lord began to speak to me again, in 2007, ten years after having this dream. During all these years, in the interim, I kept going on with a normal life, like working for a bank, taking care of the household, a husband, and two children. I also do not feel worthy of God's marvelous grace for being His servant for such an important job because I felt myself very small and incapable; I am a very common person who is not any Bible scholar, nor have I any highlighted position in a Christian community or church.

But now, after my experience in His relationship, I have learned that surely God does not require our wisdom, knowledge, and strength to fulfill His purpose, He just needs a willing heart to obey His will. Many times in history God has chosen the weakest vessel to help mankind recognize that the vain strength, knowledge, and wisdom that people depend on is worthless. As we read in 1 Corinthians 1:27: *"But God has chosen the foolish things of the world to put to shame the wise, and God has chosen the weak things of the world to put to shame the things which are mighty."*

During all these years—from the day the Lord appointed me one of His servants—He transformed me in such a way that I have developed an intimate bond with Him to a level that now I am completely separated from the world; I desire to do the job given by the Lord's messengers to help restore the lives of His people through supplication in prayers and fasting, by teaching His will from the direct counsel of the Holy Spirit and His Word, the Bible. He teaches His servants to carry the weight of the pains, sorrows, sickness, earthly miseries, and spiritual infirmities of His people on their shoulders, to bring them into His presence, and to help restore their lives in relationship with Him. This is exactly what God's messengers showed me in my vision when they told me to join His servants to build His temple that is in complete ruins at the top of the mountain.

God granted me three blessings in this dream when He appointed me His servant. I would love to share them with you.

The first blessing that the Lord gave me was the forgiveness of my sins. The Lord Jesus Christ revealed Himself to me as the King, Governor, Judge, and Savior in my dream. I did exactly, in His holy presence, what His word declares, that which we read in Acts 3:19: *"Repent therefore and be converted, that your sins may be blotted out, so that times of refreshing may come from the presence of the Lord,"* How can His appointed servants preach the gospel of repentance and forgiveness of sins without being forgiven first? Of course, it is not logical. For the same reason the Lord gave me the heart, wisdom, and choice to ask for His mercy to forgive my sins. With this grace of forgiveness of sins the Lord appointed me to be His witness in the service that is shared in Luke 24:47: *"and that repentance and remission of sins should be preached in His name to all nations, beginning at Jerusalem."* How true it is in my own life that after receiving His most precious blessing in this dream that all of my sins are shed at His feet; I have become slave of righteousness, just like Romans 6:18: *"And having been set free from sin, you became slaves of righteousness."*

I also knew while standing before the Lord Jesus Christ that I am standing among a group of people chosen for their skin to be peeled off. "In 1997 the Lord chose me for His service that I did not know about. Ten years after in 2007, the Lord called me to give His message to warn and convict mankind of their sins, and declare His judgments for this reason. *Who will not agree with me that my obedience to this call of God will not serve me with public discrimination in the likeness of the peeling of skin?"*

This concept of the peeling of skin is clearer when we learn its significance from God's directives. I will share its significance with the sacrifices offered before the Lord on the altar with the help of spiritual explanation by God's servant, Perry Stone, in his program *Manna Fest* on television. He explains the **three types of altars in the Scriptures used for three separate purposes.**

First is the Stone Altar made without iron; it is made with twelve stones representing twelve tribes of Israel. The Stone Altar is a place of a personal sacrifice to reconcile with the Lord. Thus, this first altar is the first step in the walk with God where we learn to give up our will for God's will.

Second is the Brass Altar made with wood and covered with brass. The Brass Alter was appointed where animals were slain, their skins were peeled off, and they were burned for sacrifices. 2 Chronicles 35:11: ***"And they slaughtered the Passover offerings; and the priests sprinkled the blood with their hands, while the Levites skinned the animals."*** Similarly, God's anointed servants become a living sacrifice for His service to save souls on earth. *In my dream I was blessed to be standing before the holy presence of the Lord Jesus Christ to be among His servants, who are called to serve Him by becoming a living sacrifice for Him.* For which they will be slaughtered, their skin peeled off, killed, and sacrificed by the evil of the earth and the principalities and powers of darkness—all for their obedience to God's will in His service in the exact resemblance to what Jesus did in obedience to His Father in Heaven. His servants follow the exact footsteps of their master, the Lord Jesus Christ, even to their death, for His Name sake.

ROMANS 12:1
Living Sacrifices to God
I beseech you therefore, brethren, by the mercies of God,
that you present your bodies a living sacrifice, holy,
acceptable to God, which is your reasonable service.

This is our next step to walk with the Lord, where we sacrifice our will for God's will. At this altar we win the battle of the flesh with the spirit and we learn to overcome the carnal things to gain in spiritual things. *It is an experience like peeling of skin when a battle against physical desire is won with a conversion from a physical being into a spiritual being. The Brass Altar is a place where animals were slain and their skins were peeled. Similarly, God's appointed servants are anointed to conquer the dominance of flesh and its desires.*

There were three great fires that were burning on the Brass Altar. Similarly, we learn to fight the desires of the flesh by letting the Holy Spirit burn things out of us that should not be there. *It is the Lord's mercy that I was given this gift of the peeling of skin in order to be transformed into a spiritual servant of the Lord God Almighty.*

Third is the Gold Altar that is not used for sacrifices, but for burning eleven types of incense mixed together for prayer and worship (Exodus 30:1-3). This altar represents the prayers of people going up to Heaven in an exact replica of the burning of incense lifting up to Heaven. The Golden Altar is the holy place with an intense presence of the Lord. It is the place where saints learn to worship, pray, and intercede with the anointing of the Holy Spirit. This is the point where the body of His people turns into the temple of the Holy Spirit, where only the works of the Spirit reside with removal of all impurities of the flesh.

The second blessing that was given in this dream was a washing of my feet while I was standing in ankle-deep water while two of God's messengers in white robes witnessed this incident. We understand the significance of the washing of feet from the Lord Jesus Christ when He washed the feet of His disciples in John 13:6-10.

JOHN 13:6-10
Then He came to Simon Peter. And Peter said to

Him, "Lord, are You washing my feet?"
Jesus answered and said to him, "What I am doing you
do not understand now, but you will know after this."
Peter said to Him, "You shall never wash my feet!"
Jesus answered him, "If I do not wash
you, you have no part with Me."
Simon Peter said to Him, "Lord, not my feet
only, but also my hands and my head!"
Jesus said to him, "He who is bathed needs only to wash his
feet, but is completely clean; and you are clean, but not all of you."

This story tells us that the washing of feet has the physical and spiritual implications of the purification and cleanliness of the body and soul. Peter took it like an insult of his great Master to wash his feet, and he refused to let Jesus do it for him. But Jesus warned that 'if you don't let me then you will have no part with me.' *Truly the Lord gifted me with the same privilege of the washing of feet for me to have a part with Him.* How can the Lord send His servants with the Holiest Word from His mouth to the nations of the world without their personal sanctification? Definitely not without purifying them from head to toe in His purity with the washing of their sins and removal of evil desires of flesh from every cell of their bodies. With His own hands He transforms them from a physical being into a spiritual being for His servanthood. Is it not wonderful to learn how beautiful are those feet that are washed by the master of the universe, our Lord Jesus Christ, to preach the good news of salvation? In Romans 10:15 we read, *"And how shall they preach unless they are sent? As it is written: 'How beautiful are the feet of those who preach the gospel of peace, who bring glad tidings of good things!'"* Truly I am blessed with the gift of the washing of my feet in a similar fashion for the purpose that the Lord Jesus Christ called me to do.

The third blessing is the most vital responsibility that the LORD bestowed on me, and was told by two messengers in white robes, to join His servants who are already working on the repair of His ruined Temple standing on its magnificent pillars right at the top of the mountain. The Word of God leads us to understand the significance of His house, which is established at the top of the mountains, particularly in the End Times described in Isaiah 2. You are welcome to read with me:

ISAIAH 2
Now it shall come to pass in the latter days
That the mountain of the LORD's house
Shall be established on the top of the mountains,
And shall be exalted above the hills;
And all nations shall flow to it.
Many people shall come and say,
"Come, and let us go up to the mountain of the LORD,
To the house of the God of Jacob;
He will teach us His ways,
And we shall walk in His paths."
For out of Zion shall go forth the law,
And the word of the LORD from Jerusalem.

The third and final part of my dream was about my job description for His purpose in an exact reference to Isaiah 2:2, 3. It is very clear that the LORD is describing the significance of His Temple in the latter days that would be completely restored back to its origin through His Word to concentrate His people in His companionship. The Temple is a sacred place consecrated by the presence of the Holy Lord where our oneness with Him is evident. I also viewed His Temple at the top of the mountain just like the description of Isaiah 2:2: ***"That the mountain of***

the LORD's house shall be established on the top of the mountains."

Wonderfully, I was handed the job to repair the ruins of the Temple after being anointed in the presence of the Lord Jesus Christ sitting at His throne. I saw the Temple in ruins, which indicates that the human race is shallow due to the lack of intimate relationship with their Lord. This bruised, damaged, and treasonous people are suffering for the lack of knowledge of the will of God. The existing generation has forgotten that their bodies are supposed to be Temples of God where His presence must supersede anything else, just like we read in 1 Corinthians 3:16: *"Do you not know that you are the temple of God and that the Spirit of God dwells in you?"* I can only praise the Lord God, the Most High, for choosing an insignificant person like me for such a mighty purpose to declare His Will to all the nations of the world. I know in my heart that everything is possible for Him, even to use a person like me to join His servants to repair the restless hearts with broken and damaged lives all over the globe.

Now the time is at hand when His people will seek to run to His mountain, just like a rushing wind, to find the peace, joy, restoration, and salvation at the feet of their Lord God Almighty, for His counsel would be their first priority, just like in Isaiah 2:3: *"Many people shall come and say, 'Come, and let us go up to the mountain of the LORD, to the house of the God of Jacob; He will teach us His ways, and we shall walk in His paths.' For out of Zion shall go forth the law, and the word of the LORD from Jerusalem."* We are the End Times generation that will witness the shaking of the heavens and earth with severity. We are the generation that will repent for this fear, and shall come to the desire of seeking refuge in the Temple of the Lord, where His glory surrounds us eternally.

Let's read on, in Haggai 2:6, 7:

HAGGAI 2

For thus says the LORD of hosts: "Once more (it is a little while) I will shake heaven and earth, the sea and dry land; and I will shake all nations, and they shall come to the Desire of All Nations, and I will fill this temple with glory," says the LORD of hosts.

After learning the sacred meaning of the Temple of God, you can clearly understand the vitality in the final part of this dream in 1997 in which God called me to be His servant and join laborers who are already a work-in-progress on the repair of the Temple of God on the top of the mountain. Therefore, all of God's servants are working in uniformity for the harvest of souls, for that will save the lives of multitudes from every corner of the world to proclaim eternity in the Kingdom of God.

After receiving the position of the servant of God, the Lord began a phase of preparation, sanctification, and transformation of me into a new handiwork in Him with His knowledge, love, and wisdom of heart. I can still remember how the Lord took me over, in 1997, and converted me unknowingly to become a new creation in Christ who completely lost interest in the desires of the world. How it happened, I don't know. But I do know that this is the most pleasant experience that anyone can ever experience.

Now, because of my intimate relationship with the Lord, I feel light like a feather for void of burden of sins, independent from slavery of the flesh like a cloud, carefree like a dove in Lord's holiness, and powerful like a lion in His power and strength. I could never imagine gaining it all on my own; it is the grace of the Lord Jesus Christ, who took me in my human weakness and blessed me in His love to be His child and His servant. I really cannot thank my Lord enough. Along with transforming me from the physical being into a spiritual being, the Lord also kept me growing in sacred gifts and equipped me with spiritual weapons in order to accomplish the given job, which was excruciating hardships like laborers who have to carry a container filled with soil over their head from the bottom to the top of the mountain to repair His Temple. God's servants are required to get their jobs done in the exact fashion that I saw in my dream. His servants are carrying the burden of suffering humanity in the power and strength of the Lord, equipped with the spiritual weapons from the source of all good things that is the mountain and rock of salvation, whose name is the Lord Jesus Christ.

The repair of the Temple of God synchronized with the saving salvation of humanity that the Lord created with an everlasting love. Servants of the Lord are hauling the spiritual burden in order to heal mankind from the sufferings of this world that are the result of their obedience to satan, who has trapped their souls in his clutches under the dominion of the forces of darkness. No one can do this difficult job to free anyone from the evil trap of satan without the rock and mountain of salvation, the Lord Jesus Christ, who has taught His servants well how to crush the head of serpent under their heal. I truly thank God for this great gift to be His servant and to endure the long sufferings for the sake of His people, just as we read in 2 Corinthians 6:4-10: *"But in all things we commend ourselves as ministers of God: in much patience, in tribulations, in needs, in distresses, in stripes, in imprisonments, in tumults, in labors, in sleeplessness, in fasting; by purity, by knowledge, by longsuffering, by kindness, by the Holy Spirit, by sincere love, by the word of truth, by the power of God, by the armor of righteousness on the right hand and on the left, by honor and dishonor, by evil report and good report; as deceivers, and yet true; as unknown, and yet well known; as dying, and behold we live; as chastened, and yet not killed; as sorrowful, yet always rejoicing; as poor, yet making many rich; as having nothing, and yet possessing all things."*

My conscious awakening in the Lord began with this dream, but my next dream, in 2007, about the End Time's prophecy totally shook my inner being. God spoke to me clearly about His disappointment with the whole world due to the failure of mankind for not obeying His will. I will share this testimony in chapter 2 of this book.

My Spiritual Gifts: I would love to share my experience of when I was taken in the Spirit into the darkest place I have ever seen. I saw myself entering a huge two-part wooden door about 15 feet tall and 12 feet wide. On my right hand I had a sword of the Spirit and in left hand I had the spear of the Spirit. God grants His spiritual gifts to all of His chosen servants as the Word of God puts a light on true ministry. I fought with demons which I did not see, but in the Spirit I knew that I had entered a valley of evil, which was the darkest, desolate place, exactly like what we read in Job 10:22: *"A land as dark as darkness itself, as the shadow of death, without any order, where even the light is like darkness."*

In my spirit I knew that I won the long and aggressive fight against the principalities and powers of darkness. After overcoming the demonic realm I saw myself coming out of the same door I entered, which were the gates of Hades. To my surprise I actually entered my own body the very instant I saw the door close behind me in a dream. Instantly I woke up and saw the time was exactly 3 AM. I really don't know if it was an in-body or out-of-body experience! That I don't know, but I know that when I came back to my body I instantly woke up and felt very achy and tired as if I had done heavy physical work for hours; especially the muscles of my shoulder and arms were aching. I was truly surprised to feel my spiritual faith so strong that it could move the mountains; I didn't feel this in my physical sense, for the flesh is weak, but the spirit is powerful. It came to my thoughts: *God has blessed me with a spiritual gift to triumph over the gates of the Hades.* It is a necessary tool without which the enslaved humanity under satan's rule cannot be saved. We read about this gift in Matthew 16:18: ***"And I also say to you that you are Peter, and on this rock I will build My church, and the gates of Hades shall not prevail against it."***

God's call to reach the world does not come to be fulfilled without a tremendous spiritual and physical battle with the enemy, who resisted God from the beginning and will never stop until the End of Time. The Lord proceeded to speak His heart with me with the great revelations in dreams and visions. The revelations do not come without overcoming powers of evil; therefore, the Lord sent me to the darkest place to clash with evil forces and proved that the strength of my faith in Him can move mountains. The power of the spiritual weapons in my hands will crush every evil as if they are powerless before me, because the King of the universe, Jesus, is on my side and is my strength.

In the beginning of my spiritual walk with the Lord I had a dream in which I also saw myself standing nearly at the end of a long line of people receiving spiritual blessings. This dream revealed the pattern of my personal standing before the Lord with growing and learning from Him and His word. God called me and supported and equipped me with a gift of prophesy to join His many servants to shake the souls of many all over the world at the same time as His judgments are approaching the world. The Word of God tells us the impact of the gift of prophesies supports the accomplishment of His purpose of saving humanity for eternal life in His Kingdom. In 1 Corinthians 14 God explains the effectiveness of prophesy in His church. *Prophesy is a powerful tool that draws the attention of both believers and unbelievers; ultimately, it fa-cilitates change to save the life of a sinner who God loves.* This Scripture from the Bible describes this spiritual gift that God gave me to help repair the ruins of His Temple, which would be the broken lives of His people.

1 CORINTHIANS 14
Pursue love, and desire spiritual gifts, but especially that you may prophesy. For he who speaks in a tongue does not speak to men but to God, for no one understands him; however, in the spirit he speaks mysteries. But he who prophesies speaks edification and exhortation and comfort to men. He who speaks in a tongue edifies himself, but he who prophesies edifies the church.

In conclusion I would only say that after my personal experience in a loving relation of my Creator, I feel honored to be of use to help comfort and edify the people seeking the truth. God has overwhelmed me with nonstop dreams and visions with prophecies for mankind, and the world, since 2007. Many of those predictions were fulfilled instantly and helped to build my faith in this mission to help humanity to come to God and find refuge in His arms. It is my prayer from the depths of my heart that my sufferings and sacrifices done for the work of the Lord shall not be in vain, but that all those who will read this testimony will humble themselves before the King of this universe in the spirit of re-pentance and salvation in His Name. This is as we read in Isaiah 45:23, 24: *"I have sworn by Myself; the word has gone out of My mouth in righteousness, and shall not return, that to Me every knee shall bow, every tongue shall take an oath. He shall say, 'Surely in the LORD I have righteousness and strength. To Him men shall come, and all shall be ashamed who are incensed against Him."*

I wish that my beginning in the walk of the Lord will be the end choice of all the readers to come near the Throne of the Lord Jesus Christ, as we read in Philippians 2:9-11: *"Therefore God also has highly exalted Him and given Him the name which is above every name, that at the name of Jesus every knee should bow, of those in heaven, and of those on earth, and of those under the earth, and that every tongue should*

confess that Jesus Christ is Lord, to the glory of God the Father."
Amen!

CHAPTER 2

Prophetic Warnings for Upcoming Natural Disasters

The God of Abraham, Isaac and Jacob—the Creator of the whole universe—communicated with me for the first time after assigning me to be His servant about ten years ago. God gave me an incredible vision about multiple natural disasters that our earth will face. He commanded me to witness this testimony to the whole world, which I have done since 2008 through a web ministry at www.gods-messenger.webs.com.

THE VISION

I received this vision on April 16, 2007. This is a vision that God declared to tell the whole world.

I saw a body of water that looked like a wall. I could not see the edges (ends) of the wall; neither its height nor width. I was standing in front of the wall. I was able to reach out and thrust my hand through this wall, piercing it. When I pulled my hand out not a single drop of water spilled and the gap resealed as if it had never been touched.

Then the words that came to me from the HOLY SPIRIT were:

"We are doing whatever we want to do, not thinking about the WILL OF GOD. This is not the only wall. There are several walls like this that

are held with God's strength. If this world continues to live with the same pattern; these walls will start to collapse one after the other."

I also saw a young adult man sitting on a bench facing the gigantic walls of water. He was also witnessing the same message of God. I think he is a second witness called for the same purpose of God as I.

After that vision I asked God, "Why did you choose an incompetent person like me, who is nobody? I have no resources and I do not have enough knowledge of the Word of God. I am a migrated Asian residing in the United States without any contacts to reach anyone." Being that English is not my first language, I am barely proficient enough to express my message with perfection, let alone delivering my message to the whole world. It was then that I fully understood the hardships of the task set before me by God to be one of His End Times messengers. Accomplishment of God's purpose seemed like an impossible task. I found the answer to my question from the following Scriptures.

JUDGES 6:14, 15
Then the LORD turned to him and said, "Go in
this might of yours, and you shall save Israel from the
hand of the Midianites. Have I not sent you?"
So he said to Him, "O my Lord, how can I save
Israel? Indeed my clan is the weakest in Manasseh,
and I am the least in my father's house."

MATTHEW 11:25
At that time Jesus answered and said, "I thank You, Father,
Lord of heaven and earth, that You have hidden these things
from the wise and prudent and have revealed them to babes.

MATTHEW 21:16
. . . and said to Him, "Do You hear what these are saying?"
And Jesus said to them, "Yes. Have you never read,
'Out of the mouth of babes and nursing infants
You have perfected praise?'"

After this vision I was restless because my spirit was burdened for the pain and suffering that mankind was about to have visited upon them. I started to pray for the safety of the whole world. The Lord answered my prayers, on the night of April 17, straight from His Word. The Holy Spirit led me to Jeremiah 30:23, 24 to reveal the LORD's answer to my prayer for the whole world.

JEREMIAH 30:23, 24
Behold, the whirlwind of the LORD goeth forth
with fury, a continuing whirlwind: it shall fall
with pain upon the head of the wicked.
The fierce anger of the LORD shall not return, until
he hath done it, and until he have performed the
intents of his heart: in the latter days ye shall consider it.

THE MEANING OF THIS VISION

There is an urgency for all of us to understand the meaning of this vision. The Lord God Almighty is conveying a very important message to all of mankind. Let the Holy Spirit guide us all into the understanding of it.

I saw multiple immeasurable walls of water standing straight. This stance indicates that the disasters associated with this standing wall of water will happen rapidly. I pierced my hand through a wall of water. What should have happened in the natural realm? Water should have spilled out from that very hole in the wall. Instead of spilling water, that hole resealed without a single drop of water dripping out of it; this conveys that nature is only in His sovereign control.

This is God's declaration: that multiple walls of water are standing by to fall one after the other all over the earth because no one cares to obey His will. <u>The Holy Spirit clearly spoke to me</u>: *"We are doing whatever we want to do and not thinking about the WILL OF GOD. This is not the only wall. There are several walls like this that are held with God's Strength. If the people of this world continue to live in the same pattern, these walls will start to collapse one after the other."*

The picture of a standing wall of water in my vision is very similar to Exodus 14:22: *"And the children of Israel went into the midst of the sea upon the dry ground: and the waters were a wall unto them on their right hand, and on their left."* The people of God passed through the path of the standing wall of waters, but that same wall fell over the Pharaoh and his battalion. In a similar fashion, the people of God who are living in His righteousness will pass through safely in the midst of all troubles that will befall on earth, but the unrighteous before the Lord will suffer.

The several similar walls of water symbolize "ALL NATURAL DISASTERS THAT ARE LINED UP TO FALL ON EARTH." Our Earth will <u>continuously</u> face numerous catastrophes and disasters of nature, like earthquakes, famines, cyclones or tornados, floods, volcanic eruptions, and much more . . .

The Word of God proves that the whole universe is only in God's control. For example:

MARK 4:39
And he arose, and rebuked the wind, and said unto the sea, Peace, be still. And the wind ceased, and there was a great calm.

EXODUS 14:21, 22, 26
And Moses stretched out his hand over the sea: and the LORD caused the sea to go back by the strong east wind all that night, and made the sea dry land, and the waters were divided. And the children of Israel went into the midst of the sea

upon the dry ground: and the waters were a wall unto
them on their right hand, and on their left. . . .
And the LORD said unto Moses, Stretch out thine
hand over the sea, that the waters may come again upon
the Egyptians, upon their chariots, and upon their horseman.

I am sharing this vision with you because:

First: God commanded me to witness.

Second: To help humanity comprehend that the only way to save our world is by living   according to the will of God.

Third: It is vital to understand that there is only one supreme power that rules this earth—that is the eternal God. The whole universe follows His will, with the **exception of mankind.**

This message is not for one religious group, caste, ethical background, color, or nation. This message is for ALL OF HUMANITY. **Each and every person is responsible for God's judgments.**

We place and continue to keep everything else in first place before God. We have drifted away from God, focusing instead on the pursuit and acquisition of wealth or power or the self-serving development of our own abilities.

Whom do we worship? Ask yourself.

God told Moses in advance that the Israelites would disobey Him, so He gave guidelines for punishment and forgiveness by the Law. That did not deter them from being disobedient to His Word. In exactly the same way, God knows that even with His testimony and witnesses, many people still will not obey.

DEUTERONOMY 31:16-18
And the LORD said to Moses: "Behold, you will rest
with your fathers; and this people will rise and play the
harlot with the gods of the foreigners of the land, where
they go to be among them, and they will forsake Me and
break My covenant, which I have made with them.
Then My anger shall be aroused against them in that day,
and I will forsake them, and I will hide My face from them,
and they shall be devoured. And many evils and troubles shall

befall them, so that they will say in that day, 'Have not these
evils come upon us because our God is not among us?'
And I will surely hide My face in that day because of all the evil
which they have done, in that they have turned to other gods.

Mankind needs to acknowledge who he is worshipping: physical desires, adultery, pornography, nudity, strip clubs, fornication, immoral or unethical sexual desires (even animals instinctively obey God by abstaining from unnatural sex), greed for wealth and prosperity, fulfillments of this materialistic world, and self-idolatry-like gods.

How can the Lord, who is holy, righteous, and truthful, be among such a generation filled with the filth of sins?

The Word of God revealed the characteristics of the END TIMES GENERATIONS. Please read these verses from the Bible to understand, from God's precepts, about the Last Days generation. If you read the following verses of the Bible without any partiality, you will agree that it is very common to witness this same behavior in the world today. Let's read together.

2 TIMOTHY 3:1-7
Perilous Times and Perilous Men
But know this, that in the last days perilous times will come:
For men will be lovers of themselves, lovers of money, boasters,
proud, blasphemers, disobedient to parents, unthankful, unholy,
unloving, unforgiving, slanderers, without self-control, brutal,
despisers of good, traitors, headstrong, haughty, lovers of
pleasure rather than lovers of God, having a form of godliness
but denying its power. And from such people turn away!
For of this sort are those who creep
into households and make captives
of gullible women loaded down with sins, led away by various lusts,
always learning and never able to come
to the knowledge of the truth.

If your mind is open to the things of God, you will agree that this passage is the clear picture of our generation. As for the fulfillment of the very final part of this passage, we are witnessing that the desire for learning and gaining knowledge is at its peak today, and yet this is still the most unsatisfied generation.

In all times God always gives warnings and supporting evidence from His witnesses before executing His judgments. Similarly, the Lord God Almighty is witnessing the same to our generation from the mouth of His servants sent out to the ends of the earth.

DEUTERONOMY 31:19
Now therefore, write down this song for yourselves, and
teach it to the children of Israel; put it in their mouths, that this
song may be a witness for Me against the children of Israel.

Ultimately this manmade, unstable world will be judged due to man's sinful choices. The reason for God's judgment is our own disobedience towards His will.

An important question is: what is the Will of God?

God told me that the world is not following His will.

The only hope we have is an obedient relationship with God. His will is written on our hearts. Listen to your spirit honestly and closely. It's in communion with God constantly; we simply choose to ignore it. It should be your first guideline.

In **DEUTERONOMY 30:14** God says:
But the word is very near you, in your mouth
and in your heart, that you may do it.

We can clearly understand the will of God in the verses below. It is really an urgent need to get an understanding of and follow God's directives for our own protection. Take a look at the Scripture below.

MARK 12:29-34
Jesus answered him, "The first of all the commandments is:
'Hear, O Israel, the LORD our God, the LORD is one.
And you shall love the LORD your God with all your heart,
with all your soul, with all your mind, and with all your

strength.' This is the first commandment.
And the second, like it, is this:
'You shall love your neighbor as yourself.'
There is no other commandment greater than these."
So the scribe said to Him, "Well said, Teacher. You have spoken the
truth, for there is one God, and there is no other but He.
And to love Him with all the heart,
with all the understanding, with all
the soul, and with all the strength, and to love one's neighbor as
oneself, is more than all the whole burnt offerings and sacrifices."
Now when Jesus saw that he answered wisely, He said to
him, "You are not far from the kingdom of God."

The will of God remains and constitutes itself as a mystery of pure love. It is humanly impossible to love your neighbor as yourself, because only the love of God, through His Holy Spirit, can enable us to do so, to *"love your neighbor as yourself."* God never directs us to a task that is impossible for us. Loving everyone like you is only possible through guidance of the Holy Spirit. Our spirit, which is connected to Him, knows what to do; it's our flesh that refuses to budge. The very reason every soul on earth needs to obey the first commandment—*"And you shall love the LORD your God with all your heart, with all your soul, with all your mind, and with all your strength"*—is that if you love God first, subsequently you will automatically love those whom He loves . . . but do you love Him enough? Loving God first transforms us supernaturally into a universal lover of all. We begin to love even our own enemies—just as God, who loves both the just and unjust. What an awesome God we know who majestically provides the good things to all without their input. We receive His blessings because of His indescribable loving kindness.

Overwhelming desire and passion for God and a relationship with Him can purify our souls to help us love others unconditionally, as He does. The possibility to become righteous is within our grasp. We can become transformed due to an intimate love relationship with our creator—OUR LORD GOD ALMIGHTY.

There is only one perfect way out for all of us to reach a ladder with which we can follow God's will effortlessly. Let's read the verses below to help our understanding.

ROMANS 12:2
Do not be conformed to this world, but be you transformed by the renewing of your mind, so that you may prove what is the good, and acceptable, and perfect Will of God.

It is only by having God's life dwelling in us that we can have our thinking changed to come into unity and oneness with the will and Word of God. Our minds must be renewed in Christ; we then can begin to put His ways into action in our lives, so that we can prove to ourselves that only God's way of life is good and perfect. Spiritual transformation is required to come into unity and oneness with God, His Word, and His way of life.

In response to my desperate prayers for mercy on earth on April 17, 2007, the Lord answered through Jeremiah 30:23, 24: ***"Behold, the whirlwind of the Lord goeth forth with fury, a continuing whirlwind: it shall fall with pain upon the head of the wicked. The fierce anger of the LORD shall not return, until he hath done it, and until he have performed the intents of his heart: in the latter days ye shall consider it."*** Every person on earth needs to ask a question:

Why would the Lord our God do this to the creation He made with so much love and compassion? Why is He so disappointed in us?

Why will His anger not turn away?

What can hurt our heavenly FATHER that can cause Him to separate from us?

Is the human race so self-righteous and stubborn that they will refuse to listen to GOD's voice and repent with humility? For this very reason God prophesized about His judgments that will come due to the intense sins of mankind. Disobedience to His will would cause frequent and intense natural disasters. Smaller and greater disasters like a tsunami, hurricanes, earthquakes, famines, floods, and other of nature's turmoils will follow in Heaven and earth—and we are witnessing them to come to pass.

Prophecies of Intensified Natural Disasters

God called me to be His witness before the whole world to testify to His will and the progression of tribulations on earth in similarity to a woman in birth pains, before the second coming of the Lord Jesus Christ.

MARK 13:8
For nation will rise against nation, and kingdom against kingdom. And there will be earthquakes in various places, and there will be famines and troubles. These are the beginnings of the birth pains.

1 THESSALONIANS 5:3
For when they shall say, "Peace and safety"; then sudden destruction cometh upon them, as travail upon a woman with child; and they shall not escape.

The Word of God predicts that the natural disasters and wars will grow in correlation to a woman's labor pains. Labor pains increase more and more in frequency and in intensity as the time draws near for a baby to be born. Similarly, the earth will go through the same phase of contractions before the second coming of the Lord Jesus Christ, with the shaking of the earth. The last extreme contraction brings the child out of the woman's womb. The earth will quake globally and the powers of Heaven will shake at the coming of a Messiah of the Universe: the *Yeshua Ha'Mashiach – the Lord Jesus Christ* – to earth. Rejoice that the day of the redemption of saints will come.

Remarkably, the Lord of the universe spoke to me again on November 10, 2009, to warn of the increase in the intensity of all natural disasters. God reveals His messages to me through dreams, visions, voice, and His Word. That night the Lord revealed the upcoming future devastations in a unique experience with the Holy Spirit.

I had an amazing experience on the night of November 10, 2009. I was overwhelmed with the overpowering presence of the Holy Spirit around me. I never had the connection and presence of God on this level before. I was completely immersed in the fire of the Holy Spirit. This experience had given me the wisdom and knowledge of what King David and King Solomon felt when they were inspired by the Holy Spirit of God to write the books of Psalms, Proverbs, and The Song of Solomon. The Word of God was continuously pouring onto me. I was completely enveloped and immersed in the passion of God. I kept expressing my love for God ceaselessly. *I could not stop uttering my love for the Lord God Almighty. Honestly, I wanted this experience to continue forever.* I will share one expression of the praise and worship in the presence of God's throne: "I am a burned out candle that is completely worn out like a melted wax. It is only You, my Lord God, who has made a brand new candle out of a worn out wax to burn and shine only for you."

The Holy Spirit made me aware that I had lost my identity completely, just like a completely dissolved wax candle. The heavenly Father is my identity now, for He has transformed me to burn and shine for His glory, to shine His light so as to remove the darkness of sins from people's life by witnessing His will to them. There is no darkness in the presence of light. Similarly, there is no existence of dark sin in the presence of God's light of righteousness. Many other words of wisdom kept pouring on me like a flowing spring of water. It is so hard to explain. I was completely immersed in the depth of the ocean of God's passion and love. This experience of the love of God is the most desirable sensation you can ever imagine. You will not regret leaving any love or relationship of this earth to experience this passion in God. I went to sleep with this joy of the Holy Spirit within me.

The very same night God showed me another incredible vision concerning to our earth and mankind.

Vision on the Night of November 10, 2009

I am viewing a flood that completely drowned everything. I observed an isolated town that is under water up to the ceiling of the houses. It looks as if the city has turned into an ocean with no life. There is an air of isolation and depression everywhere. Only infants and young children were left alive. I saw a girl of about five years of age. She was looking for something to tie her hair. I bent a piece of stick and dried it in the sunlight. It turned into a perfect hair band for the little girl.

On the other hand, I saw few children less than three years of age. One child was sleeping very peacefully and it was revealed in the Spirit that his parents had drowned. I started to search for food because I was concerned that the child would be hungry after he woke up. But there was no food anywhere. I felt in the Spirit that God Himself would provide for these children.

The Meaning of this Vision

God is revealing that the upcoming disasters will be more intense than the past experiences of 2009 and those before. The last disasters did not result in a soaring number of deaths and devastations; but upcoming natural disasters on earth like earthquakes, floods, cyclones, and other of nature's turmoils will be more extensive and intense. The floods and other natural disasters will come at a very high magnitude as cities are converted into ocean. Isolation and depression will be everywhere.

God showed that only those who are like children will be saved. Their needs will be met with the supernatural resources from God. Their survival will be the mercy of God. God will provide for their needs and food.

In my vision, I saw a baby sleeping peacefully; the child's parents had drowned in a flood. God is revealing to the whole world in advance that many families will be broken by the disasters and devastation because of the death of family members. In the vision it is very clear that technology is completely lost. People will be relying only on the natural resources available in the affected areas of disasters. Deaths due to disasters will surpass our imagination. It will be a time of great depression.

One obvious question that comes to our minds is why only innocent children are saved in my dream.

MARK 10:14
When Jesus saw this, he was indignant. He said to them. "Let the little children come to me, and do not hinder them, for the Kingdom of God belongs to such as these."

MARK 10:15
I tell you the truth, anyone who will not receive the kingdom of God like a child will never enter it.

God desires His people to have the characteristics of children. This vision indicates that the only survivors will be the people who are pure and innocent at heart like children. The more you look at a child, the more goodness you will find in them. This is what God wants us to be. God has gifted us with the beautiful nature of a child, but we have ruined it with our own creativity and with the help of satan. We all need to reject satan and walk with our Lord God Almighty. He is waiting with open arms to save and protect us all. Once we decide to change our paths toward God, we will receive the gift of Holy Spirit through the acceptance of Jesus Christ as our Lord and Savior. The Holy Spirit will guide and teach us the will of God; then obedience to the perfect Will of God will change us physically, emotionally, and spiritually into a perfect human being. This perfect man or woman will be a perfect replica of the children that I saw in my vision, who will be the only survivors in the midst of tribulations on earth.

I will repeat this again: God is revealing that we can only survive and be protected in these tribulations and judgments if we are like a child.

The Lord called me to witness before mankind about the **"Global Warning for Upcoming Natural Disasters."** The Lord also shared the reason for these happenings and provided the way out for those who will repent and strive to seek His counsel, and learn to obey His will. Are you willing to come and join His congregation in the name of the King and Savior of the universe, the Lord Jesus Christ?

Prophecies Came to Pass

My journey to obey God's calling began just after an awakening voice that I heard in 2008, saying, "Ezekiel, chapter 12, verse 24." At that time, I was not an avid reader of the Bible, and I didn't know that a book of Ezekiel even existed. This voice from God urged me to share Lord's messages with the whole world without any more delay.

EZEKIEL 12:24, 25
For there shall be no more any vain vision nor flattering divination within the house of Israel.

When you read the next verse, the understanding becomes clearer.

*For I am the LORD: I will speak, and the word
that I shall speak shall come to pass; it shall be no more
prolonged: for in your days, O rebellious house, will I say
the word, and will perform it, saith the Lord GOD.*

Vision of December 19, 2010

I was worshiping and praising the Lord on Saturday night, December 19, 2010. At about 2:30 AM, when I was completely soaked in praises to the Lord, I saw a vision about the future catastrophe and devastation that our earth will face.

I saw a footlong hoagie sandwich. I lifted the top half of the bread and it was spotted with black mold. Surprisingly, the bottom half of sandwich was edible with deli meat, lettuce, tomatoes, and onions on it. *This vision divulges that half of the food harvest will be destroyed all over the world, especially grains.*

I also saw a huge mall parking lot. The sky was filled with heavy-looking snow clouds. Also, the parking lot had a very smooth layer of about an inch of snow. There was no mark of anyone's footsteps or tire tracks. I was the only one in my car in the whole parking lot. It felt like a ghost town with a feeling of isolation and depression in the air.

Meaning of This Vision

The Lord is letting us know about the increase in the intensity of natural disasters that we will face on Earth in the form of famine, freezing cold, and snowstorms.

FAMINE: Half of the world's harvest will be destroyed due to drastic climate changes and other scourges like bugs and diseases. I saw half of the bread spoiled due to black mold. Black indicates death of grains, and mold represents the source of the spoilage of crops. We know that mold grows due to moisture. Therefore, rain and snowstorms will be the main source to wipe out grains all over the world. As we are heading toward a great famine all over the world, start to preserve food as Joseph did.

FREEZING OF THE EARTH, SNOWSTORMS: The storm clouds indicate excessive rain and snowfall will encompass the world. The empty snow-covered parking lot warns us of severe emergency situations, in which people will be confined in their homes and businesses will be forced to close. God is revealing that our earth will face greater catastrophes and devastation.

Remember, only God is in control of the forces of nature. God is giving these warnings to help mankind recognize their sins and repent. It is imperative to seek the face of the LORD and fall on our knees with humble hearts. Our overwhelming amount of sins and rebellions against the will of God will only ensure His righteous judgment.

Prophetic Fulfillment from the Vision of December 19, 2010
The Signs of Future Famine

God showed me that half of the grains (harvest of food) will be destroyed. The following news articles prove the beginning of the eradication of the crops all over world.

The Coming Famine: Risks and Solutions for Global Food Security
Julian Cribb
Saturday, 17 April 2010

Then there is the slice of farm water that climate change is already stealing, whether it is rainfall over the great grainbowls, evaporation from storages, shrinking rivers and groundwater, or the loss of meltwater from mountain regions. The Himalayan glaciers are disappearing—the only debate is how fast. And the North China Plain is running out of water. These two regions feed 1.7 billion people now and must feed twice that many in future. If they fail, the consequences will affect everyone.

The International Food Policy Research Institute has warned of a potential 30 % drop in irrigated wheat production in Asia and 15% in rice, due to climate factors. The World Bank fears African productivity could halve and India's drop by as much as 30 %, unless urgent steps are taken.

Leslie Kaufman
updated June 3, 2011

As the surging waters of the Mississippi pass downstream, they leave behind flooded towns and inundated lives and carry forward a brew of farm chemicals and waste that this year — given record flooding — is expected to result in the largest dead zone ever in the Gulf of Mexico.

Government studies have traced a majority of those chemicals in the runoff to nine farming states, and yet today, decades after the dead zones began forming, there is still little political common ground on how to abate this perennial problem. <u>Scientists who study dead zones predict that the affected area will increase significantly this year, breaking records for size and damage.</u> (Emphasis mine. – I.N.)

Half of Texas Now Under 'Exceptional' Drought
— Articles and blogs about drought published by *U.S. News & World Report*

Our world is truly under the threat of a global famine as the Lord revealed in my dream of December 19, 2010. Signs of the future famine are evident before our eyes and are published in news on a daily basis.

Occurrences of Extreme Snowstorms as Revealed in My Vision of December 19, 2010

The Lord showed me that snowstorms will isolate life out of places where it will strike. We can witness that all came to pass as the LORD exposed, just after this vision.

Updated: Dec. 30, 2010 – A rare December blizzard unleashed its fury on the East Coast on Dec. 26, 2010, centering its force on the New York metropolitan area, where <u>it shut down the three major airports and stopped commuter trains and some subway lines. Knee-to-thigh-high snows were common, and officials said it would probably take days to dig out.</u>

New Zealand Snowstorm Believed To Be Heaviest In 30 Years .
— www.huffingtonpost.com/2011/.../new-zealand-snowstorm....

Posted on 27 June, 2011, by Jeff Masters in Skeptical Science:

A series of remarkable snow storms pounded the Eastern U.S., with the "Snowmageddon" blizzard dumping more than two feet of snow on Baltimore and Philadelphia. Western Europe also experienced unusually cold and snowy conditions, with the UK recording its eighth-coldest January. A highly extreme negative phase of the NAO and AO returned again <u>during November 2010, and lasted into January 2011</u>. **Exceptionally cold and snowy conditions hit much of Western Europe and the Eastern U.S. again in the winter of 2010–2011.**

Vision of March 10, 2011

I had a vision while praying and worshipping on March 10, 2011. I saw a kitchen sink, filled to the brim with water. I looked at the floor under the sink, concerned that water may leak down the sink. To my surprise, the water started to seep out of the floor right below that sink, and it kept rising. The sink was already filled to its capacity—another drop would cause it to overflow. The ground was so saturated that it could not absorb any more water. The floor was expelling the excess water from its depth.

Meaning of This Vision

This vision represents the increased intensity and amount of storms headed our way. Heaven is loaded with water (rains) to such a level that more showers will lead to extreme flooding. The grounds will be saturated with water and will have no capacity left to absorb any more rain. Our earth is entering into the next stage of a contraction of birth pains with storms, tornadoes, and floods after March 10, 2011. Severity of such disasters will become overwhelming for mankind; every eye will become anxious to observe the overfilled clouds in the heavens and the flooded grounds below.

Prophetic Fulfillment from the Vision of March 10, 2011

This prophecy that the Lord gave me on March 10, 2011 did come to pass. Let's review some of the news articles proving this outrageous severity of flooding all over the world.

Natural disasters across the globe have made 2011 the costliest on record in terms of property damage, and that's just six months in, according to a report released Tuesday by a leading insurer that tracks disasters.

A day after of my prophetic vision:

faithenvironmentcollide.wordpress.com/2011/.../japan-earthquaketsu...

March 11, 2011 – *As you likely know by now, Japan was hit by an earthquake and ... Right now, tsunami warnings are in effect all over the Pacific - endoftheamericandream.com*

http://endoftheamericandream.com/archives/why-are-there-so-many-natural-disasters-in-2011

May 27, 2011– *So far in 2011, we have seen a record number of tornadoes, unprecedented flooding, rampant earthquakes, disturbing volcanic eruptions, and a tsunami in Japan that none of us will ever forget. So why are there so many natural disasters in 2011? Our top scientists seem to be at a complete loss to explain what is happening. It just seems like there is one disaster or emergency after another.*

Dream on April 22, 2011

I saw a dream on Friday night, April 22, 2011 that hailstones the size of eggs were falling on my roof. We were not scared to sit on the first floor, right under the ceiling. My family was sitting, talking, and completely relaxed without any fear of disaster over our heads. Hail was falling hard on the roof, but we were not concerned about it at all. Nothing was damaged and we were safe.

Meaning of This Dream

The Lord showed me a dream about imminent disasters at my home, which represents the United States. The storms will be strong, with egg-sized hail. Hailstones can signify capital punishment.

LEVITICUS 24:23
Then Moses spoke to the Israelites, and they took the blasphemer outside the camp and stoned him. The Israelites did as the LORD commanded Moses.

As the corruption increases, so does the size of the judgment. All obedient and righteous children of God will be sheltered in the midst of these natural disasters. Within one week of this revelation the whole country experienced storms of the same intensity. We all witnessed the hailstorms with hail the size of an egg as shown in my dream from the Lord. The true Church of God will be safe in the midst of these storms, because God is their shepherd. I trust in my Lord more and more every day. I honor His works, purpose, and judgments with passion, and I have no doubt that His people are sheltered in the midst of all troubles. His mighty hand is powerful to protect His people miraculously in the midst of a deadly storm. But the unrighteousness cannot escape His righteous judgments that will befall on them suddenly as they rebel against His counsel to follow the works of darkness and evil.

Prophetic Fulfillment of a Dream on April 22, 2011

Storm, hail, reported tornadoes pummel parts of South

By the CNN Wire Staff

A tornado struck an Air Force base, military officials said, and prompted the Arkansas governor to declare a state of emergency. According to the agency's Storm Prediction Center, there were 29 tornado reports -- many in northeast Texas -- by late Tuesday, but the actual number had not been confirmed.

'Awful, terrible, disturbing'

"An awful, terrible, disturbing, and deadly day of tornadoes unfolded on Wednesday, April 27, 2011, with more than 100 reported tornadoes striking several states in the South and even a few areas in the Mid-Atlantic," the Weather Channel said in an article written by three of its meteorologists.

*NORTH TEXAS (CBSDFW.COM) – CBS Local Media: Another afternoon of severe storms left many North Texans cleaning up following multiple reported tornado touchdowns Tuesday night. The storms also brought several inches of rain and **very large hail** to the area. A viewer photo from Peeltown in Kaufman County showed a piece of hail the size* *of a softball with spiked edges.*

We all have witnessed that the prediction of upcoming disasters in a dream of April 22, 2011 did came to pass instantaneously.

Dream on May 21, 2011

The Lord showed me a dream on Friday, May 21, 2011 pertaining to natural disasters related to fires and accompanied with extreme unexpected emergencies. I saw that I was driving on a highway. Traffic on my side of the road was moving steadily at an average speed. It was a very peaceful and typical highway. But on the opposite side of the highway, fire trucks were coming down one after the other with emergency lights on. It seemed like there was no end to the line of the fire trucks. The opposite side was under complete chaos.

The Meaning of This Dream

The Lord showed me that many emergencies are heading our way, signified by the fire trucks and their sirens. Our Earth will see consistent fire emergencies as shown by fire trucks emerging one after the other. But these tragedies will not impact the children of God, because they have surrendered their lives to walk in the path of righteousness in His will.

The opposite side of the highway represents all those who have chosen the path of sin and unrighteousness. *Mankind will suffer and experience tragedy and turbulence due to unexpected emergencies of fire-related accidents, volcano eruptions, disorientation of the planet earth causing major fire threats and other accidental emergencies, arms and ammunitions fires due to war, and conflicts of many forms of nature.* It means that any kind of accident will emerge causing unexpected crises. I saw fire trucks keep coming speedily with sirens and emergency lights on. It signifies that fire-related emergencies will keep emerging all over the world, ceaselessly. <u>The next phase of God's righteous judgments on earth will come in the form of fires and fire related emergencies</u>.

Prophetic Fulfillment of a Dream of May 21, 2011

I have listed a few news articles that prove the fulfillment of the revelation that God gave me on May 21, 2011. A tremendous amount of fire emergencies will continue to arise all over the globe after this vision.

World Natural Hazards Website Natural Disaster Management
26-May-2011 – *Powerful Typhoon Threatening the Western Pacific, Typhoon Songda, now approaching the Philippines, is predicted to veer north to the Philippines and Japan.*

NBC News.com: updated 6/6/2011 5:28:19 PM ET
An erupting Chilean volcano sent a towering plume of ash across South America on Monday, forcing thousands from their homes, grounding airline flights in southern Argentina and coating ski resorts with a gritty layer of dust instead of snow. Booming explosions echoed across the Andes as toxic gases belched up from a three-mile-long (five-kilometer long) fissure in the Puyehue-Cordon Caulle volcanic complex .

Arizona wildfires fueled by high winds, low humidity
Weather is of great concern as fires spread toward New Mexico. There are "several difficult days of firefighting ahead," U.S. Forest Service chief says.

June 8, 2011 | By Michael Muskal | Los Angeles Times
Driven by fierce winds and single-digit humidity, wildfires on Wednesday continued their spread from Arizona toward New Mexico as thousands of firefighters struggled to control the blazes.

http://www.euronews.com/tag/forest-fires/

The World's Worst Forest Fires
Australia: firefighters battle wildfires near Sydney as more extreme weather forecast Australian firefighters are working against the clock to contain wildfires on the outskirts of Sydney. The huge blazes have burned through more than 120,000 . . . October 22, 2013

BBC NEWS ASIA - 26 April 2012
More than 220 forest fires spread across Nepal

Updated 3 May 2012: Protected areas in Nepal and northern India have been affected by forest fires, with at least one suffering huge wildlife losses, officials have said. They say nearly 70% of Nepal's Bardiya National Park has been consumed by fire in the past few days.

The Lord continuously communicates with me through dreams and visions with His messages to the world. Such as: God foretold a warning about the Hurricane Sandy on October 24, 2012. In a dream of August 20, 2012 the Lord revealed about the Earthquake of Iran and their condition.

God has anointed me with a spiritual gift of predicting upcoming tribulations that comes to pass in a very short time.

EZEKIEL 12:25
*For I am the LORD: I will speak, and the word
that I shall speak shall come to pass; it shall be no more
prolonged: for in your days, O rebellious house, will I say
the word, and will perform it, saith the Lord GOD.*

I am now sharing the most recent prophetic revelation that also came to pass.

Dream of October 27, 2013

The LORD GOD gave me a prophetic dream on October 27, 2013, about the severity in natural disasters that is more than mankind has experienced before. I saw the worse after-effects of disasters in comparison to my previous dreams, just like the labor pains of women intensify before delivery. I saw rains stronger than the ones I have seen in my past dreams and visions. For the first time in this prophetic dream of natural disasters, the Lord showed me the filthy muddle left after flood. Thus from this date onward our earth will proceed to face more intensified natural catastrophes such as floods, tornadoes, earthquakes, fires, volcanic eruptions, and more, than ever before.

Prophetic Fulfillment of This Dream

Doyle Rice and Alia E. Dastagir, USA TODAY – November 8, 2013

Super Typhoon Haiyan, which slammed into the Philippines early Friday morning, is one of the strongest storms ever recorded on the planet. Here are some fast facts about the storm:

- *Super Typhoon Haiyan had winds of 195 mph and gusts of 235 mph. This is one of the highest wind speeds ever recorded in a storm in world history.*
- *The storm [is] over 300 miles wide: The width is about equal to the distance between Boston and Philadelphia.*

The Lord specifically revealed in this dream that the great amount of damage, filth and shamble will be left after this disaster leaves. Please read how exactly it came to pass.

By BECKY EVANS
PUBLISHED: 15:45 EST, 11 November 2013 | UPDATED: 12:45 EST, 12 November 2013
www.usatoday.com/story/news/world/2013

Bodies piled in the streets as makeshift mortuaries are overrun and Philippine typhoon rescue teams warn death toll will 'rise sharply' from the 10,000 already confirmed

- *Typhoon Haiyan was a maximum category-five storm with gusts of up to 235mph*
- *Authorities say in the city of Tacloban, Leyte, alone, 10,000 could be dead and 'two out of five bodies' are children*
- *Tens of millions of pounds worth of aid has been pledged by countries around the world*
- *Aid agencies say as many as 10million people could be in need of shelter, clean water and food*
- *Mortuaries set up in remaining buildings like churches are overrun with bodies.*

According to my prophetic dream, our earth has entered into a next level of contractions like the birth prangs of a woman in labor. From this stage onward our earth will experience more disasters similar to Super Typhoon Haiyan—until the next, greater, contraction in the deeps emerges.

Now with all these proven facts of the fulfillment of the dreams and visions that the Lord God Almighty gave me to witness before the world, how can anyone deny the sovereignty of the One who created the universe, the principalities and powers, the earth, and the things in it such as the oceans, the mountains, the valleys, the birds, the animals, the humans, the air, the fires, and the winds. God proves to us His existence and His power out of the beauty of His creations everyday. We see His beauty and love in all the good things He bestowed for our benefit, nourishment, life, and enjoyment. What is there that He did not do for His beloved humanity? But why can't the same human race see His loving kindness, His love, His heart, His will, and His care for them? God do not desire to see mankind suffer. Our denial, separation, sinful desires, and pride brings us into the troubles like pains, sufferings, death, and tribulations. Now is the hour to repent and seek God for mercy and salvation.

We will not drive at a high speed for a fear of getting a speeding ticket. We do not steal for fear of going to jail. We know how to honor man's laws and decrees, but we have no honor of God's laws and judgments. Fear of the Lord is the beginning of wisdom. If fear and obedience of man-made law can save us from earthly troubles, then fear, honor, and obedience to God's Laws will definitely lead us to safety, prosperity, and peace on this Earth. And then, when our physical life will end here, our eternity with the LORD will begin in His Kingdom.

It would be foolish to reject God's protective shield.

It would be unwise to continue with our ungodly way of life.

It would be great misfortune to live without God's love.

PSALM 46:1-11

God is our refuge and strength, a very present help in trouble.
Therefore will not we fear, though the earth be removed, and
though the mountains be carried into the midst of the sea;
Though the waters thereof roar and be troubled, though
the mountains shake with the swelling thereof. Selah.
There is a river, the streams whereof shall make glad the city
of God, the holy place of the tabernacles of the most High.
God is in the midst of her; she shall not be moved:

God shall help her, and that right early.
The heathen raged, the kingdoms were moved:
he uttered his voice, the earth melted.
The LORD of hosts is with us; the God
of Jacob is our refuge. Selah.
Come, behold the works of the LORD, what
desolations he hath made in the earth.
He maketh wars to cease unto the end of the
earth; he breaketh the bow, and cutteth the spear
in sunder; he burneth the chariot in the fire.
1Be still, and know that I am God: I will be exalted
among the heathen, I will be exalted in the earth.
The LORD of hosts is with us; the God
of Jacob is our refuge. Selah.

Survival in the Middle of Troubles

God gave me a revelation about His judgments for correction of mankind. Who will survive by the supernatural intervention of the Lord, and what makes them different from the rest of the world? Let's understand this great knowledge from the heart of the Father in Heaven, revealed in this dream.

Dream on July 10, 2011

The Lord showed me a dream on July 10, 2011 about the growing severity and intensity of natural disasters compared to our previous experiences.

In the first scene, I am sitting with my daughter in front of my house. Winds from the west started to blow so strongly that they pushed a trunk of a pine tree at about a 45-degree angle. Winds were about 60 to 100 miles per hour from west to east.

In the second scene, I saw two trees fall on my neighbor's house. My house was completely unharmed; not one branch fell on my property.

In the third scene, I went to my neighbor to help her clean the mess. She told me that she saw my sister praying through our window just before this damage on her house. I discerned in my spirit while hearing the neighbor's story that my sister knelt down humbly and lifted her hands towards Heaven to seek Lord's mercy at this hour of trouble, and her prayers left the window toward Heaven like a fire.

The Meaning of This Dream

In the first part of the vision, the Lord God Almighty is showing us that the natural disasters will grow in force compared to our previous experiences. Winds, floods, storms, tornados, earthquakes and other natural disaster will come with greater frequency and power.

Just before the year 2010, God showed me the strength of disasters, such as a nearly 30-foot tree moving in circles. We have all witnessed the magnitude of previous global natural disasters. Today the LORD showed me that not one, but two, trees fell on my neighbor's house. Therefore, the earth will experience a double potency of natural disasters in comparison to what we have seen before July 10, 2011.

In the second and third part of the vision I saw that trees fell on my neighbor's house, but my house was completely unharmed. My neighbor shared that she witnessed my sister's prayers lifted up to the heavens in the form of a fire, and for this reason we were saved by the Lord's supernatural protection.

The prayer action of my sister in a dream is a revelation for those who want to be saved at times of tribulations. The only deed that can save us in times of troubles is seeking the face of the Lord with extreme humility (she knelt down to pray), and lifting our spirit high with a desire to depend only on God, our Creator (she lifted her hands toward Heaven). These conducts of meekness combined with completely relying on the Lord will definitely bring your needs before the throne of God in Heaven with purity and force (her prayers left toward Heaven in the form of a fire). The final result will be our supernatural protection in the midst of floods, tornadoes, hurricanes, storms, earthquakes, fires, and wars. Who is more trustworthy than our Lord God Almighty? Yes, all those who seek the face of the Lord will be saved in the midst of troubles.

Praise the Lord God Almighty for the next phase of global contractions. God's judgment will bring correction among many peoples around the world. The miraculous rescue of God's people will be a testimony to those who do not seek God for their protection and do not know Him personally. These eye-opening experiences will save multitudes all over the earth.

Keep praying to the Lord and let the Holy Spirit be with you always. Each and every child of God will be used as a testimony to save those who have never experienced the Lord's existence. Nothing can save us from these disasters on earth but our faithful relationship with the creator of this universe, the Lord God Almighty.

A Great Mystery

It is important to understand the significance of the Holy Spirit, because the Lord showed it in this dream. The Holy Spirit is the only helper sent from our Father in Heaven to sustain, protect, and lead His people.

JOHN 14:26
But the Helper, the Holy Spirit, whom the Father will
send in My name, He will teach you all things, and bring
to your remembrance all things that I said to you.

JOHN 14:6
Jesus said to him, "I am the way, the truth, and the life.
No one comes to the Father except through Me."

The finality of man to approach the heavenly Father for his protection is only through the Lord Jesus Christ: *"No one comes to the Father except through Me."* The Lord Jesus Christ is the only salvation and rescue in all circumstances for everyone because He completed the requirements of God's laws; as He said: "It is finished."

JOHN 19:30
So when Jesus had received the sour wine, He said, "It is
finished!" And bowing His head, He gave up His spirit.

Jesus did away with the curse that began due to Adam and Eve's disobedience in the Garden of Eden. The Law of God teaches that the punishment of sin is death. Therefore, the Savior of the universe, the Lord Jesus Christ, fulfilled this law in our place and died on the cross to end this curse. His blood that was shed on the cross replaces death with life. He won the battle of death and darkness to give us the free gift of life and light. What a marvelous and perfect plan God has for His people. Who can love us more than He?

The Holy Spirit wants to share a great mystery of the power of the blood of Jesus, to save His people at this hour of judgments on the earth. History is repeating itself in our time. We all know the story when Moses took the Israelites out of Egypt. God sent the series of judgments on Egypt when Pharaoh hardened his heart and refused to let His people go. The last judgment was the death of the firstborn of Egypt. Let's read the reference verses from the Bible.

EXODUS 12:5-7, 12, 13

"Your lamb shall be without blemish, a male of the first year. You may take it from the sheep or from the goats. Now you shall keep it until the fourteenth day of the same month. Then the whole assembly of the congregation of Israel shall kill it at twilight. And they shall take some of the blood and put it on the two doorposts and on the lintel of the houses where they eat it. . . .

"'For I will pass through the land of Egypt on that night, and will strike all the firstborn in the land of Egypt, both man and beast; and against all the gods of Egypt I will execute judgment: I am the LORD. Now the blood shall be a sign for you on the houses where you are. And when I see the blood, I will pass over you; and the plague shall not be on you to destroy you when I strike the land of Egypt.

Our generation is passing the final phase of the judgment. The Lord Jesus Christ is our Passover Lamb whose blood needs to be on the two doorposts and on the lintel of our house. Jesus said, *"No one comes to the Father except through Me."* How can you expect to be saved physically and spiritually without Him? No one can! In Exodus 12:13 we read that God said, *"When I see the blood, I will pass over you; and the plague shall not be on you to destroy you when I strike the land of Egypt."* How can we say that God is passing us today?

1 KINGS 19:11-12

And he said, Go forth, and stand upon the mount before the LORD. And, behold, the LORD passed by, and a great and strong wind rent the mountains, and brake in pieces the rocks before the LORD; but the LORD was not in the wind: and after the wind an earthquake; but the LORD was not in the earthquake: And after the earthquake, a fire; but the LORD was not in the fire: and after the fire a still small voice.

These verses prove that the Lord is passing by us today. Are you experiencing the great strong winds, an earthquake, or a fire? The stronger they get, the more intense the power of the Holy Spirit will be around His people on earth to seal and protect them. Therefore, God's promise is still the same for all mankind. All those who have accepted the Lord Jesus Christ as their Lord will not perish, because He is the perfect Lamb of God whose blood was shed for us. Now, anyone who has put the blood of the Lamb on the doorposts and lentil of his or her heart, mind, and soul will be saved in the midst of tribulations. These plagues will only destroy the land of Egypt, which is quite similar to our sinful world today. God is passing by us today. Are you ready to accept the Lord Jesus Christ as your Lord and Savior? Only He can save you!

ROMANS 8:9

You, however, are not in the flesh but in the Spirit, if in fact the Spirit of God dwells in you. Anyone who does not have the Spirit of Christ does not belong to him.

My dear friends, your safety is a relationship with your Father in Heaven through His son Jesus Christ. GOD is holy; our good deeds are not sufficient to help us get close to His throne. A single lie will make you unholy enough to get you out of His holiest presence. Don't take God for granted. Try to understand the seriousness of your choices in this life on earth. The only way is the washing of your sins through the blood of the Lord Jesus Christ. Why did God have to send His only be-gotten son to die on the cross? He must have some good reason! Please, try to seek the truth. As God showed me in this dream, only the people in relationship with Him in sprit and truth will be saved from upcoming disasters.

Hour of Repentance Has Arrived

In the last week of August 2011, God led me to Jonah 3. The Holy Spirit is letting us know that there is a desperate need to do what the people of Nineveh did.

Our earth is moving forward to the more advanced stage of its contraction of birth pains before the coming of our Lord Jesus Christ. There is a desperate need for people to be completely humble with repentance, just like the people of Nineveh. Let us read together to understand God's will for the correction of mankind.

JONAH 3:1-4
And the word of the LORD came unto Jonah the second time, saying,
Arise, go unto Nineveh, that great city, and preach
unto it the preaching that I bid thee.
So Jonah arose, and went unto Nineveh, according
to the word of the LORD. Now Nineveh was an
exceeding great city of three days' journey.
And Jonah began to enter into the city a day's journey, and he cried,
and said, Yet forty days, and Nineveh shall be overthrown.

In this passage we learn that the Lord sent the warning through His servant Jonah that the great city of Nineveh will be judged and over-thrown in forty days. History tells us that God never judges the world without sending His servants with a gospel of repentance. The Lord's servants are shouting all over the world to help save multitudes. Let's read more of God's message to understand the desire of His heart for us.

JONAH 3:5, 6
So the people of Nineveh believed God, and proclaimed a fast, and
put on sackcloth, from the greatest of them even to the least of them.

For word came unto the king of Nineveh, and he arose
from his throne, and he laid his robe from him, and
covered him with sackcloth, and sat in ashes.

In verses 5 and 6 we learn the most important lesson, because it is the only seed that grows the tree of hope and salvation. *This seed is self-denial; yes, we all need to deny our selves, from greatest to least, and fall down at the feet of our Creator-Lord God Almighty to ask that He would forgive our sins, which are many.*

It is an urgent hour, one in which we need to do exactly what the people of Nineveh did.

<u>Believe God</u>: trust the warning from the mouth of Jonah.

<u>Proclaim a fast</u>: empty ourselves before the Lord of our pride, self-worshipping, hypocrisy, evil doings, idol worshipping, and every sin that ever ruled our lives.

<u>Put on sackcloth</u>: remove our pride and ego to have a humble heart, which God desires so much.

We must do what the king of Nineveh did. He arose from his throne, put on sackcloth, and sat on the ashes. It is the only way for us to be saved at this hour of God's judgment all over the earth. Rich, poor, mighty, and weak people of this earth have to deny themselves, cry, repent, and sit in ashes to receive the mercy and grace of the Lord God Almighty. *The abundance of our sins has called for God's righteous judgments; similarly, a surplus of repentance from our hearts will save us from the sufferings that will come to pass in the form of global disasters all over the earth.*

Your Lord Jesus Christ is welcoming you to deny yourself, pick up your cross, and follow Him. It is the only way for your salvation.

MARK 8:34
When He had called the people to Himself, with His disciples
also, He said to them, "Whoever desires to come after Me, let
him deny himself, and take up his cross, and follow Me.

Continuation of Jonah 3
JONAH 3:7-10

*And he caused it to be proclaimed and published through Nineveh by
the decree of the king and his nobles, saying,
Let neither man nor beast,
herd nor flock, taste any thing: let them not feed, nor drink water:
But let man and beast be covered with sackcloth, and cry
mightily unto God: yea, let them turn everyone from his
evil way, and from the violence that is in their hands.
Who can tell if God will turn and repent, and turn
away from his fierce anger, that we perish not?
And God saw their works, that they turned from their
evil way; and God repented of the evil, that he had said
that he would do unto them; and he did it not.*

What a powerful message we get from verses 7-10! These verses dis-
close the only possible way of salvation for the human race. If each and
every person living on the face of this earth would unite with humility
and repentance, with fasting and prayers before the Lord God Almighty
in an exact manner as the people of Nineveh did, God *will* forgive and
spare us from His judgments.

But, we all know that not everyone will do this. All those who follow
God's will individually will be saved individually. Let's see what we need
to do.

- Be covered with sackcloth
- Cry mightily unto God
- Turn from evil ways
- Turn from the violence of our hands

Then we will be able to hope that we will not perish like the people
of Nineveh.

JONAH 3:9
*"Who can tell if God will turn and repent, and turn
away from his fierce anger that we perish not?"*

CHAPTER 3

End Times Tribulation

God communicated with me through a dream in 2008 about the reason and the timeline of the End Times Tribulations.

THE VISION

I am standing on top of a building with objects rotating on top of my head at an extremely fast pace, in circles. Glimpses of rapidly developing devices are changing at a speed like a "blink of an eye." Then I see a messenger of the Lord wearing a white robe standing on a pristine beach, where the sand is powder white and the serene atmosphere is filled with an unimaginable peace. The ocean is extremely calm—without a single wave. I am overwhelmed by the calmness and tranquility of it. A wall made from precious White Mountain rocks is set beside the messenger of God. This exquisite white wall is erected amid this scene of the ocean and a messenger.

She speaks to me and says: **"It's going to be over in few years."**

The Meaning of This Vision

The Lord exhibited three things in this dream.

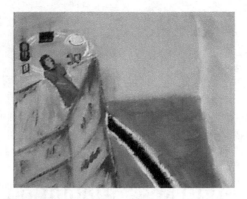

The First Symbol is the fast pace of technology. God wants us to know that upcoming judgments will be accelerated with the progression of technological growth and development. Be ready to face the unrest of nature as advanced devices and gadgets will be introduced in the market at a virtually unnoticeable rapid pace.

I saw that I am standing on top of the high-rise building wrapped with the latest technology. The tools of technology are rotating above my head in circles at a very high speed. The Lord is imparting to me that the new advanced technology (computers, cell phones, all kinds of high-tech gadgets) are the idols of today's generation. These things are placed as first priority and as people's most valuable gods. The majority of people living on the face of this earth are completely engrossed in worshipping these items day and night, similar to the idolaters in the Bible who worshipped idols engraved in the high places. I also saw varieties of high-tech devices moving speedily in circles above my head, which reveals the fact that these things are hanging over people's heads senselessly. Truly, we are all observing it happen in our generation. We witness that so many are engrossed completely in the things of the world like cell phones, computer, television, radio, and more. We have broken the First Commandment of the Bible and replaced God with idols that are the things of this world. Truly, the majority is devoted to the latest technology more than worshipping The Lord God Almighty.

PSALM 78:58
For they provoked him to anger with their high places,
and moved him to jealousy with their graven images.

2 KINGS 21:3

*For he built up again the high places which Hezekiah
his father had destroyed; and he reared up altars for
Baal, and made a grove, as did Ahab king of Israel; and
worshiped all the host of heaven, and served them.*

Mankind will be judged severely because of their *idol worshiping and lust*. The **global disasters** are being accelerated to coincide with the rapidity of modern technology . . . the waves of waters will be under complete chaos.

<u>The Second Symbol</u> that the Lord showed me was an incredibly peaceful ocean. I did not notice a single wave on it. The ocean symbolizes balance of nature. God is the only one who can keep the tranquility of nature.

Natural disasters will fall all over mankind. The world will be affected by and suffer with nature's turmoil in Heaven and earth. Oceans will leave their borders on a massive and gigantic scale that the human race has never encountered before. Earthquakes, famines, tornados, floods, and other disasters will come with unimaginable rapidity and force. When you will notice extreme escalation and acceleration of technology, be ready to face these End Times Tribulations! As the messenger of the Lord said, *"It's going to be over in few years."*

We always argue against the authenticity and truth of God's revelations through human reasoning, and by scientific and human knowledge, which is limited. The concept of "global warming" is spreading like a wildfire. Detractors will deny the fact that this so-called global warming was already prophesized thousands of years ago.

REVELATION 7:1
"After this I saw four angles standing at the four corners of the earth, holding back the four winds of the earth to prevent any wind from blowing on the land or on the sea or on any tree."

REVELATION 11:13
In the same hour there was a great earthquake, and a tenth of the city fell. In the earthquake seven thousand people were killed, and the rest were afraid and gave glory to the God of heaven.

REVELATION 8:6-13
So the seven angels who had the seven trumpets prepared themselves to sound.

FIRST TRUMPET: VEGETATION STRUCK
The first angel sounded: And hail and fire followed, mingled with blood, and they were thrown to the earth. And a third of the trees were burned up, and all green grass was burned up.

SECOND TRUMPET: THE SEAS STRUCK
Then the second angel sounded: And something like a great mountain burning with fire was thrown into the sea, and a third of the sea became blood. And a third of the living creatures in the sea died, and a third of the ships were destroyed.

THIRD TRUMPET: THE WATERS STRUCK
Then the third angel sounded: And a great star fell from heaven, burning like a torch, and it fell on a third of the rivers and on the springs of water. The name of the star is Wormwood. A third of the waters became wormwood, and many men died from the water, because it was made bitter.

FOURTH TRUMPET: THE HEAVENS STRUCK
Then the fourth angel sounded: And a third of the sun
was struck, a third of the moon, and a third of the
stars, so that a third of them were darkened. A third
of the day did not shine, and likewise the night.
And I looked, and I heard an angel flying through
the midst of heaven, saying with a loud voice, "Woe,
woe, woe to the inhabitants of the earth, because
of the remaining blasts of the trumpet of the
three angels who are about to sound!"

Revelation chapters 9 and 16 also speak about global warming, together with many more reference from the Bible.

Mankind suffers only when God separates from them due to their extensive sins. We know that anything outside of God's Laws brings failures. The fact is that the sin rooted in the flesh of man always goes contrary to the will of God, and causes separation from Him. Bible history proves that people always suffered by their wrong decisions; God separated from them due to their evil works, which resulted in their own self-annihilation. Today mankind will suffer the consequences of the global warming due to their unprincipled wisdom, which is being used for the satisfaction of the flesh with greed and lust.

Man's scientific advancement has caused climate changes and gravitation alienation, which will also bring suffering for the whole world. History also has proven that the people of any nation or kingdom have always prospered when they lived in obedience to the Lord. God designed the principles and commandments to discipline our lives. His disciplinary structure bestowed mankind with riches of life in abundance of love, peace, joy, security, and wealth. God will not guide us with His constructive wisdom anymore—not until we purify ourselves by removing ourselves from the things of the world (our idols) and evil works, as He is pure.

1 CORINTHIANS 1:20
Where is the wise? Where is the scribe? Where is the disputer of this
age? Has not God made foolish the wisdom of this world?

Though mankind is suffering tremendously due to his evil works, and rejecting God, many will still **not repent** because they love to obey the lust of their flesh rather than the **Lord God Almighty**.

> **REVELATION 9:20, 21**
> *But the rest of mankind, who were not killed by*
> *these plagues, did not repent of the works of their*
> *hands, that they should not worship demons, and*
> *idols of gold, silver, brass, stone, and wood, which*
> *can neither see nor hear nor walk. And they*
> *did not repent of their murders or their sorceries*
> *or their sexual immorality or their thefts.*

The Third Symbol in this dream was the final statement of God's messenger: *"It's going to be over in few years."*

I experienced two things in my spirit when the messenger said, *"It's going to be over in few years."* One was the overwhelmingly high pace of technology, and other was the extraordinary serene water at the beach. It means that the peace of nature will be over in few years—when we experience the exceedingly advanced technology before us like the blink of an eye. It is very important to understand why God would give us a warning of a few years! The reason is that the Lord has assigned these years for all of His servants to be sealed for His discipleship, as mentioned in Revelation 7:1-3.

REVELATION 7
*After this I saw four angels standing at the four corners of the
earth, holding back the four winds of the earth to prevent any
wind from blowing on the land or on the sea or on any tree.
Then I saw another angel coming up from the east, having
the seal of the living God. He called out in a loud voice to the four
angels who had been given power to harm the land and the sea:
"Do not harm the land or the sea or the trees until we put
a seal on the foreheads of the servants of our God."*

These verses clearly indicate that God is in control of nature as "four angels standing at the four corners of the earth, holding back the four winds of the earth to prevent any wind from blowing on the land or on the sea or on any tree." In verse 3, these angels are instructed not to harm nature until the servants of God are sealed on their foreheads. The messenger in my vision said, **"It's going to be over in few years,"** which is indicating the fulfillment of Revelation 7:3, when a seal will be placed on the foreheads of the servants of the LORD.

The Perception of This Revelation

The Lord revealed His ideology through His Word. He led me to 2 Chronicles 36 to identify the grounds for the upcoming judgments on Earth. This passage draws a comparison between our societies at present with the works of kingdoms in the past. Concentrate on this undisclosed mystery and learn the facts from God's perception.

2 CHRONICLES 36:1-4
THE REIGN AND CAPTIVITY OF JEHOAHAZ
*Then the people of the land took Jehoahaz the son of
Josiah, and made him king in his father's place in Jerusalem.
Jehoahaz was twenty-three years old when he became king,
and he reigned three months in Jerusalem. Now the king of
Egypt deposed him at Jerusalem; and he imposed on the land a
tribute of one hundred talents of silver and a talent of gold.
Then the king of Egypt made Jehoahaz's brother Eliakim king
over Judah and Jerusalem, and changed his name to Jehoiakim. And*

Necho took Jehoahaz his brother and carried him off to Egypt.

From verses 1 through 4 we learn that the king of Egypt replaced the king of Judah, Jehoahaz, with his evil brother, king Eliakim, to rule over Judah and Jerusalem. The king of Egypt enthroned him with a new name—Jehoiakim—and took Jehoahaz captive to Egypt. Likewise, satan, who rules the land of sin (Egypt symbolizes the world) has removed the righteous rulers from every corner of our world; he has replaced them with evildoers appointed by him, with new names, ordained to war against the will of God.

Let's continue to read the passage to understand the roots of the troubles, because they are the same in all ages.

Continuation of 2 CHRONICLES 36

2 CHRONICLES 36:5-16

THE REIGN AND CAPTIVITY OF JEHOIAKIM

Jehoiakim was twenty-five years old when he became king, and he reigned eleven years in Jerusalem. And he did evil in the sight of the LORD his God. Nebuchadnezzar king of Babylon came up against him, and bound him in bronze fetters to carry him off to Babylon. Nebuchadnezzar also carried off some of the articles from the house of the LORD to Babylon, and put them in his temple at Babylon. Now the rest of the acts of Jehoiakim, the abominations which he did, and what was found against him, indeed they are written in the book of thekings of Israel and Judah.
Then Jehoiachin his son reigned in his place.

THE REIGN AND CAPTIVITY OF JEHOIACHIM

Jehoiachin was eight years old when he became king, and he reigned in Jerusalem three months and ten days. And he did evil in the sight of the LORD. At the turn of the year King Nebuchadnezzar summoned him and took him to Babylon, with the costly articles from the house of the LORD, and made Zedekiah, Jehoiakim's brother, king over Judah and Jerusalem.

ZEDEKIAH REIGNS IN JUDAH

Zedekiah was twenty-one years old when he became king, and he reigned eleven years in Jerusalem. He did evil in the sight of the LORD his God, and did not humble himself before Jeremiah the prophet, who spoke from the mouth of the LORD. And he also rebelled against King Nebuchadnezzar, who had made him swear an oath by God; but he stiffened his neck and hardened his heart against turning to the LORD God of Israel. Moreover all the leaders of the priests and the people transgressed more and more, according to all the abominations of the nations, and defiled the house of the LORD which He had consecrated in Jerusalem.

THE FALL OF JERUSALEM

And the LORD God of their fathers sent warnings to them by His messengers, rising up early and sending them, because He had compassion on His people and on His dwelling place. But they mocked the messengers of God, despised His words, and scoffed at His prophets, until the wrath of the LORD arose against His people, till there was no remedy.

Verses 5 through 14 addresses that King Jehoiakim, King Jehoiachin, and King Zedekiah *"did evil in the sight of the LORD."* This act result-ed in their captivity to the king of Babylon, who took them along with the costly articles from the house of the Lord. God is highlighting an important factor here—their pattern of evil works continuing from one generation to the next. Similarly, the human race is living in sin today from generation to generation. Satan (the King of Babylon is a symbol of him) gets a legal right (from us, by our behavior) to enslave sinners under his authority and to snatch away the treasures that the Lord has entrusted to our possession. Today, mankind is suffering with financial depression because we are enslaved by satan. The prophet Jeremiah was sent to king Zedekiah to guide, to warn, and to correct all evil works. This was due to God's unconditional love toward the Hebrews, but Ze-dekiah did exactly what mankind is doing today: many have stiffened their necks and hardened their hearts and resisted turning back to the Lord.

Moreover, many of the leaders, priests, and the people have transgressed in a progressive fashion, according to all the abominations of malevolence and so, herewith, have defiled the will of God. But God will keep sending messengers who will speak from His mouth because of His compassion and mercy for mankind. However, when people continue to mock the messengers of God and despise His words intensely, the **wrath of God** will arise and there will be no remedy left.

Mankind will face the same judgments as he did in the past. Our earth will fall exactly the same way as Jerusalem fell for its evil works. Let's read the next verse to understand God's warning for all mankind.

Continuation of 2 CHRONICLES 36
2 CHRONICLES 36:17

Therefore He brought against them the king of the Chaldeans, who killed their young men with the sword in the house of their sanctuary, and had no compassion on young man or virgin, on the aged or the weak; He gave them all into his hand.

History will repeat itself with the dominance of the ruthless king of the Chaldeans over all the nations of the world. It will be the cause of great trouble. These enemies of the Lord and His people will have no compassion on young man or virgin, or on the aged or the weak, because of their great sins and rejection of God's messengers who are sent for their guidance and correction. Satan can control and empower over the human race only when the Lord is not with man anymore as his Ruler, Shepherd, and Savior.

God will not tolerate mankind installing and worshiping idols at high places because high places belong to Him. They are meant for us to habitate so God can dwell with and among us. We invite His wrath when we rip off **His** place in order to position satan with our graven idols in high places.

The occupation of the high place was the very first rebellious desire of corrupted hearts, just as we read in Isaiah 14:13, 14.

ISAIAH 14
"For you have said in your heart:
'I will ascend into heaven,
I will exalt my throne above the stars of God;
I will also sit on the mount of the congregation
On the farthest sides of the north;
I will ascend above the heights of the clouds,
I will be like the Most High.'"

Lucifer speaks of his desire to occupy the personal habitation place of God. That was his primary obsession, and it still is. He accomplishes this act of defiance because we allow him to blind us to the fact that he craves the worship that belongs to God. He deceived Adam and Eve and he is deceiving us even now. This desire has survived through the ages and is resident in every degenerate heart. It is functioning in our midst through technology. You will agree that, truly, technology has become our primary obsession and nations are completely lost in its lust. We will be judged similar to the nation of Israel when the Israelites perpetrated the abomination against God with their graven images. Finally, the Lord will bring a shaking to bring down the idols that men have placed before Him. Remember: God's messenger told me, *"It's going to be over in few years."*

Are we ready to destroy altars used for idolatry and remove them from the high places of our hearts, minds, and souls?

DEUTERONOMY 12:2, 3
You shall utterly destroy all the places where the nations which
you shall dispossess served their gods, on the high mountains
and on the hills and under every green tree. And you shall
destroy their altars, break their sacred pillars, and burn their
wooden images with fire; you shall cut down the carved images
of their gods and destroy their names from that place.

God has blessed us with a forewarning. When technology increases rapidly into highly advanced devices, our Earth will go through major shakings. The peace of nature will be shaken. Mankind will experience an outbreak of natural disasters in Heaven and on earth; this will happen together with the conflict between the nations of the world.

Please do not blame God for all these tribulations toward mankind. Our sins are the reason for everything. The sooner we recognize our sins, the sooner we can repent and surrender our lives to God. With that, the eternal death, hell, and God's judgment will not rule over us because our sins will be washed through the blood of the Lord Jesus Christ.

ACTS 4:12
"Nor is there salvation in any other, for there is no other name under heaven given among men by which we must be saved."

Please do not allow the Father in Heaven to grieve at His creation, which He made with extreme compassion and care.

GENESIS 6:6
And the LORD was sorry that He had made man on the earth, and He was grieved in His heart.

CHAPTER 4

God's Final Verdict

The Lord communicated to me the third time about His final Day of Judgment. In the morning worship of Monday, April 7, 2008, the Holy Spirit led me to Zephaniah chapter 1. God is conveying about whom, why, and what type of people will be judged. It is my humble prayer that no one falls among such group of people, who will be destroyed due to their deeds, which are unacceptable in the eyes of the Lord. It is extremely important to comprehend this message in order to save our selves and our loved ones.

ZEPHANIAH 1:1-3
The word of the LORD which came to Zephaniah the son
of Cushi, the son of Gedaliah, the son of Amariah, the son of
Hezekiah, in the days of Josiah the son of Amon, king of Judah.

The Great Day of the LORD
"I will utterly consume everything
From the face of the land,"
Says the LORD;

"I will consume man and beast;
I will consume the birds of the heavens,
The fish of the sea,
And the stumbling blocks along with the wicked.
I will cut off man from the face of the land,"
Says the LORD.

Verses 2 and 3 indicate the intensity of God's judgment, which will utterly consume everything on earth due to the stumbling blocks of evil works on earth. They rejected the voice of God for sake of their own, self-stimulated beliefs. The end of all evil will come.

How—and with what—can everything be utterly consumed from the face of the land?

- A single and powerful volcano?
- A giant earthquake?
- A fire from heaven?
- A giant asteroid?
- The powers of Heaven will shake to fall on the earth?

My dear brothers and sisters, do not live in denial. Have we ever considered . . .

- What if this will happen in our lives?
- Where do we stand in the eyes of the Lord?
- What is the true righteousness that God desires?
- Are we "good enough" to get saved from this judgment?
- Do we believe, trust, love, and worship God 100 percent?

Let us all be honest and look at our selves not from our standpoint, but from God's perception. Let's discern God's message from the rest of the verses of this chapter.

Continuation of ZEPHANIAH 1
ZEPHANIAH 1:4-6
"I will stretch out My hand against Judah,
And against all the inhabitants of Jerusalem.
I will cut off every trace of Baal from this place,

The names of the idolatrous priests with the pagan priests—
Those who worship the host of heaven on the housetops;
Those who worship and swear oaths by the LORD,
But who also swear by Milcom;
Those who have turned back from following the LORD,
And have not sought the LORD, nor inquired of Him."

These verses explain what kind of **worship God does not desire**.
God is rejecting the types of people listed below. He will stretch out His hands against them:

- Those who are the idolatrous and pagan priests. God will pull out the seed of mischief that has grown the tree of evil and brought the fruit that misguided and destroyed million of souls that He made with extreme care, love, and for His purpose. Yes, God's justified hand will stretch against all hypocrite and evil preachers, teachers, and counselors first. The Lord will not spare the pagan priests who misguided innocent mankind toward idol worshipping in defiance against their Creator.

- Those who do not believe in God's existence. They worship idols made with their own hands or the host of heaven. These people worship everything in the heavens and earth that benefit them, but refuse to worship the Creator.

- Those who are the hypocrites, are simply double-minded, who call upon the name of the Lord but do not trust God completely because their confidence in other gods is greater than the one who created them. The reason is that they are devoid of His love.

- Those who have turned their backs to the Lord and do not even care to know about Him. They will also face God's judgment. Such people are completely lost in the things of the world. They live, eat, drink, and are merry. They will not bother to inquire about God and His will, even until the last day, when they will be utterly consumed from the face of the land.

Let's **look at our idols**—or *Milcom*—of whom we swear and worship, in reality:

- A great number of humanity worship engraved images made from their own hands that they honor and rely on. They defy their own Creator and the Creator of all those things that they bow down to, like the sun, moon, stars, animals, trees, plants, and more.

- Mankind counterfeits the only true Lord God Almighty with man-made gods. For example, we pretend to believe in the Lord but seek psychics, astrologers, white witches, black witches, and many other kinds of idols installed at high places that we depend upon, more than God.
- Our idols are also materialistic strengths like wealth, prestigious status, pride, beauty, intelligence, knowledge, talents, and **our power.**
- We love and trust people more than God, such as a father, mother, husband, wife, son, or daughter, or any other human relationship.
- We honor and obey man-made governments and their laws more than the Lord's commandments.
- Simply, anything that we put in first place before the Lord is our idol.

Continuation of ZEPHANIAH 1
ZEPHANIAH 1:7, 8
Be silent in the presence of the Lord GOD;
For the day of the LORD is at hand,
For the LORD has prepared a sacrifice;
He has invited His guests.
"And it shall be,
In the day of the LORD's sacrifice,
That I will punish the princes and the king's children,
And all such as are clothed with foreign apparel."

Verse 7 illustrates the blessed people who belong to God and are clothed as His guests. God has bid His obedient children to be protected from His day of judgment.

Verse 8 portrays those people who are princes and king's children. They love, rely on, and worship the wealth and the riches of this world because they falsely believe that they are princes and kings who own this world. All those who are clothed in foreign apparel are the ones who do not belong to God. They are dressed in denial and disobedience to the will of the Lord. They reject God's will for living a lifestyle to satisfy their selfish and evil desires of the flesh. They are called the princes and the king's children because the only voice they heard and obeyed all the days of their lives was of the prince of the air (satan). As we read in Ephesians 2:2, *"in which you once walked according to the course of this world, according to the prince of the power of the air, the spirit who now works in the sons of disobedience."*

In Matthew 22 the Lord Jesus Christ mentioned the exact incidence of Zephaniah 1:7, 8 that will happen at the Great Day of the Lord. Let's read Matthew 22 for clearer understanding.

Matthew 22:1-13

And Jesus answered and spoke to them again by parables and said:
"The kingdom of heaven is like a certain king who arranged marriage
for his son, and sent out his servants to call those who were
invited to the wedding; and they were not willing to come.
Again, he sent out other servants, saying, 'Tell those who are invited,
"See, I have prepared my dinner; my oxen and fatted cattle are killed,
and all things are ready. Come to the wedding."'
But they made light of it and went their ways, one to his own farm,
another to his business.
And the rest seized his servants,
treated them spitefully, and killed them.
But when the king heard about it, he was furious. And he
sent out his armies, destroyed those murderers,
and burned up their city.
Then he said to his servants, 'The wedding is ready, but those who
were invited were not worthy.
Therefore go into the highways,
and as many as you find, invite to the wedding.'
So those servants went out into the highways and gathered together
all whom they found, both bad and good.
And the wedding hall was filled with guests.
"But when the king came in to see the guests, he saw a man
there who did not have on a wedding garment.

So he said to him, 'Friend, how did you come in here
without a wedding garment?'
And he was speechless.
Then the king said to the servants, 'Bind him hand and foot, take him
away, and cast him into outer darkness; there will
be weeping and gnashing of teeth.'"

In this parable God wants us to understand those who are worthy to be a part of the great heavenly celebration of the salvation of saints in His Kingdom. Many who are chosen are found unworthy due to lack of their knowledge about God's will. They made light of God's messages and went their ways to earthly chores. The rest seized His servants, treated them spitefully, and killed them. Therefore, God will send His armies to destroy them on His Great Day.

God will ceaselessly send out His servants to publish the invitation at every corner and with every soul on earth to come and join the great celebration for their salvation that the Lord has given freely to all those who will accept His calling. Multitudes came to join this great heavenly feast, but some did not bother to dress appropriately according to the banquet's requirements. For they are found dressed in the rags of their spiritual filthiness in spite of such an awesome privilege to join the Kingdom of God in holiness. Finally the King of kings and the Lord of lords will tell His servants to bind them hand and foot, take them away, and cast them into outer darkness, where there will be weeping and gnashing of teeth.

Continuation of ZEPHANIAH 1
ZEPHANIAH 1:9
In the same day I will punish
All those who leap over the threshold,
Who fill their masters' houses with violence and deceit.

On the Great Day of the Lord every misconduct and evil of mankind will be judged. God will punish all those who have filled His house (earth) with violence, deceit, abuse, misuse, and torture to slaughter the innocent. That day will be the end of child molesters, drug and child sex traffickers, evil politicians, sex addicts, and every other evildoer (the list of sins is very long).

In **ZECHARIAH 8, VERSES 16 AND 17,** God says:
"But this is what you must do: Tell the truth to each other. Render the verdicts in your courts that are just and that lead to peace. Don't scheme against each other. Stop your love of telling lies that you swear are the truth. I hate all these things, says the Lord."

Praise the Lord for such a fair judgment against the evil on earth. Rejoice all you pure and innocent people who are abused and tortured from the hands of evildoers; the Master of this house (world) has come to avenge every violence and deceit. He will give you the permanent shelter where peace, joy, and love will prevail forever.

Continuation of **ZEPHANIAH 1**
ZEPHANIAH 1:10, 11
"And there shall be on that day," says the LORD,
"The sound of a mournful cry from the Fish Gate,
A wailing from the Second Quarter,
And a loud crashing from the hills."
Wail, you inhabitants of Maktesh!
"For all the merchant people are cut down;
All those who handle money are cut off."

Listen, all ye the inhabitants of this earth, for the Great Day of the Lord has come that will bring forth the mournful cry and a loud crashing from the hills. The Lord will cut off the eminent merchant people, money hoarders, and money handlers, who desire to be the kings and queens to rule the world. They have rejected the Great King Lord due to their pride in the wealth and treasures that has blinded them to see the truth. Therefore, the King of kings will cut off all money worshippers from the face of the earth.

Continuation of ZEPHANIAH 1
ZEPHANIAH 1:12
"And it shall come to pass at that time
That I will search Jerusalem with lamps,
And punish the men
Who are settled in complacency,
Who say in their heart,
'The LORD will not do good,
Nor will He do evil.'"

Verse 12 is pointing out to those who always lived in contentment of their self-righteousness, under a false impression that God will not judge nor will do right, that they misguide themselves and love to live as their heart desires. They deny the truth because they do not want to give up their blinded, sinful lifestyle to acknowledge God's will, which leads to repentance, and helps transform to the holiness of the LORD; that would be too boring and dry for them. Therefore, God will search them with lamps (no one can hide) to be judged fairly on the Day of the Lord.

Continuation of ZEPHANIAH 1
ZEPHANIAH 1:13
Therefore their goods shall become booty,
And their houses a desolation;
They shall build houses, but not inhabit them;
They shall plant vineyards, but not drink their wine.

Verse 13 helps us to understand the vanity of things that man trusted and worshipped. Our plans of life will be shattered because we did not seek the Lord's communion and His participation in our lives. We have thrown God behind our backs and have become gods in our own eyes. We have rejected the ruler of this universe and have become the ruler of our own lives. There is no room for God in our home, work, or hearts. We have built a room full of greed and lust right in the center of our lives to rule us and destroy our relationship with God. The Lord wants to rule our lives only to give us peace and joy and to rescue us from the hands of the enemy. Our enemy is our trust in the work of our own hands that we build to buy security and prosperity. Such works and things are merely shallow, unreliable, and perishable. Man's trust in himself will be shaken and destroyed. They will build houses but not inhabit them. They shall plant vineyards but not drink their wine. Praise the Lord for His righteous judgments.

Continuation of ZEPHANIAH 1
ZEPHANIAH 1:14-17

The great day of the LORD is near;
It is near and hastens quickly.
The noise of the day of the LORD is bitter;
There the mighty men shall cry out.
That day is a day of wrath,
A day of trouble and distress,
A day of devastation and desolation,
A day of darkness and gloominess,
A day of clouds and thick darkness,
A day of trumpet and alarm
Against the fortified cities
And against the high towers.
"I will bring distress upon men,
And they shall walk like blind men,
Because they have sinned against the LORD ;
Their blood shall be poured out like dust,
And their flesh like refuse."

Verses 14 to 17 is the voice of the LORD crying to the cities that, "you will be judged for the sins you have done against Me." The Great Day of the Lord is very near, in which mighty men shall cry for their inequities. They sold themselves into the hands of satan and did evil against the innocent. They were blinded with the shimmering gold, deaf with the sound of devil's false promises. Their mouths opened in self-worshiping and shut to praise the one who created them. The Lord called them all their lives through the voices of His servants to repent to find salvation in their Savior—their God. But they rejected the voices of repentance due to their hypocrisy, pride, and ego. They became puppets in the hands of their master, satan, to hurt and kill God's servants. In spite of their extreme cruelties, God gave them multiple chances out of His unconditional love, but they refused constantly.

Alas, the Great Day of His Judgment is near, which will be:

- The day of wrath
- A day of trouble and distress
- A day of devastation and desolation
- A day of darkness, gloominess, clouds, and thick darkness
- A day of trumpet and alarm against the fortified cities and high towers

That day will be so distressing that mankind will walk like a blind man, completely confused and stressed. That day will be a day of death for sinners and evildoers. On that day their blood will be poured out like dust and their flesh like refuse. That day will be the end of all evil.

Continuation of ZEPHANIAH 1

ZEPHANIAH 1:18

Neither their silver nor their gold
Shall be able to deliver them
In the day of the LORD's wrath;
But the whole land shall be devoured
By the fire of His jealousy,
For He will make speedy riddance
Of all those who dwell in the land.

Verse 18 helps mankind with an awareness of the worthlessness of the riches of this earth. Men hoard wealth with faith in its power to protect them in times of need and trouble. Many lose their souls for the love of wealth and prosperity in this materialistic world. Their trust is in their own capabilities and riches, instead of the Lord God Almighty. Neither their silver nor gold will deliver them from the day of the Lord's wrath. That day will be the end of every idol that men have worshipped, including themselves. Only God and His righteousness will prevail forever, because He is alpha and omega—the beginning and the end. His rule remains forever because He is the King of kings and the Lord of lords.

Dear friend, I beg of you to separate yourself from this list of people mentioned in Zephaniah chapter 1. You still have time until this Day of Judgment of the Lord, which is coming very soon. Humble yourself and repent. Seek God's mercy in the only Savior and Messiah—the Lord Jesus Christ. He is the only way to your salvation. He came to earth only to save you! Read His promises, which are the light, life, and truth for each and every person living on earth.

JOHN 14:6

Jesus said to him, "I am the way, the truth, and the life.
No one comes to the Father except through Me."

JOHN 10:9

"I am the door. If anyone enters by Me, he will be saved,
and will go in and find pasture . . . I have come that they may
have life, and that they may have it more abundantly."

JOHN 11:25

Jesus said to her, "I am the resurrection and the life. He
who believes in Me, though he may die, he shall live. And
whoever lives and believes in Me shall never die."

JOHN 8:12

Then Jesus spoke to them again, saying, "I am the
light of the world. He who follows Me shall not
walk in darkness, but have the light of life."

Our covenant faith and relationship in the Lord Jesus Christ can save us from the Day of Judgment.

CHAPTER 5

Jeremiah 24's Relevance in the End Times

The HOUR of your DECISION has arrived

The Holy Spirit revealed to me at about 3 AM on January 14, 2011 that, *"A camera has arrived that can focus inside-out of a human body. It is so powerful that it can gaze at every cell of a human body. Nothing can be hidden that cannot be revealed."*

The living Word of God in Hebrews 4:13 agrees with the spiritual manifestation that the Lord imparted to let mankind be aware that no one must live in deception, that their evil works cannot be concealed under superficial humanitarian pretense, because all things are naked and open before the Lord. An hour of judgment has arrived when all the hidden works of mankind will be revealed and judged.

HEBREWS 4:13
And there is no creature hidden from His sight,
but all things are naked and open to the eyes of
Him to whom we must give account.

I did not know the significance of this vision; therefore I asked the

Lord to help me with its understanding. The Lord led me to His Word in Jeremiah 24, which is a picture of this dream. Let's read and understand it together with the guidance and wisdom of the Holy Spirit.

JEREMIAH 24:1
The LORD shewed me, and, behold, two baskets of figs were set before the temple of the LORD; after that Nebuchadrezzar king of Babylon had carried away captive Jeconiah the son of Jehoiakim king of Judah, and the princes of Judah, with the carpenters and smiths, from Jerusalem, and had brought them to Babylon.

In verse 1 the figs represent each and every individual living on earth. The temple of the Lord is a portrayal of the Kingdom of God; King Nebuchadrezzar represents the captivity of satan and that Babylon is our cursed Earth. The individuals are brought down in two separate baskets before the Lord during the season of their captivity under satan's dominion all over the earth. These people will be brought before the temple of the Lord from every class, caste, and creed.

Continuation of **JEREMIAH 24:2, 3**
One basket had very good figs, even like the figs that are first ripe: and the other basket had very naughty figs, which could not be eaten, they were so bad. Then said the LORD unto me, What seest thou, Jeremiah? And I said, Figs; the good figs, very good; and the evil, very evil, that cannot be eaten, they are so evil.

Verses 2 and 3 clearly signify an intense contrast between good and evil. Near the end of times the world will witness extremes of both. The urgent hour of our decision has come; a path of righteousness or unrighteousness. It is very important to understand that there is no mixture of good and bad. All those who decide to put their feet in both baskets are foolish. A person cannot afford to choose to play this dangerous game anymore. Revelation 3:14-17 confirms this statement. Please read this passage carefully.

REVELATION 3:14-17

"And to the angel of the church of the Laodiceans write,
'These things says the Amen, the Faithful and True
Witness, the Beginning of the creation of God:
"I know your works, that you are neither cold
nor hot. I could wish you were cold or hot.
So then, because you are lukewarm, and neither
cold nor hot, I will vomit you out of My mouth.
Because you say, 'I am rich, have become wealthy,
and have need of nothing'—and do not know that you
are wretched, miserable, poor, blind, and naked"

Revelation 3:14-17 goes hand in hand with Jeremiah 24:2, 3. The Lord will spit out the lukewarm who are hypocrites, as described by the Lord Jesus Christ in Matthew 23:27: *"Woe to you, scribes and Pharisees, hypocrites! For you are like whitewashed tombs which indeed appear beautiful outwardly, but inside are full of dead men's bones and all uncleanness."* The Lord will discard the cold: those who have denied God and harden their hearts towards His love and mercies. Blessed are the hot who desire His intimate love relationship that gives merciful salvation through the Lord Jesus Christ. Finally, the Lord is dividing a margin line to pick and choose good for the Kingdom of God, and the rest will be cast out among people (figs) that *"could not be eaten, they were so bad"* for eternal damnation. The people (figs) that the Lord chooses are *"like the figs that are first ripe."* God will embrace all that are humble and meek, for their hearts are pure like fresh, ripe figs.

Continuation of JEREMIAH 24
JEREMIAH 24:4-7

Again the word of the LORD came unto me, saying,
Thus saith the LORD, the God of Israel; Like these
good figs, so will I acknowledge them that are carried
away captive of Judah, whom I have sent out of this
place into the land of the Chaldeans for their good.
For I will set mine eyes upon them for good, and I will bring
them again to this land: and I will build them, and not pull

them down; and I will plant them, and not pluck them up.
And I will give them a heart to know me, that I am the
LORD: and they shall be my people, and I will be their
God: for they shall return unto me with their whole heart.

Verses 4-7 are overpowered with Lord's love and mercy for the captives of Judah who are living in the land of the Chaldeans (our earth). They are called and chosen out of the whole world for the Lord's purpose, which benefits them as well as others through their obedient discipleship. Don't be disheartened, for the Lord has left you in your assigned position for a great purpose. As in verse 5 we read, " . . . whom I have sent out of this place into the land of the Chaldeans for their good." Yes, the Lord has left us here for our own good, because we are the work of His precious hands designed for His glory to become good figs, just like verse 2: *"One basket had very good figs, even like the figs that are first ripe."*

Are you ready for the Lord's great plans for you?

YES! The Lord will set His eyes upon you. He will bring you to this land of His dominion to build and plant you. The Lord will give you a heart of flesh that will know and understand Him. You shall return to your Lord God with your whole heart.

God's decision is a very serious matter. There is no stopping the Lord's plans. God's love is calling you LOUD and CLEAR. Do not rebel and take pride in human wisdom. Our perception cannot prevail before the WISDOM OF THE MOST HIGH GOD. It is not wise to shut our eyes and ears to the truth, especially during these times of great disasters and tribulations that will inevitably come. Get rid of all hypocrisy. If we still resist God's love and mercy with the obstinate choice to repudiate, then verses 8-10 are for us.

Continuation of **JEREMIAH 24**
JEREMIAH 24:8-10
And as the evil figs, which cannot be eaten, they are so evil;
surely thus saith the LORD, So will I give Zedekiah the king
of Judah, and his princes, and the residue of Jerusalem, that
remain in this land, and them that dwell in the land of Egypt:

And I will deliver them to be removed into all the kingdoms
of the earth for their hurt, to be a reproach and a proverb, a
taunt and a curse, in all places whither I shall drive them.
And I will send the sword, the famine, and the
pestilence, among them, till they be consumed from off
the land that I gave unto them and to their fathers.

In verse 8 we learn that the evil fig that cannot be eaten symbolizes the people who love their evil ways and reject God's righteousness. Everyone—no matter whether ruler or slave, prince or beggar, famous or common, or rich or poor—will become slaves of sin in the land of Egypt (the world), because they rejected the liberty given in faith in the Lord.

In verse 9, the Lord said that He will deliver them to the kingdoms of the earth. We need to understand what the kingdoms of the earth are and who rules them. The Bible proves that satan is the king of the demonic kingdoms of this earth. In Matthew 4:1 we read: *"Then Jesus was led up by the Spirit into the wilderness to be tempted by the devil."* During this hour of temptation, satan showed Him all the kingdoms of the world and their glory that are under his dominion and power that he stole from Adam and Eve in the Garden of Eden. They chose to disobey the Lord God Almighty and lost their right and inheritance over all things that God put under Adam's supervision. Let's read the reference verses for clearer understanding.

MATTHEW 4:8-10
Again, the devil took Him up on an exceedingly high
mountain, and showed Him all the kingdoms of the world and
their glory. And he said to Him, "All these things I will
give You if You will fall down and worship me."
Then Jesus said to him, "Away with you, Satan!
For it is written, 'You shall worship the LORD
your God, and Him only you shall serve.'"

We have come to the conclusion that the Lord separates from us when we are the evil figs, because people have succumbed to what satan offered to the Lord Jesus Christ. Satan told Jesus, *"All these things I will* give You if You will fall down and worship me." All mankind is suffering under his slavery, for he causes the hardships of life. The people of this world have fallen down to worship the earthly pleasures. Therefore, the Lord has finalized their destinies under the kingdoms of earth by saying, *"And I will deliver them to be removed into all the kingdoms of the earth for their hurt, to be a reproach and a proverb, a taunt and a curse, in all places whither I shall drive them."*

The last verse of Jeremiah 24 gives a warning to satan's worshippers that God will send the sword, the famine, and pestilence till mankind is consumed from the surface of this earth, because the fruit of sin is death.

NO EVIL CAN BE ACCEPTED BEFORE THE THRONE OF GOD.

In Revelation 22:10, 11 the Bible says, *"And he saith unto me, Seal not the sayings of the prophecy of this book: **for the time is at hand. He that is unjust, let him be unjust still: and he which is filthy, let him be filthy still: and he that is righteous, let him be righteous still: and he that is holy, let him be holy still."***

Praise the Lord God Almighty, who has won the war of man's slavery for the salvation of His children through the sacrifice of the Lord Jesus Christ at the cross. Satan has lost his powers and his rule from all those who have chosen the King of kings as their savior. They will stand strong to destroy and win the battle against all powers of evil that can rule only over the sinners of this earth.

JOHN 18:36
Jesus answered, "My kingdom is not of this world. If my kingdom were of this world, my servants would have been fighting, that I might not be delivered over to the Jews. But my kingdom is not from the world."

DANIEL 2:44
And in the days of those kings the God of heaven will set up a kingdom that shall never be destroyed, nor shall the kingdom

*be left to another people. It shall break in pieces all these
kingdoms and bring them to an end, and it shall stand forever.*

According to the revelation in my vision of January 14, 2011, an invisible line is drawn between good and evil. The hearts, minds, and souls of every individual will be scrutinized and tested. *Those who are found humble and meek through a relationship with the Lord Jesus Christ will find a refuge and salvation.* Daniel 2:44 reveals that His Kingdom shall break the pieces of all these kingdoms of satan to bring them to an end. Only His rule will stand forever.

* * * * *

Finally, we have come to the knowledge that the dividing wall is under installation between the good and evil, between good figs and evil figs, between holy and unholy, between wise virgins and foolish virgins, and between God's followers and satan's followers. God will judge the hearts, minds, and souls of all humanity. Nothing can be hidden from the Lord God Almighty that will not be revealed on the day of His judgment. Rise and wake up to live according to the Godly consciousness before it's too late.

CHAPTER 6

The Year 2012

The Lord God Almighty showed me a vision on March 5, 2011.

I saw two numbers ascending down from Heaven. I could not read the number at the top, but I read the number underneath it. It read, "11-11-12." This number is November 11, 2012, because the Holy Spirit revealed that the number ascending from Heaven is a date. Thus, November 11, 2012 is the date of a great significance.

God always gives me an understanding of dreams and visions from His Word or straight from an interpretation of a vision. I received no other revelation besides this number and an understanding in Spirit that it is a date. I asked God what I would tell the world about this. I had no idea what would happen that day.

The Lord led me to Scripture in the Bible and revealed that November 11, 2012 coincided with Isaiah 5. This Scripture will open our minds to an understanding of Lord's loving heart for His people and a prediction of what the date 11-11-12 stands for. Let's read and understand it together with the guidance of the Holy Spirit.

ISAIAH 5:1-7
God's Disappointing Vineyard
Now let me sing to my Well-beloved
A song of my Beloved regarding His vineyard:
My Well-beloved has a vineyard
On a very fruitful hill.
He dug it up and cleared out its stones,
And planted it with the choicest vine.
He built a tower in its midst,
And also made a winepress in it;
So He expected it to bring forth good grapes,
But it brought forth wild grapes.
"And now, O inhabitants of Jerusalem and men of Judah,
Judge, please, between Me and My vineyard.
What more could have been done to My vineyard
That I have not done in it?
Why then, when I expected it to bring forth good grapes,
Did it bring forth wild grapes?
And now, please let Me tell you what I will do to My vineyard:
I will take away its hedge, and it shall be burned;
And break down its wall, and it shall be trampled down.
I will lay it waste;
It shall not be pruned or dug,
But there shall come up briers and thorns.
I will also command the clouds
That they rain no rain on it."
For the vineyard of the Lord of hosts is the house of Israel,
And the men of Judah are His pleasant plant.
He looked for justice, but behold, oppression;
For righteousness, but behold, a cry for help.

We will try to understand the message of the Lord God Almighty, who created this earth with great care with an expectation of an abundance of good works of mankind in His loving relationship, just like a gardener who builds a vineyard with an expectation of a great harvest of good quality grapes. Isaiah 5 is referring to God as a builder of a vineyard.

Isaiah 5:1 is an expression of God's sentiment for mankind. God brought forth this earth from the depths of waters and formatted it for us to dwell in within the righteousness of His will. We are His well-beloved, formed over a very fruitful hill that is the Lord Jesus Christ. As we read in John 1:3: *"All things were made by him; and without him was not anything made that was made."*

John 15: 1-6 goes hand in hand with **Isaiah 5:1-6** to inscribe on hearts that the Lord Jesus Christ is a true vine in whom all who abide bear good fruit and that those who reject Him are cast out of His presence. Let's read what Jesus said in these verses for our better understanding.

JOHN 15:1-6

I am the true vine, and my Father is the husbandman.
Every branch in me that beareth not fruit he taketh away: and every
branch that beareth fruit, he purgeth it,
that it may bring forth more fruit.
Now ye are clean through the word which I have spoken unto you.
Abide in me, and I in you. As the branch cannot bear fruit of itself,
except it abide in the vine; no more can ye, except ye abide in me.
I am the vine, ye are the branches: He that abideth
in me, and I in him, the same bringeth forth much
fruit: for without me ye can do nothing.
If a man abide not in me, he is cast forth as a
branch, and is withered; and men gather them, and
cast them into the fire, and they are burned.

John 15:1-6 is relating the same message as Isaiah 5:1-6, which points to the truth about man's position in life, that he perishes without God and His relationship.

We also learn in these verses that in the midst of His creation, we are given a tower, the Lord Jesus Christ, before whom every knee shall bow. It is said in Isaiah 5:2 that *"He built a tower in its midst."* Surely the Lord Jesus Christ is our tower. No one can comprehend, nor can obey, the will of the Heavenly Father without abiding in the Son of God, because the Lord Jesus Christ was justified in saying, in John 15:5, that *"I am the vine, ye are the branches: He that abideth in me, and I in him, the same bringeth forth much fruit: for without me ye can do nothing."* Surely no other name is given in Heaven, on earth, and under the earth by which righteousness can rule over our lives. The attributes of the Lord Jesus Christ fulfill all the Holy Scriptures because He is a tower in the midst of universe, a tree of life in <u>the Garden of Eden</u>, and a <u>true vine of earth</u>.

The Lord has expressed His disappointment over His vineyard in Isaiah 5:1-7. All those who refuse to abide in one true vine that can bring forth good fruit will be cast into the Hell of fire due to their self-righteousness. These are people whose evil works are like wild grapes. The wisdom, teachings, and the counsel of God will be withdrawn from them because of His separation from ungodliness. God's communion helps to prune His people to bring plentiful good works (the grapes in a vine). Alas, the evil of this world will be left alone to live in their filth and sins like briers and thorns. God will not shower His Word, which nourishes mankind like a fresh rain. He will eventually separate from sinners according to His words in Isaiah 5:6: *"I will lay it waste; it shall not be pruned or dug, But there shall come up briers and thorns. I will also command the clouds that they rain no rain on it."* God has entrenched His vineyard with indescribable love, but heartbreakingly, His disappointing vineyard brings forth only wild grapes instead of the wonderful works of righteousness. It is painful to recognize God's hurtful statement about mankind in Isaiah 5:4: "What could have been done more to my vineyard, that I have not done in it? Wherefore, when I looked that it should bring forth grapes, brought it forth wild grapes?"

Would you not agree with the following woes pronounced on wicked humanity, that has trodden the love and works of the Lord under foot?

Continuance of **Isaiah 5**
Isaiah 5:8-11
Impending Judgment on Excesses
Woe to those who join house to house;
They add field to field, Till there is no place
Where they may dwell alone in the midst of the land!
In my hearing the LORD of hosts said,

"Truly, many houses shall be desolate,
Great and beautiful ones, without inhabitant.
For ten acres of vineyard shall yield one bath,
And a homer of seed shall yield one ephah."
Woe to those who rise early in the morning,
That they may follow intoxicating drink;
Who continue until night, till wine inflames them!
The harp and the strings,
The tambourine and flute,
And wine are in their feasts;
But they do not regard the work of the LORD,
Nor consider the operation of His hands.

In these verses we learn about man's wicked heart, which always desires to go against the will of the Lord. We will learn in detail what sort of insanity of mankind that God removes from His holy presence.

- Woe to those whose bellies burst out with the greed and loot of the things of this world while they overlook their neighbor's needs. Harshly in their blinded greed they *"join house to house; They add field to field, Till there is no place."*

- This hardhearted and selfish characteristic of mankind against his neighbor removes the peace and joy from the world. No wonder God will judge righteously for such behavior by desolating the house of greed and removing the abundance of blessing from them, as God said, *"Truly, many houses shall be desolate, Great and beautiful ones, without inhabitant. For ten acres of vineyard shall yield one bath, And a homer of seed shall yield one ephah."*

- Woe to those who begin and end their days worshipping idols. Man's gigantic idol is self-worship and the satisfaction of the sinful desires of the flesh. Every kind of evil gives birth from such insanity. Yes, mankind is blinded to God's perfect will and therefore accepts no counsel and guidance from Him. Our world is exceedingly intoxicated and blinded in immorality, similar to: *"That they may follow intoxicating drink; Who continue until night, till wine inflames them! The harp and the strings, The tambourine and flute, And wine are in their feasts."* Mankind is obstinate to regard God's will: *"But they do not regard the work of the LORD, Nor consider the operation of His hands."*

Continuance of ISAIAH 5

ISAIAH 5:13

Therefore my people have gone into captivity,
Because they have no knowledge;
Their honorable men are famished,
And their multitude dried up with thirst.

Isaiah 5:13 is enlightening us that mankind plunges into the captivity of sin, death, and damnation only when the Lord God Almighty is insignificant in their lives. Naturally, people who consider God as trivial would not care to know about Him or His commandments. This is why God said, *"Therefore my people have gone into captivity, Because they have no knowledge."* Such people are easily captivated into the works of evil. Truly, ignorance of God diverts our attention to the knowledge of man's deadly and fatal wisdom of the fulfillment of the sinful desires of the flesh. God has clearly made us aware that mankind needs Him to be free from the captivity of sin. How awful mankind turns when he is malnourished spiritually. We truly need spiritual food, consistently, on a daily basis. If our physical bodies can die without food, then why would our spiritual bodies not die without the Word of God? How realistically God illustrates the fact that multitudes are famished without the food of His loving commandments and dried with thirst without a water of life. *"Their honorable men are famished, And their multitude dried up with thirst."*

Continuance of ISAIAH 5

ISAIAH 5:14

Therefore Sheol has enlarged itself
And opened its mouth beyond measure;
Their glory and their multitude and their pomp,
And he who is jubilant, shall descend into it.

Verse 14 indicates that Sheol has enlarged itself beyond measure, because greater is the number of those who are following lucifer, for whom Hell was originally made. Sadly, the multitudes who have adopted the nature of satan to live under his obedience are equally yoked to his characteristics. They will be thrown away from the holy presence of the Lord just like lucifer. The Lord has rightfully warned that they shall descend into Hell due to the evil in their heart.

PSALM 55:15

Let death come upon them; let them go down alive to Sheol; for evil is in their homes and in their hearts.

In contrast, all those who abide in the Lord—all these will be delivered from the depths of Sheol.

PSALM 86:13

For great is Your steadfast love toward me; You have delivered my soul from the depths of Sheol.

The majority of people do not agree with God's judgment with the common argument that "if God is a good God, then why is He letting humanity suffer in Hell?" We definitely appreciate a fair judgment in man's court of law against any criminal, but many will stand against God's judgment of a serial killer, murderer, thief, child molester, rapist, and others of this type. Why such a biased argument against God's unbiased judgments? *Because many don't want to repent and give up their evil works.* Would you tell a police officer that he is being unfair by giving a speeding ticket for speeding? BUT WE WILL DEFINITELY SAY THAT GOD IS UNFAIR TO LET SINNERS GO INTO HELL FOR THEIR EXTENDED SINS. Truthfully, God doesn't want anyone to go to Hell; He died on the cross to save us all. But followers of satan will accompany the fallen angel into Hell, as God's righteous Law cannot judge unjustly. Our whole world can transform into a heavenly place if we acknowledge our weaknesses. Restoration is impossible without the knowledge of the causes of the problem.

Continuance of ISAIAH 5
ISAIAH 5:15-17
People shall be brought down,
Each man shall be humbled,
And the eyes of the lofty shall be humbled.
But the LORD of hosts shall be exalted in judgment,
And God who is holy shall be hallowed in righteousness.
Then the lambs shall feed in their pasture,
And in the waste places of the fat ones strangers shall eat.

Wonderfully, all self-exalted, proud, and lofty people will be brought down to be humbled on the Day of the Lord. The same day, the Lord of hosts will be exalted in His righteous judgment; their hoarded treasures will become a waste that they worshipped and honored all the days of their life.

Continuance of ISAIAH 5
ISAIAH 5:18-23
Woe to those who draw iniquity with cords of vanity,
And sin as if with a cart rope;
That say, "Let Him make speed and hasten His work,
That we may see it;
And let the counsel of the Holy One of Israel draw near and come,
That we may know it."
Woe to those who call evil good, and good evil;
Who put darkness for light, and light for darkness;
Who put bitter for sweet, and sweet for bitter!
Woe to those who are wise in their own eyes,
And prudent in their own sight!
Woe to men mighty at drinking wine,
Woe to men valiant for mixing intoxicating drink,
Who justify the wicked for a bribe,
And take away justice from the righteous man!

November 11, 2012 became the shift into a season when sinners of the world drifted swiftly into the depths of sins to embrace the desires of their hearts. Thus, those who are persistent in sin and reject the counsel of the Lord will be judged. The detailed woes are for those whose character is the same as described in Isaiah 5:19-23. We will review all these woes that the Lord has assigned, and we will also evaluate the reasons for them.

- Woe to those who bring injustice and iniquity with pride and arrogance. They take delight in their sins without a fear of the Lord. Truly, the fear of the Lord is the beginning of wisdom when we honor and respect Him as a Father in Heaven and obey His commandments as a son to a father's authority. (Isaiah 5:18)

- Woe to those who challenge God's purposes and will. These people are gods in their own eyes. These egotistic and self-centered people reject God by saying, *"Let Him make speed and hasten His work, that we may see it; and let the counsel of the Holy One of Israel draw near and come, that we may know it."* (Isaiah 5:19)

- Woe to hypocrites and the crooks of this earth. They are those whose religion is self-righteousness. They are blinded to call evil "good" and good "evil," "darkness" for light and "light" for darkness, "bitter" for sweet, and "sweet" for bitter. They are wise and prudent in their own eyes. Their overconfidence has blinded their sight to the truth, and made themselves deaf to hear the voice of God. Woe to such people, as they have lost the hope of joy, peace, and love in the Lord. (Isaiah 5:20-21)

- Woe to those who are mighty at drinking wine and fearlessly mix intoxicating drinks. It represents all those who are completely drunk in the joyous fulfillment of fleshly intoxicating desires. Woe to such humanity who influence many others in similar lifestyles of every kind of evil works. They are completely wrapped up in immorality. (Isaiah 5:22)

- Woe to those who are unjust and unfair to others. God is referring to the injustice of a society that is driven by money. Laws can be twisted to favor the wicked and evildoers because their bulging pockets can get them out of anything they do. The innocent are being tortured and hurt every day in a money-worshiping society. This looks like our world today—without a fair law and order. What would a just and a fair Lord of hosts think about such an unfair society? (Isaiah 5:23)

Let's see what the Lord, who owns a court of law to govern the whole universe fairly, will do to the evil of our earth.

Continuance of **ISAIAH 5**

ISAIAH 5:24

Therefore, as the fire devours the stubble,
And the flame consumes the chaff,
So their root will be as rottenness,
And their blossom will ascend like dust;
Because they have rejected the law of the LORD of hosts,
And despised the word of the Holy One of Israel.

Desolation will fall all over mankind in fire and brimstone in those days because man has rejected the law of the Lord God Almighty and despised the word and testimony of Jesus. Yes my friends, the word of God has been severely rejected by the majority. Alas, many have shut their eyes and ears to Him. I wonder why?

Continuance of **ISAIAH 5**

ISAIAH 5:25

Therefore the anger of the LORD is aroused against His people;
He has stretched out His hand against them
And stricken them,
And the hills trembled.
Their carcasses were as refuse in the midst of the streets.
For all this His anger is not turned away,
But His hand is stretched out still.

Verse 25 explains that our excessive evil deeds will culminate with an explosion of the Lord's anger on such a level that mountains will tremble and dead bodies will be strewn in the midst of streets like garbage. Alas, this judgment of God will not end here because mankind will still continue to reject and blaspheme the Lord God Almighty . . . *"For all this His anger is not turned away, But His hand is stretched out still."*

Continuance of ISAIAH 5
ISAIAH 5:26-29
He will lift up a banner to the nations from afar,
And will whistle to them from the end of the earth;
Surely they shall come with speed, swiftly.
No one will be weary or stumble among them,
No one will slumber or sleep;
Nor will the belt on their loins be loosed,
Nor the strap of their sandals be broken;
Whose arrows are sharp,
And all their bows bent;
Their horses' hooves will seem like flint,
And their wheels like a whirlwind.
Their roaring will be like a lion,
They will roar like young lions;
Yes, they will roar
And lay hold of the prey;
They will carry it away safely,
And no one will deliver.

Verses 26 to 29 are predicting a picture of mighty forces ready to attack mankind. Players gear up for a game when the referee whistles. Similarly, potent and mighty forces will gather together when God *"will hiss unto them from the end of the earth."*

Verse 27 explains the strength and power of these forces. Not a single warrior is weary or tired. They do not slumber and fall, for their sandals are strapped up firmly with belts tight and sturdy around their waist. This verse exposes the power, strength, sturdiness, and swiftness of these forces.

Verse 28 shows us the readiness and strength of their weapons. They are equipped with sharp and fierce weapons for mass destruction.

Verse 29 tells us about the capability and attitude of these strong warriors. They are like roaring lions whose prey no one can snatch away. Truly no one can snatch away from this roaring enemy except God. As many have rejected the relationship with the Lord, then who else can intervene to save humanity? Therefore, mankind will not be delivered from these robust forces, for their sins are great. Only the Lord can restore them back, only if all would *repent*.

Continuance of Isaiah 5

Isaiah 5:30

In that day they will roar against them
Like the roaring of the sea.
And if one looks to the land,
Behold, darkness and sorrow;
And the light is darkened by the clouds.

Those days will come like a roaring sea and surround men with darkness of clouds and sorrow, pains, and suffering. I wish that each and every person living on earth would humble themselves, repent, and cry before the Lord for the forgiveness of their sins. This is the only way to receive His mercies.

Acts 4:12

Nor is there salvation in any other, for there is no other name
under heaven given among men by which we must be saved."

Has the prophecy of November 11, 2012 come to pass?

Sharing future prophetic revelations takes the faith of moving a mountain. It was a daring step of faith for me to obey the voice of the Lord. I obeyed His voice because my love relationship with Him helps me to obey my call.

The Holy Spirit led me to Isaiah 5 when I inquired of the Lord
about the significance of the date "11-11-12."
Are we seeing the Scriptures come to pass?

We are witnessing that the secular and religious leaders are standing to support the lawlessness and unrighteousness. The daily news articles testify that the commandants of God are broken as never before. It looks like that the world has gone mad to legalize abortion and same-

THE LORD'S VOICE CRIES TO THE CITY . . .

sex marriage and partnership laws. The desire to remove the Creator from legislature has never been as in demand as it is today. The world is on fire—from November 11, 2012 on—to call evil good and good evil . . . more than ever before. The prophesized date "11-11-12" was a turning point to a next phase in human history. The gloominess portrayed in Isaiah 5 does not only portray a physical death, but also a spiritual death.

ISAIAH 5:20, 21

Woe to those who call evil good, and good evil;
Who put darkness for light, and light for darkness;
Who put bitter for sweet, and sweet for bitter!
Woe to those who are wise in their own eyes,
And prudent in their own sight!

Many will comment that sin has been around from the beginning. I completely agree with you if you say that righteousness and unrighteousness have been around from the beginning. All generations have dealt with similar issues, but unlikely to the extent that we see in the present age. The world received its judgments at different times, such as with Noah and with Sodom and Gomorrah. Do you witness that the wickedness and the hardness of heart of today's generation is matching the people of Sodom and Gomorrah, where God could not find even ten righteous people? The goodness from our earth is being eradicated, exactly like Sodom and Gomorrah.

The LORD told me that 11-11-12 is a fulfillment of Isaiah 5. His judgments are increasing at a parallel scale to the amount of evil on earth. This will conclude with Isaiah 5:30: "In that day they will roar against them like the roaring of the sea. And if one looks to the land, Behold, darkness and sorrow; and the light is darkened by the clouds."

May the LORD GOD ALMIGHTY give us the wisdom to repent and a desire to seek safety and salvation in the name of the LORD JESUS CHRIST!

PHILIPPIANS 2:10

. . . that at the name of Jesus every knee should bow, of those in

heaven, and of those on earth, and of those under the earth,
Amen!!

CHAPTER 7

The Year 2023

God communicated to me in a vision on December 28, 2009.

In the first scene I saw a business executive in a black suit standing in center of his office supervising the replacement of the entire office system with the latest version of technology for business growth and development. He had an air of arrogance and self-importance, as if he was a god in his own eyes. He looked completely determined to achieve worldly success to such an extent that everything else in his life lacked importance.

In a second scene, I saw another young man wearing a black suit, working on software. He was anxiously trying to restore God's message, which I am seeking to share with the world through a web ministry at www.gods-messenger.webs.com. The young man was unsuccessful to load the page, and I felt in my spirit that God's message via this web link was completely disconnected and cannot be reached by the world any more. His personality was totally opposite from the other arrogant man consumed in his worldly accomplishments. He seemed to be humble and down to earth.

The third thing that I saw was a number: 2023. The Holy Spirit revealed that it is indicating the year 2023.

The Meaning of This Vision

The **first part of this vision** symbolizes the people who are engrossed in worshiping themselves and their desires. I saw this conceited-looking executive wearing a black suit, because he portrays the death of all such people. Their entire lives are focused on achieving materialistic success, which transforms them from simple humans into gods who wish to rule their lives like kings in superciliousness. For the very same reason, they do not care to know the real King of kings, who rules the world in reality.

This man in my dream looked like an arrogant king, who builds a palace made of glass with extreme care, and is totally engrossed in its beauty. He shuts every door of his palace, from which he can get a warning that this palace he is relying on will collapse. He does not even care to know because he only loves, believes, and trusts his idols—himself and the things of this world. These people let pass their opportunities to hear God's witnesses who proclaim the gospel of salvation of the Lord Jesus Christ. They do not have the desire to acknowledge the truth, even on the last day of their life, as the wages of sin is death.

ROMANS 6:23
For the wages of sin is death; but the gift of God
is eternal life through Jesus Christ our Lord.

In a **second part of this vision** I saw that this young man, in spite of being kind and humble, was also wearing a black suit. His desperate attempt failed to restore my website; this represents the communication lines that connect the gospel of the Lord Jesus Christ to the people. He also represents all those whose religion is humanity, whose trust is not in the righteousness through God, but by the works of their own hands. They refuse to acknowledge that a simple liar cannot stand before the holiness of God. They rejected God's plan designed for their salvation. This young man in a black suit was trying to connect with God's message, but it was too late, because the gospel cannot reach anyone anymore, just as in the days when Noah was told to shut the door to the ark. People outside Noah's ark despairingly screamed to have gates opened for their safety, but the time of calling for the repentance of sins was ended. Alas, history will repeat again. Just as in the days of Noah, God's servants are calling mankind with the good news of repentance and salvation. The wise will listen and get inside the ark of life with the LORD, and the foolish will be left out.

The death of a man eliminates his chance to be saved by means of the gospel of salvation. Sadly, our last chance of a hope and refuge in the Lord Jesus Christ ends at our last breath. Multitudes will cry outside the Kingdom of God because they prioritized perishable things over a permanent redemption with the Lord. They did not listen to God's servants declaring the gospel of salvation. Therefore, *the Judgment of death will be the fate of all the self-righteous.*

God did not show me anyone praying or doing His work in this vision. Therefore, it is very much evident that the Bride of Jesus Christ, which is the children of God, will not face death.

In a **third part of my vision**, the Lord revealed the year 2023.

2023 is the year for the death of all those who didn't care to know their Lord. They contemplated themselves as wiser than their Creator. They worshipped themselves instead of the Lord because of their odious pride. The death of all these is admissible, all these who were satisfied with their inadequate good works and did not care to know about the holy righteousness which God desires. They never comprehended in all the days of their lives that a true humanity births only through an intimate love relationship with the Heavenly Father of this universe— but not by the works of their own hands.

Is 2023 a Year of Rapture?

My answer to this question is, "I don't know." I am not a theologian to understand the depth of Bible prophecies. I just know that Lord calls His servants to speak according to the instruction of the Holy Spirit, and I am doing so. I am called to share the revelations that the Heavenly Father gives me through His son, the Lord Jesus Christ, with an inspiration of the Holy Spirit. I might not understand it all, but I trust the Lord, and believe all He declares is the virgin truth. God's servants understand that all learning and knowledge comes only from the Lord; the Lord Jesus Christ instructed His disciples what to speak in Matthew 10:19, 20. He said, *"But when they deliver you up, do not worry about how or what you should speak. For it will be given to you in that hour what you should speak; for it is not you who speak, but the Spirit of your Father who speaks in you."* Therefore, after seeing this vision, I immediately shared it on my web ministry. *Though I simply shared the interpretation of this vision as I did with you, many people pointed to this vision as a declaration of Rapture.* Many comments were left on the web page by visitors, such as:

joie

08:05 AM on February 07, 2010

I am not sure to believe you that the year 2023 is the time of rapture. In our dispensation today we are living in perilous times. Many Bible studies around the globe today as Apostle say that in the book of II Timothy 3:7 always learning and never able to come to the knowledge of truth. It is a stern warning from Apostle Paul. GOD in this new era will not reveal the future through humans, not like before he spoke to the Prophets and the called ones. So, I will not believe that the year 2023 is the end of time. Only the Father which is in Heaven knows, not even the son.

Joie and many other visitors on the web page were right when they commented that, "Only the Father in Heaven knows the day and the hour." I would never dare to contradict the Word of the Lord, because I honor it over my life.

MATTHEW 24:36
"But of that day and hour no one knows, not even the angels of heaven, but My Father only.

I shared this vision straightforwardly, not speaking of Rapture or the End of the World, but still, many more misinterpreted my vision and raised similar questions. To clarify again, this vision is portraying the death of self-worshippers and the self-righteous in the year 2023.

Would that be the season of tribulation as prophesied in the Bible? Is this how and when death will come to pass? Only God will know!

Still, due to such inquiries from many, one day I asked God while working in my kitchen: *"What does the year 2023 stand for?"* God led me to turn the television on. Minister of God Perry Stone was giving a sermon on Rapture. You can also witness this by visiting http://www.voe. org/. Perry Stone was explaining how the whole earth will shut down at the time of Rapture. God showed me the same thing in my vision in which the Internet connection was completely ceased. As we read in Matthew 24: 27: *"For as the lightning comes from the east and flashes to the west, so also will the coming of the Son of Man be."* This lightning will totally obstruct and freeze the world communication systems like satellites, cell phones, and the Internet.

Even though the Lord led me to the Perry Stone sermon on television to answer my inquiry, the huge criticism and arguments kept me asking God what the year 2023 stands for. God answered me on February 3, 2010, through a vision, showing me a single grain of wheat in a center of a palm of a hand. God did not show me the wheat on its stalk or wrapped in its kernels, but the Lord showed a completely threshed grain that is separated from the wheat kernels after the harvest. The single grain of wheat on the palm of a hand is the one ready to be preserved in a barn.

As we all know, wheat symbolizes the Bride of the Lord Jesus Christ. We are living in the season of a great harvest of souls. At present, wheat is growing strongly on its stalks, just like His church is rejoicing and dancing with a breeze of the Holy Spirit flowing around it. At present, the great harvest is wrapped in its kernels, just as the arm of the Lord is protecting His people. Read the parable of wheat and tares that the Lord Jesus Christ gave for our learning and counsel.

MATTHEW 13:24-30
Another parable He put forth to them, saying: "The kingdom of heaven is like man who sowed good seed in his field; but while men slept, his enemy came and sowed tares among the wheat and went his away. But when the grain had sprouted and produced

a crop, then the tares also appeared.
So the servants of the owner came and said to him, "Sir, did you
not sow a good seed in your field? How then does it have tares?
He said to them, "An enemy has done this." The servants
said to him, "do you want us then to go and gather them up?"
But he said, "No, lest while you gather up
tares you also uproot the wheat with them."
Let both grow together until the harvest, and
at the time of harvest I will tell the reapers, "First
gather together the tares and bind them in bundles to
burn them, but gather the wheat into my barn."

The Lord Jesus Christ explained the meaning of the parable of wheat
and tares when His disciples asked, because they could not comprehend
what it meant (and means).

MATTHEW 13:36-50
Meaning of: The Parable of the Tares
Then Jesus sent the multitude away and went into
the house. And His disciples came to Him, saying,
"Explain to us the parable of the tares of the field."
He answered and said to them, He who sows
the good seed is the Son of Man.
The field is the world, and good seeds are the sons of the
kingdom, but the tares are the sons of the wicked one.
The enemy who sowed them is the devil, the harvest
is the end of the age, and the reapers are the angels.
Therefore as the tares are gathered and burned
in the fire, so it will be at the end of the age.
The Son of Man will send out His angels, and
they will gather out of His kingdom all things that
offend, and those who practice lawlessness,
and will cast them into the furnace of fire.
There will be wailing and gnashing of teeth.
Then the righteous will shine forth as the sun in the kingdom
of their Father. He who has ears to hear, let him hear!

*So it will be at the end of the age. The angels will
come forth, separate the wicked from among the just,
and cast them into the furnace of fire. There
will be wailing and gnashing of teeth.*

This parable of the wheat and tares given to us by the Lord Jesus Christ clearly explains that the wheat will be gathered and the tares will be thrown away at the "End of the Age," as we read: *"So it will be at the end of the age. The angels will come forth, separate the wicked from among the just."*

The Lord gave me a similar revelation in dreams of December 28, 2009, and of February 3, 2010.

The Holy Spirit also led me to Joel chapter 3 for understanding what the year 2023 stands for. Let's read it together to understand.

JOEL 3:1-3
God Judges the Nations
*"For behold, in those days and at that time,
When I bring back the captives of Judah and Jerusalem,
I will also gather all nations,
And bring them down to the Valley of Jehoshaphat;
And I will enter into judgment with them there
On account of My people, My heritage Israel,
Whom they have scattered among the nations;
They have also divided up My land.
They have cast lots for My people,
Have given a boy as payment for a harlot,
And sold a girl for wine, that they may drink.*

God is declaring the day when He will bring the captives of Judah and Jerusalem (people who are saved) as well as all the nations of the world (people who are unsaved) to the Valley of Jehoshaphat (Court of the Judgment). On that great day the Lord will judge the nations for all the injustices done against His faithful, obedient, and loving heritage, Israel (saved Jews and Gentiles from every corner of the earth), who are abused, killed, tortured, and hated with passion. The enemies of the Lord did not fear to divide His land, stealing the rights, possessions, and heritage of His people.

Continuation of **JOEL 3**

JOEL 3:4-8

"Indeed, what have you to do with Me,
O Tyre and Sidon, and all the coasts of Philistia?
Will you retaliate against Me?
But if you retaliate against Me,
Swiftly and speedily I will return your retaliation upon your own head,
Because you have taken My silver and My gold,
And have carried into your temples My prized possessions.
Also the people of Judah and the people of Jerusalem
You have sold to the Greeks,
That you may remove them far from their borders.
"Behold, I will raise them
Out of the place to which you have sold them,
And will return your retaliation upon your own head.
I will sell your sons and your daughters
Into the hand of the people of Judah,
And they will sell them to the Sabeans,
To a people far off;
For the LORD has spoken."

In verses 4 to 8 God is questioning His adversaries about their embezzlement with His Word, treasures, and the possessions of His people; to sacrifice to their idols that they worshipped and obeyed to retaliate against God's will. The Lord declared in verse 4 that, *"Swiftly and speedily I will return your retaliation upon your own head."* Praise the Lord God Almighty, who will rightfully avenge all those who demoralize, hurt, and enslave His people. This spiritual hatred against the faithful people of God will be justified by the ruler of this universe—our Lord.

Continuation of **Joel 3**
Joel 3:9-17
Proclaim this among the nations:
"Prepare for war!
Wake up the mighty men,
Let all the men of war draw near,
Let them come up.

Beat your plowshares into swords
And your pruning hooks into spears;
Let the weak say, 'I am strong.'"

Assemble and come, all you nations,
And gather together all around.
Cause Your mighty ones to go down there, O LORD.

"Let the nations be wakened, and come
up to the Valley of Jehoshaphat;
For there I will sit to judge all the surrounding nations.

Put in the sickle, for the harvest is ripe.
Come, go down;
For the winepress is full,
The vats overflow—
For their wickedness is great."

Multitudes, multitudes in the valley of decision!
For the day of the LORD is near in the valley of decision.

The sun and moon will grow dark,
And the stars will diminish their brightness.

The LORD also will roar from Zion,
And utter His voice from Jerusalem;
The heavens and earth will shake;
But the LORD will be a shelter for His people,

And the strength of the children of Israel.

"So you shall know that I am the LORD your God,
Dwelling in Zion My holy mountain.
Then Jerusalem shall be holy,
And no aliens shall ever pass through her again."

Lift up your hands to praise the Lord your God, for the day of your redemption has come. Verses 9 to 17 are good news for the righteous—and bad news for the unrighteous. This chapter is the voice of God crying to the world, for their wickedness is great against His people. The day of the Lord has come when multitudes will be gathered in a valley of decision to be judged, because the Lord said, *"For the day of the LORD is near in the valley of decision."*

Saints sharpen the weapons of spirit and fight this final spiritual war of hatred against God and His will. All those who make a choice to worship and obey God will always be opposed by the unbelievers. God directs His people in verse 9: *"Proclaim this among the nations: 'Prepare for war! Wake up the mighty men, Let all the men of war draw near, Let them come up.'"* This war between good and evil that began at birth of satan is ready to come to an end on the Lord's Day. Praise the Lord, for the day of the redemption of His faithful heritage is near.

It is so painful to see multitudes fallen in satan's deceit because of their lack of knowledge of a spiritual warfare that existed from the beginning. They don't want to know the truth because of their pride in their own foolish wisdom, because they consider themselves gods, just like satan. The time of their judgment will come, as the Lord said in verse 12: *"Let the nations be wakened, and come up to the Valley of Jehoshaphat; For there I will sit to judge all the surrounding nations."* That will be a day when the universe will shake under the tremendous power, might, and strength of the Lord, just like verse 15 describes: *"The sun and moon will grow dark, And the stars will diminish their brightness."* The Lord's voice from His judgment seat demonstrates His powers to the level that "The heavens and earth will shake." On the other hand, the Lord's gentle love will embrace His people forever, because it is promised that " . . . *the LORD will be a shelter for His people.*" The Lord will also cherish and nourish His people with an everlasting love and protection, one in which no one can hurt them anymore, because the Lord said, *"And no aliens shall ever pass through her again."*

Continuation of **JOEL 3**

JOEL 3:18-21

God Blesses His People

And it will come to pass in that day

That the mountains shall drip with new wine,

The hills shall flow with milk,

And all the brooks of Judah shall be flooded with water;

A fountain shall flow from the house of the LORD

And water the Valley of Acacias.

"Egypt shall be a desolation,

And Edom a desolate wilderness,

Because of violence against the people of Judah,

For they have shed innocent blood in their land.

But Judah shall abide forever,

And Jerusalem from generation to generation.

For I will acquit them of the guilt of

bloodshed, whom I had not acquitted;

For the LORD dwells in Zion."

Finally all the blessings, peace, and joy that anyone could ever imagine will be bestowed from the Heavenly Father to those who worshipped, loved, and cherished Him in their lives on earth, and patiently endured all the pain and sufferings for His Name's sake, from His, and their, enemies who hated and tortured them fiercely. The Lord their God will wipe their tears away and cherish them dearly in His Holy presence with an abundance of unimaginable treasures of Heaven on earth and with a passionate word of life that will gift them with eternity forever. This is because His word said, in verse 18, *"And it will come to pass in that day That the mountains shall drip with new wine, The hills shall flow with milk, And all the brooks of Judah shall be flooded with water; A fountain shall flow from the house of the LORD And water the Valley of Acacias."*

The opposite will be the destiny of all those who rebelled against the Lord and His will. In their rebellion and violence against the Lord, they shed the blood of His servants and followers till the last day of judgment. Yes, they have filled this earth with the blood of the innocent. God will bring complete desolation on this earth (of which Egypt is a metaphor). As the word said in verse 19: *"Egypt shall be a desolation, And Edom a desolate wilderness, Because of violence against the people of Judah, For they have shed innocent blood in their land."*

Praise the Lord our God for His ultimate decision for His people that is mentioned in verse 20: *"But Judah shall abide forever And Jerusalem from generation to generation."*

The Lord Jesus Christ declared His decision, similar to Joel Chapter 3, which refers to the judgment of the nations of the world. Our Shepherd will gather together His sheep on His right hand and the goats on the left. Sheep symbolize those people who have the same characteristics of an actual sheep, such as a total dependence, obedience, being affirmative, a follower, innocent, harmless, and having purity. The Lord will cherish them and keep them in His presence forever. On the other hand, the goats will be gathered together on His left hand to be removed from His presence for eternity. The goat symbolizes those people who easily stray to temptations and distractions. Such a category of people as those who have fallen into the wrongdoings of the world. They have strayed away from the Lord and into the malicious deceit of satan.

MATTHEW 25:31-33
The Son of Man Will Judge the Nations
"When the Son of Man comes in His glory, and all the holy angels with Him, then He will sit on the throne of His glory. All the nations will be gathered before Him, and He will separate them one from another, as a shepherd divides his sheep from the goats. And He will set the sheep on His right hand, but the goats on the left.

For this reason sheep are the righteous ones who will inherit the Kingdom of God, and the goats are the unsaved ones who will enter into the eternal punishment in Hell. Now we all have to make a choice.

The Lord related to me the significance of the year 2023 in three ways. First, through a vision of December 28, 2009, in which I saw two categories of mankind destined for death in the year 2023. They would be the self-worshippers and the self-righteous. The second source the Lord used to explain the happenings in the year 2023 was Scripture, specifically Joel chapter 3. The third source was another dream, this one on February 3, 2010, which showed a grain of wheat picked up in a palm of a hand; this proves that His people are not destined for the punishment of death because God is their shield and rescue.

Would the year 2023 lead us into a season of Great Tribulation, Rapture, or the End of the Age as prophesied in the Bible? Only the Lord of all creations knows His perfect plans for us. The Lord speaks to us in parables, in prophecies, and in His Word to sanctify His Bride and to judge the sinners. All the prophecies that the Lord gives me come to pass. The Lord has given the prophetic revelation for the year 2023 to prepare His church to watch and pray. Satan knows that his days are numbered, and he is working aggressively to devour God's people, as we read in Revelation 12:12: *"Therefore rejoice, O heavens, and you who dwell in them! Woe to the inhabitants of the earth and the sea!* **For the devil has come down to you, having great wrath, because he knows that he has a short time."**

How important is it to understand the times and seasons. God knows their importance and He is relating them to His beloved Bride through His chosen servants. It is not a time to doubt, but one to pray and seek the face of the Lord—until we see Him again face to face on His Day.

REVELATION 15:4
Who shall not fear You, O Lord, and glorify Your name?
For You alone are holy.
For all nations shall come and worship before You,
For Your judgments have been manifested."

CHAPTER 8

Rapture Is at Hand

Rapture is the biblical term for "caught up" or "translation." On the day of Rapture, the Lord will receive His bride. His bride is His church, the members of which accepted Him as their Lord and Savior, and became holy in their spiritual walk with Him. His church will be taken away to its permanent home, which He prepared exactly as He promised before leaving this earth two thousand years ago.

JOHN 14:1-3
Let not your heart be troubled: ye believe in God, believe also in me.
In my Father's house are many mansions: if it were not
so, I would have told you. I go to prepare a place for you.
And if I go and prepare a place for you, I will come again, and
receive you unto myself; that where I am, there ye may be also.

Rapture is not symbolic, but a practical promise. Mankind will experience its happening in a similar manner as to that which we read in Matthew 24:30, 31: "*Then the sign of the Son of Man will appear in heaven, and then all the tribes of the earth will mourn, and they will see the Son of Man coming on the clouds of heaven with power and great glory. And He will send His angels with a great sound of a trumpet, and they will gather together His elect from the four winds, from one end of heaven to the other."*

The LORD gave me a life-changing message for His beloved Church in these Last Days. The LORD spoke to me His heart through several dreams, only to relate His concerns for His believers. What our Lord desires is shared in the light of my dreams, like: betrothal of the bride of Christ, grooming of His bride before a wedding day, and lastly, good news of His second coming on the day of Rapture.

JOHN 3:29
He who has the bride is the bridegroom; but the friend of the bridegroom, who stands and hears him, rejoices greatly because of the bridegroom's voice. Therefore this joy of mine is fulfilled.

Betrothal Ceremony of the Bride of Christ

My first dream was about getting engaged with my first love; this dream came on March 23, 2011. I saw that my first love had finally agreed to get engaged with me. He and his guests are ready and waiting for me to be prepared to get betrothed. I rushed to get ready. I wore a beautiful bridal dress made with a fabric like silky brocade, adorned with bridal jewelry made of gold embedded with magnificent turquoise. My dress and jewels looked very orthodox, classic, expensive, and extremely beautiful. I got completely dressed and looked lovely in my engagement accessories, but I completely forgot to adorn my nails. They looked very plain without nail polish, especially in comparison to the remainder of the gorgeous adoration I had prepared in for this ceremony. I felt panicked that it was time to join my fiancé and I was not completely ready. Then, I heard that *my fiancé and his guests would wait for me a little bit longer to allow me to get ready.*

PSALM 45:13, 14
The royal daughter is all glorious within the palace; Her clothing is woven with gold.

She shall be brought to the King in robes of many colors;
The virgins, her companions who follow
her, shall be brought to You.

The Meaning of This Dream

GOD is the first love of His bride: His church. He desires a complete, intimate dedication of His chosen church exactly as it is portrayed in Deuteronomy 6:5: *"you shall love the LORD your God with all your heart, with all your soul, and with all your strength."* My dream reveals that the Lord has chosen His church to be betrothed to. The Groom and His guests are ready and waiting patiently for the bride to get ready for an engagement ceremony. The bride knows that she is accepted and must adorn herself quickly for uniting with her first, passionate love, but the bride is depressed to see that she missed garnishing her nails and that she does not look like a perfectly prepared bride for her first love. But she then feels relaxed to hear that the groom will give her a little bit more time to finish up the things that are missing. Now the bride is working diligently to finish the last job on her nails.

This dream predicts that the Lord Jesus Christ has chosen His bride, His church. He is ready and waiting for His church to get prepared to receive her position as the Lord's fiancée. The church is rushing and trying her best to be ready, but still more righteousness and purification is required, as is an intimate heart for the Lord. His people need to seek His Word, His commandments, teaching and counseling diligently to repair the weaknesses of the spirit and flesh. The Lord is waiting patiently and has granted a little bit more time to let His bride, His church, be completely ready. *This dream warns His people to be alert and not lax in their relationship with the LORD.* The church of Christ is chosen to be betrothed for its redemption and salvation, to be glorified eternally with her lover and King: the Lord Jesus Christ.

2 CORINTHIANS 11:2
For I am jealous for you with godly jealousy. For I
have betrothed you to one husband, that I may
present you as a chaste virgin to Christ.

The Bridal Preparation Before the Great Wedding Day

The dream about getting married; this dream came on April 3, 2011:
I saw a dream that I am going to get married. I saw a house crowded with people. Children are sitting down on a floor, playing with rocks, carefree of what is going on. Multitudes of people have gotten together for a wedding ceremony and are witnessing a bridal bath. I am taking this bridal shower in the presence of this gathering of natives. When I get up after bathing, I see some hair on my leg that I didn't clean up. I realize that I should have cleansed myself well for my groom, but I felt in spirit that my groom will accept me in spite of my imperfection.

Now I am in a bridal chamber, getting ready in my bridal accessories. All things needed for the bridal grooming are wrapped in individual boxes of various sizes. I have not opened any of them yet, but I am ready to start working on them soon. I saw Romel (my husband) looking at me sitting at the edge of a bed in my bridal chamber, getting ready for my wedding. I am thinking with sadness that my relation with him will end very soon. An hour of separation from this earthly relationship is coming soon.

The Meaning of This Dream

This dream is in exact picture of Ephesians 5:25-27:

> *Husbands, love your wives, even as Christ also*
> *loved the church, and gave himself for it;*
> *That he might sanctify and cleanse it with*
> *the washing of water by the word,*
> *That he might present it to himself a glorious church,*
> *not having spot, or wrinkle, or any such thing; but*
> *that it should be holy and without blemish.*

The Bride of Christ needs to be cleansed for a washing away of the sins of her flesh and soul through a baptism of water. The living water that sanctifies is His Word in communion with His Holy Spirit. In my dream I am taking a bridal shower in front of heavenly beings. All principalities and powers of Heaven are witnessing the selection and purification of the Church of God. I finished my bridal shower, but a few hairs are left which should have been removed. I didn't feel sanctified enough for my groom. In this vision in my dream, the Church of God is taking every measure to get ready for coming of the Lord Jesus Christ, but human efforts always leave some errors. The church will not be 100 percent pure, even on the day of His arrival, but the love and mercy of the Lord restores His Church. In my dream I felt in my spirit that the Lord will accept me in spite of my imperfection. *God clearly related that He will welcome all those who are diligently seeking to wash off their sins ingrown deep in their flesh through the water of His Word, who seek Him faithfully and humbly, who have a deep desire in their hearts to be as holy as He is holy.* Who can desire to do this all without love? The love of God rooted deep in the heart of His church will help to come near the Throne of God.

I saw that the bride has moved to her bridal chamber. The bridal dress, jewelries, and other accessories are sitting in front of the bride, wrapped in their individual boxes. *It signifies that **the church of God is bestowed with the spiritual gifts and talents that need to be opened and used in order to be fully groomed into an enchanting bride for Christ.*** I have not opened any box yet in my dream, but I am going to do it. ***The church of Christ is ready to enter into a great phase of revival when His chosen bride will use her spiritual gifts and talents with full strength and force.*** A mighty wind of the Holy Spirit will surround His church to help it use all its spiritual gifts in such a magnitude that a tremendous transformation and the saving of millions of souls will be done to the ends of the earth. I can feel a great awakening coming among His people. Similar to this revival, **the church of Christ is getting ready to get adorned and look pleasantly beautiful in His righteousness, purification, perfection, intimate passion, and love of her redeeming husband, Yeshua Ha'Mashiach—the Lord Jesus Christ.**

I saw Romel (my husband) looking at me getting ready for my wedding. I felt sad with this knowledge in my spirit that an hour of our separation is coming very soon. ***The last part of my dream shows that an hour of separation of the church of God from this earth is arriving very soon.*** The church will be separated from her earthly loved ones to unite with her first love: the Lord Jesus Christ. The day of Rapture of the saints is coming very soon.

Dear church of God, we do not know when our bridegroom, the Lord Jesus Christ, is coming back to receive His adorned bride. God is coming in our lifetimes for the celebration of the Great Wedding Day. That day He will embrace His bride for eternity. Now they are bounded together forever in each other's passionate love. This vision is good news for His church, that Her Lord is coming soon.

REVELATION 19:7-8

Let us be glad and rejoice and give Him glory, for the marriage of the Lamb has come, and His wife has made herself ready." And to her it was granted to be arrayed in fine linen, clean and bright, for the fine linen is the righteous acts of the saints.

Wake-up Call to the Church of God

The Lord gave an awakening call for His church to prepare for His arrival. I received a message for the church of God. It is urgent not to stumble and fall due to blindness, overconfidence, and carelessness. Please read what the Lord wants His Church to know.

My Dream on October 12, 2011

I saw that we are getting ready for a wedding ceremony of my first love. He is not marrying me, but someone else. I am sitting with the groom's mother, who wanted me to marry her son. I am wearing a beautiful white shirt, but I had on a carelessly adorned unevenly matched scarf and pants with it. Later on, I changed my mind and wore all white. Now my dress looks perfect due to careful selection. I also wore bright colored lipstick, but the groom is not even looking at me. It broke my heart. His focus is only on the girl who he has chosen to be his bride. Her wedding dress is too tight on her as if it did not belong to her, and she did not look pretty at all. I thought that this girl got the chance to marry him because she lived next door and I lived far away. It was very heartbreaking that my first love had chosen someone else over me, even though I was more beautiful, in love with him, and now perfectly dressed. He did not even look once at me, but was completely lost in the passion for his wife. I am inconsolable because I lost my right and chance to marry him due to my carelessness, and also because I moved far away from him.

The Meaning of This Dream

The Lord is conveying to His church to be vigilant and strive to receive their rightful position in the Kingdom of God. God is warning us about major weaknesses that are found in the churches today. I noticed these deficiencies in me in this dream.

- Lost the significance of my lover from the heart
- Carelessness in a selection of attire for a wedding ceremony
- Separation, or living far away from my lover

In this dream I was very lackadaisical when it came to my first love. Until I saw him on his wedding day, my heart did not desire to be his only love. I was not even hurt when I heard about his wedding with another girl. I was a complete picture of an ignorant and careless fiancée. I did not even dress with care to be a guest of honor in his wedding.

This dream clearly shows how our Lord sees His church today: ignorant and careless of His love for them. The church has lost its desire for her savior due to its over-confidence that it is the chosen people of God. The church will lose its position as the bride of Christ. I beg you to wake up now and let the love for your Lord burn in your hearts. Awakening from your overconfidence and clumsiness is necessary. If you do not hear these warnings and change your ways, disappointment and misery will be your fate. The church should not think that its inheritance in the Kingdom of God is guaranteed in spite of its negligence. Your first preference and focus must be a search of righteousness through your master, the Lord Jesus Christ. The church will be disappointed to see its inheritance taken away and given to those who searched diligently and lived closer to the Lord, even though they seemed unworthy.

Wake up, church, and completely bathe yourself in the Scriptures of His Word for the saving of your crown. The church of God is needed to be diligently searching the face, heart, and will of her LORD. *His chosen bride needs to strive to obey His will and the calling in her life with faithful obedience, with love and passion in His relationship. His bride must seek to come closer to the first love of her life, which is the Lord God*

Almighty. A little careless separation of the heart will cost members of the church an eternal separation with God.

How awesome is the right of His bride that strives to seek her Lord. A crown of righteousness will be presented on the glorious Day of the Lord. Come, church, rise up and do all that is taught in the verses below to receive your crown of glory.

2 TIMOTHY 4:7, 8

I have fought the good fight, I have finished the race, I have kept the faith. Finally, there is laid up for me the crown of righteousness, which the Lord, the righteous Judge, will give to me on that Day, and not to me only but also to all who have loved His appearing.

Another experience in my dream was the separation from my first love. I have moved and lived far from him; therefore, the girl that lived next door to him received the privilege of being his wife. The Lord is warning that the heart of His church is also separated from Him.

Let's review all the weaknesses that the Lord sees in His people today:
- We have drifted away and lost our focus to the things of this world
- We are overconfident that we own our position of His bride, and our pride has blinded us to see and seek our lover
- We have forgotten that we cannot claim our entitlement, as God says in Matthew 3:9: *"And do not think to say to yourselves, 'We have Abraham as our father.' For I say to you that God is able to raise up children to Abraham from these stones."*

The church of God is divided in the similar pattern as the wise and foolish virgins presented by the Lord Jesus Christ in this parable. Let's read the following Scripture passage to understand God's perspective for the dangerous position where the church can be.

MATTHEW 25:1-13

The Parable of the Wise and Foolish Virgins
"Then the kingdom of heaven shall be likened to ten virgins who took their lamps and went out to meet the bridegroom.

Now five of them were wise, and five were foolish.
Those who were foolish took their lamps and took no oil with them,
but the wise took oil in their vessels with their lamps.
But while the bridegroom was delayed, they all slumbered and slept.
"And at midnight a cry was heard: 'Behold, the bridegroom is
coming; go out to meet him!'
Then all those virgins arose and trimmed their lamps.
And the foolish said to the wise, 'Give us some of your oil,
for our lamps are going out.'
But the wise answered, saying, 'No, lest there should not be enough
for us and you; but go rather to those who sell,
and buy for yourselves.'
And while they went to buy, the bridegroom came,
and those who were ready
went in with him to the wedding; and the door was shut.
"Afterward the other virgins came also, saying,
'Lord, Lord, open to us!'
But he answered and said, 'Assuredly, I say to you,
I do not know you.'
"Watch therefore, for you know neither the day nor
the hour in which the Son of Man is coming.

The Lord relates through this dream that His church is behaving like the five foolish virgins, who took their lamps yet had no oil with them. The body of Christ is represented with lamps in this parable; these are called to light the dark world of sin through His righteousness. The oil is a source that burns the lamp to illuminate in the dark. The oil in this parable is an intimate love with God. No one can light and shine for the Lord to remove the darkness of sins, pains, and suffering, and the root of misconduct of the hardened heart of the world—no one can do this without the oil of an intimate love of God.

The Lord is calling out of His love to revive and breathe life into His children. *I cannot express the hurt and disappointment belonging to this dream. It will be too late to renew your passion for God on the Last Day. You will find yourself outside the door. For this reason I have delivered the Lord's message for the church to wake up. The disappointment of rejection as His bride will be unbearably heartbreaking. Thus, the Holy Spirit is addressing His lovely bride to wake up, to thirst for His love, and to rise up to witness His second coming for the salvation of all mankind. Rise up, church. Your Lord is waiting for you with open arms to embrace in His loving kindness, His protection, and His everlasting communion forever.*

The Great Day of the Wedding Is Coming Soon

I saw another dream the very night I opened my forty days fast after sunset, on February 9, 2012. This dream was about the Rapture.

I saw one of my coworkers, who is a born again Christian, come to me in excitement and tell me that his wife got pregnant. I replied to him with an authority in spirit that **"the day she delivers the baby would be a day of Rapture."** In this dream, I experienced urgency in my spirit to go out on streets to share the good news of the gospel of the Lord Jesus Christ with each and every person who I got in touch with, because His coming was at hand. At the very moment that I woke up, I saw the time on the clock was 3:21 AM.

This dream is an alert to the servants of God about the urgency to share the message of the Lord Jesus Christ with the whole world with a serious effort and at full force. The woman is impregnated in my dream on February 10, 2012. It means that the Lord is telling His people to be ready for His arrival as He is coming very soon. His bride, the church of God, must prepare herself to get together with her groom. This dream is a signal for His people to be likewise to the virgins who were ready with their lamps, filled with oil, to go to meet the groom (reference Matthew 25:1-13). The church of God needs to get ready to welcome its Lord and Savior—the Lord Jesus Christ. I felt panicked in my dream with the thought that I do not have time left to organize a big ministry to share the good news of salvation in the name of Jesus. I felt an urgency to go out on the streets and ask everyone passing by me if they knew Jesus.

This dream is an appeal to every child of God to go and spread His Word to the ends of the earth. The church of God also needs to acknowledge that it does not have much time left. Therefore, wake up and do the work of the Lord. It is urgently important that each and every soul must hear the message that Jesus Christ is his or her Lord and Messiah. It is urgent to pay attention to this message of the Lord.

The Word of God also supports this vision of February 10, 2012, within the Scriptures, when the Lord is giving a revelation of a woman giving birth to a child. We read this in Revelation 12:1-5.

REVELATION 12:1-5
The Woman, the Child, and the Dragon

Now a great sign appeared in heaven: a woman clothed with the sun,
with the moon under her feet,
and on her head a garland of twelve stars.
Then being with child, she cried out in labor and in pain to give birth.
And another sign appeared in heaven: behold, a great, fiery red
dragon having seven heads and ten horns,
and seven diadems on his heads.
His tail drew a third of the stars of heaven
and threw them to the earth.
And the dragon stood before the woman who was ready to give birth,
to devour her Child as soon as it was born.
She bore a male Child who was to rule all nations with a rod of iron.
And her Child was caught up to God and His throne.

The dream I saw on February 10, 2012 is declaring that the day of Rapture is at hand. The important thing for the saints is to be ready for the Lord with a total acceptance of willingness to seek His will and desire to shelter under His counsel.

I have shared everything that the Lord reveals because I understand what happened to a servant who hid his talent under the ground and responded to his master's inquiry in this way: *"And I was afraid, and went and hid your talent in the ground. Look, there you have what is yours"* (Matthew 25:25). What will happen to such disobedient servants of the Lord? Exactly the same as Jesus made clear in Matthew 25:26-28: *"But his Lord answered and said to him, 'You wicked and lazy servant, you knew that I reap where I have not sown, and gather where I have not scattered seed. So you ought to have deposited my money with the bankers, and at my coming I would have received back my own with interest. Therefore take the talent from him, and give it to him who has ten talents."*

The Bible teaches us to examine the prophecies and determine whether they will come to pass—then it is confirmed that they are from the Lord God Almighty.

JEREMIAH 28:9
As for the prophet who prophesies of peace, when the word of the prophet comes to pass, the prophet will be known as one whom the LORD has truly sent."

I will ask everyone to seek the face of the Lord for their salvation, and to do so diligently. It is important to acknowledge that our Lord will come to take His bride. The important factor is to have an intimate love relationship with the Lord Jesus Christ. We all are witnessing that the signs of the End Times are fulfilling, speedily, the Bible prophecies. His coming is at hand; therefore stand alert so that the enemy cannot devour us from our walk in faithfulness to the Lord God Almighty.

1 THESSALONIANS 4:16, 17
For the Lord Himself will descend from heaven with a shout, with the voice of an archangel, and with the trumpet of God. And the dead in Christ will rise first. Then we who are alive and remain shall be caught up together with them in the clouds to meet the Lord in the air. And thus we shall always be with the Lord.

Praise the Lord for His perfect plans for His children who are waiting for their reward after a long race, under the scorching hot sun, filled with the tribulations on earth, which they endured for His name's sake.

CHAPTER 9

Revelation of War

The Lord God Almighty showed me a dream with a revelation of a Great War.

MARK 13:8

For nation will rise against nation, and kingdom against kingdom. There will be earthquakes in various places; there will be famines. These are but the beginning of the birth pains.

The LORD showed me a dream on August 29, 2011 about a war that will involve the nations of the world.

<u>First</u>: I saw fighter planes warring in the skies. They are launching bombs and missiles at each other. It seemed like an ongoing war. The only thing that filled the sky was the firing of the fighting planes.

<u>Second</u>: I saw people of different countries who have some major political differences sheltered together in refugee camps out in the wilderness. I did not see that they had any shelter over their heads, like tents; but they were lying on vast open ground under an open sky. The sky above their heads was nothing but a ceiling of fire. I walked from

within to the border of this camp and looked around. We were completely surrounded by the military forces, which were absolutely alert like eagles and swift like dogs. They were armed with weapons. One soldier looked directly at me. His hostile stare scared me because these soldiers were ordered to kill any suspicious person. As I was separated from my camp, I could be deemed a suspicious person and shot down. Therefore, I walked back immediately to the camp.

Third: I saw some military officers who were letting people go to other places of shelter with better accommodations. One officer was looking at me favorably and allowed me to leave the distressing camp in the wilderness to an enhanced and comfortable shelter.

The Meaning of This Dream

The Lord God Almighty has revealed a very deep wisdom of upcoming global war. Heaven and Earth will turn into a complete war zone.

According to a first scene of the dream, the military and the air forces have completely covered the ground and sky. They are heavily armed. I saw air forces incessantly attacking at each other, nonstop, with missiles. Military forces are ordered to kill anyone suspicious and dangerous to them. This war will be so devastating that multitudes will suffer and die.

According to a second scene of the dream, we discern that multitudes will be desolate and without homes during this war. We will be facing a nerve-wracking war in which the roofs over the heads of the nations will be replaced with an open sky of firing planes. I saw people of countries like India, Pakistan, South Korea, and North Korea together in refugee camps. The troubles facing mankind due to the major global conflicts will be so severe that the disputes between nations will be disregarded to deal with problems of greater magnitude that will arise during this Great War.

I saw the brutality, strength, capacity, and swiftness of the forces involved in the upcoming Great War. They see like an eagle, are swift like snake, and attack like vicious dogs. No one can escape their eyes. Anyone dangerous and suspicious is immediately destroyed.

According to the third scene of this dream, the church of God will receive favors miraculously, in the midst of war, by the mighty power of

God. In other words, you can say that those whose trust is in the Lord with an intimate relationship, with obedience to His teaching and counsel, will have supernatural favors during the war. His presence is a guaranteed restoration for mankind. But all those who either don't believe in God's existence or consider Him insignificant will not experience the miraculous protection of the Lord that He faithfully provides in all ages. Unfortunately, people devoid of Him will suffer greatly in this perilous time of war and be vulnerable and without any shelter.

PSALM 46:1-3
God is our refuge and strength,
A very present help in trouble.
Therefore we will not fear,
Even though the earth be removed,
And though the mountains be carried into the midst of the sea;
Though its waters roar and be troubled,
Though the mountains shake with its swelling. Selah

The Derivation of War

It is vital to understand the root of **peace** and **war**. By knowing the cause of all troubles, we might make corrections and restore our peace. The Bible gives us a logical explanation of when and how can we go from the phase of harmony and prosperity to sufferings, poverty, and troubles.

It is important to acknowledge these facts and find ways to restore peace. Surely, it is as practical today as thousands of years ago because God's promises are unchangeable and true in all eras.

DEUTERONOMY 28:1-3, 7
Blessings of Obedience
"Now it shall come to pass, if you diligently obey the
voice of the LORD your God, to observe carefully all His
commandments which I command you today, that the LORD
your God will set you high above all nations of the earth.
And all these blessings shall come upon you and overtake you,

because you obey the voice of the LORD your God:
"Blessed shall you be in the city,
and blessed shall you be in the country. . . .
"The LORD will cause your enemies who rise against
you to be defeated before your face; they shall come out
against you one way and flee before you seven ways.

The Bible is the book of God's lawful counsel and is proven historically, in all eras, that people prevailed only when they put God first in every area of their administrative affairs. Bible history establishes the fact that the blessings sustained over nations were under the rule of God-fearing governments led by men like King David, King Solomon, King Hezekiah, and King Josiah.

EXODUS 34:10
And He said: "Behold, I make a covenant. Before all
your people I will do marvels such as have not been done
in all the earth, nor in any nation; and all the people
among whom you are shall see the work of the LORD.
For it is an awesome thing that I will do with you."

We will take the example of the United States of America in the current age of the human history. We have all witnessed the peace and prosperity of this country. It was established as "One Nation under God"; therefore, America was established as a covenant nation. The USA became the leader of the free world. Its enemies could not stand before it due to the power that the Lord bestowed for its obedience to His will. Exodus 34:10 is a practical reality that still exists among His covenant nations of both Jews and Gentiles. The same principal applies to all nations of the world.

PSALM 33:12
Blessed is the nation whose God is the LORD,
the people he chose for his inheritance.

We have learned the reason for blessings; now we will evaluate the reason for the troubles that sweep away the peace, security, prosperity, wisdom, and morality of the nations. The Word of God is a truth that sets us free, and our obedience to His Word can restore our world.

Deuteronomy 28:15, 16, 25, 36
Curses of Disobedience

"But it shall come to pass, if you do not obey the voice
of the LORD your God, to observe carefully all His
commandments and His statutes which I command you today,
that all these curses will come upon you and overtake you:
"Cursed shall you be in the city, and
cursed shall you be in the country. . . .
" . . . The LORD will cause you to be defeated before
your enemies; you shall go out one way against them
and flee seven ways before them; and you shall become
troublesome to all the kingdoms of the earth. . . .
" . . . The LORD will bring you and the king whom you set
over you to a nation which neither you nor your fathers have
known, and there you shall serve other gods—wood and stone".

We will continue to understand the consequences of disobedience from the comparative illustrations of the kings of Israel and the United States of America.

We know the history of the kings of Israel when their nation suffered greatly under their administration. The disobedience of King Saul, King Hoshea, King Jehoshaphat, and many others to God's commandments is disclosed in the Word of God. They compromised with the neighboring nations' immorality and provoked the Lord through their evil deeds. They served idols—this the Lord had forbidden them to do. They worshipped other gods at high places and eliminated the Lord their God from their lives, their hearts, and their minds.

Many disasters in Israel's history came not at the hands of her ene-
mies, but as a result of her own disobedience.
(See Deuteronomy 31:29)

In our current example of the United States of America, God has been taken away from every corner of administration: from schools, Congress, judicial courts, and all legislative departments. Where God was honored in the past, the mere mention of His name is now forbidden in public settings. We can see the outcomes of leaving God behind. All the blessings that used to pour from Heaven have been eroded. We are suffering natural disasters, crop failures, and economic ruin. Just look what has happened since the USA removed God from its public settings: the country is now bankrupt, its enemies have financial dominion over it, and the economy is on the brink of collapse. America is no longer the head anymore—her enemies control her. This is leading the country to a steep decline in peace, prosperity, and security. Continuation of the rebellion against the will of God will result in complete destruction. Every nation on earth is under the same command of God. No one is exempt: Disobedience of the laws of God has the same consequences for everyone; this is because Jew and Gentile are the same for Him. We are all made by His hands with the same love, purpose, and principles.

Why Such a Pressure to Obey His Will?

The Lord God Almighty created the universe to relate to Him through worship and obedience. God desires us to obey His will so that He can save and protect us. God knows that satan and his rebellious followers want to devour every human on earth. We will not see this fact without our spiritual eyes open because man can scrutinize only what's in his humanly limitations. Therefore, man is incapacitated without the infinite competence of God. The human race can be eradicated without God's intervention and support.

God is pure and departs from us when we live in sin. *Man's decline begins when God separates due to his sins.* God's companionship furnishes us with constructive wisdom that helps us to make wise decisions and grow intelligently. The wisdom in His commandment leads us to prosperity. Similarly, the evil of man will separate him from God. This separation releases from God's constructive counsel to man's imprudent, foolish decisions. Man's self-destructive "wisdom" leads to failures. The fact is that in all times, mankind needs to honor God with a proper reverence and understanding of His worth—not to benefit God, but for his good will.

Possibly, we are heading into a Third World War.

Does Bible prophesy predict that there will be world wars before the End Times and one Final Conflict (the war to end all wars, possibly World War III) at the end?

MATTHEW 24:6-8, 15-22

"And ye shall hear of wars and rumors of wars: see that ye be not troubled: for all these things must come to pass, but the end is not yet.
For nation shall rise against nation, and kingdom
against kingdom: and there shall be famines, and
pestilences, and earthquakes, in divers places.
All these are the beginning of sorrows. . . .
. . . When ye therefore shall see the abomination of
desolation, spoken of by Daniel the prophet, stand in the
holy place, (whoso readeth, let him understand:)
Then let them which be in Judaea flee into the mountains:
Let him which is on the housetop not come
down to take anything out of his house:
Neither let him which is in the field return back to take his clothes.
And woe unto them that are with child, and
to them that give suck in those days!
But pray ye that your flight be not in the
winter, neither on the sabbath day:
For then shall be great tribulation, such as was not since the
beginning of the world to this time, no, nor ever shall be.
And except those days should be shortened, there should no flesh
be saved: but for the elect's sake those days shall be shortened.

REVELATION 6:4

And there went out another horse that was red: and
power was given to him that sat thereon to take peace
from the earth, and that they should kill one another:
and there was given unto him a great sword.

My dear friends, these verses from the Bible prove the occurrence of a global war. This war will be awfully destructive, because in Matthew 24:22 we read that, *"And except those days should be shortened, there should no flesh be saved: but for the elect's sake those days shall be shortened."*

The Lord's voice is crying to the nations of the world to come into the protective arms of its Father in Heaven, away from the land of death and damnation destined only for the antichrist and his followers. Come and begin a new life full of grace, peace, and restoration within the will of the Creator of all and all.

CHAPTER 10

God's Hand Over Israel

Only the hand of God can restore the peace on Earth.

God has predestined through a nerve-wracking dream about the threats and menacing intentions of terrorists against the United States of America, as well as all the other nations that support Israel. God is warning mankind through this dream for many reasons. First, and most important, the purpose is for man to repent and seek only God for protection. A nation's self-jurisdiction and self-strategies to establish peace on earth will not be successful. Our eyes must focus only on the Lord's powerful hand, which is a confident refuge to those who obey His will.

God Revealed the Act of Terrorists Through a Dream on September 8, 2010

I saw a young man—about 18 years old—with an ambition to come to the USA for a better life and career. He falls into a scheme of terrorists. The terrorists offered to help him to get inside the USA only if he will carry a machine with him. I saw this young man get inside the USA illegally, through the borders of the sea, along with this machine. I saw an old, white couple that seemed angelic and kind sailing in their boat.

They saw him floating on the surface of a deep ocean. They immediately helped this young man get inside their boat to save his life—this was symbolic of their act of caring for humanity.

Now I saw another adult man, this one about forty years of age. He has actual control and possession of this machine that arrived inside the USA's borders through the clueless young man. This machine functions like a chopper that can kill any adult into something just like ground beef, within seconds. I saw the same young man who came, initially, along with the killer machine through the USA borders, and he is now accompanied by this adult man—but the young man is without the knowledge of his companion's intentions. He is also unfamiliar with the use and function of this murderous tool. This "chopper" sort of machine is a great secret. If anyone comes to know its secrecy, they will be instantly killed, insanely so. I discerned in my spirit that several white folks (these signify European nationals) are already killed in the same manner because they witnessed this life- threatening tool in the hands of terrorists.

The Meaning of This Dream

God is warning us about many consequences and outcomes through this dream. I will share what the Holy Spirit has revealed.

I saw a naive young man who is an ambitious dreamer get involved in an illegal act foolishly to accomplish the desire of his heart. Terrorists will use such young men to achieve their motives. These terrorists will make grounds in foreign lands for fulfilling their evil plans against Israel and its affiliates. Many naïve people will support these terrorists and their cause in order to accomplish their personal ambitions such as financial gains or a better future, unaware that their support will result in the death of innocent people all over the world.

I saw the very humanitarian act of the old white couple who helped this young man and saved his life from the deep waters of the ocean. This part of the dream represents America and other nations that support Israel. They are doing everything in their power to maintain peace for all nations for a long time. (This is symbolized by the aged couple who are doing the rescuing in my dream). They will keep supporting because of their extreme humanitarian acts, oblivious to evil intentions behind the false commitments at the surface, and the hidden, deadly plans like a deep, dark ocean, which is difficult to unearth. Terrorism supporters will continue to get inside the protective land of peaceful nations due to the aged, humanitarian policies in place. This will benefit the evil cause of terrorists just like a rescuing sailing boat on the top of a deep, dark ocean. Terrorists will establish a stronghold of their evil motives in lands of peace.

Now we will enter into the main course of this dream. I saw three things.

- Established a control center of attack: I saw the terrorist entered inside the United States borders, along with the tool of killing, to accomplish their evil plans and schemes of terrorism all over the world.
- Characters of terrorists: These terrorists are brutal, slaughterers, inhuman, heartless, and cold-blooded. God has exposed their extreme insanity of mental illness through the manner of their killing people in my dream.
- Secrecy of their plans and resources: Their plans are kept in deadly secrecy to such a level that if anyone gets a minor clue about it, they are killed, brutally, just like ground meat.

I saw only white folks getting killed by them. God revealed that this terrorist regime is against the United States of America and all other nations that support Israel. They killed them in such a manner that no evidence is left to trace a murder. They work in extreme secrecy, which is impossible to unearth.

MATTHEW 10:28

"And do not fear those who kill the body but cannot kill the soul. But rather fear Him who is able to destroy both soul and body in hell."

Answer of my prayers to the LORD

This dream left a scar of a deep sore in my spirit. My heart was hurt, tense, and nervous about the inhumanely brutal motives of the enemy of mankind. I prayed ceaselessly with a deep love for Israel as well as every other nation of the world. I begged the Lord for the protection of His people against such evil intentions. God gave me a hope in a dream that I saw on October 1, 2010.

I saw an Israeli man (Jewish faith) sitting on a chair. He looked like a man of decisive power and dignity. He looked very sophisticated and, interestingly, about the same age as the terrorist in my previous dream. He is wearing a splendid quality suit of a blue color, similar to the star in the Israeli Flag. There is serene air of trust, confidence, and hope. I saw pressure poured on him from every direction by great men of earth. But he was sitting very calm, composed, and unflustered. His demeanor is like an unshakable mountain that cannot be moved with any kind of influences and pressures. **The Holy Spirit revealed that God's hand is on him.**

There is a great hope when God's hand is the reinforcement, help, and protection. We know the power of God's hand, which the Bible history proves. His prophets, kings, and nations prevailed and stood strong in a rightful position when the LORD was their God. God's answer to my prayers took my anxiety away because the Lord has shown the stability of Israel (His people) in spite of uncertainty around them; as I saw the Israeli representative sitting with complete confidence instead of the chaos and stress poured over him. The Lord gave an affirmation in the end of this dream that His hand is on His man of honor (His people). It is only God's hand that would be able to save mankind from the evil plans of terrorists. Please uplift your hands and call the name of Jehovah-Jireh for your protection, and praise Him for His love and mercies.

Why do enemies rise up to kill and destroy?

It is prudent to understand why enemies are rising up against America and the rest of Israel's allies. We cannot comprehend the reason of judgments without knowing the basis of blessing from the Lord. Let's see what Bible teaches about the similar situations that arose in the past. We will also learn the biblical emphasis for the reason of this never-ending rival, which the Lord showed me in this dream.

LEVITICUS 26:3-7
Promise of Blessing and Retribution
'If you walk in My statutes and keep My
commandments, and perform them,
then I will give you rain in its season, the land shall yield
its produce, and the trees of the field shall yield their fruit.
Your threshing shall last till the time of vintage, and
the vintage shall last till the time of sowing;
you shall eat your bread to the full, and dwell in your land safely.
I will give peace in the land, and you shall lie
down, and none will make you afraid;
I will rid the land of evil beasts,
and the sword will not go through your land.
You will chase your enemies, and they
shall fall by the sword before you.

Verses 3 to 7 in this passage demonstrates God's promises of un-mitigated blessings for those who obey His teachings and counseling; and then God Himself will bestow His people with the abundance of food, fullness of peace, joy, protection, and restoration. Their enemies become powerless in spite of their deadly hatred against them because the Lord God is their guard whose hand surrounds them protectively. Who can hurt those who receive the favor of the Father in Heaven—the Lord God Almighty!

Now we will read about the justice of God, when mankind revokes His teachings and counseling intentionally. Being a perfect Father in Heaven, He will discipline His people to help them come back to their rightful position as the children of God.

Continuation of **LEVITICUS 26**
LEVITICUS 26:14-17
'But if you do not obey Me, and do not
observe all these commandments,
and if you despise My statutes, or if your soul
abhors My judgments, so that you do not perform all
My commandments, but break My covenant,

I also will do this to you:
I will even appoint terror over you, wasting disease and fever
which shall consume the eyes and cause sorrow of heart.
And you shall sow your seed in vain, for your enemies shall eat it.
I will set My face against you, and you shall
be defeated by your enemies.
Those who hate you shall reign over you, and
you shall flee when no one pursues you.

These verses help us to understand that God desires the obedience of His commandments. He is warning us that if we despise His statutes, His judgments will be poured on us.

Many will say:

- Why such a pressure to obey?
- If we do not obey, why judgments?
- God is not love. He punishes and lets sufferings come on us.

Dear friends, the answers are found in these questions.

- Will you let your children drink any harmful drink or food like bleach, medicine, etc. that could kill them?
- Will you let your innocent children put their little finger in an electrical outlet?
- Will you let your child run into traffic?

Of course, your answer is NO.

I will ask you another question:

- Will you not be strict in disciplining your child if he or she is stubborn to disobey you, intentionally, and does evil forcefully?

You will definitely try everything in your power to discipline your child to help them recognize the things that can hurt them, and make sure that they will not attempt to do wrong even in your absence because of your overpowering love for them. Why do we refuse to accept the similar chastisements from our Heavenly Father—the Lord God Almighty?

Because <u>we</u> have not given Him a place of HEAVENLY FATHER!

Truth is that we are like a child in God's eyes. Just like a child cannot see the danger as clearly as a parent can, due to their wisdom and maturity, God knows satan's deceitful plans against us. Satan hates us because God has made us in His image with an overpowering love of a Father. God will keep disciplining us until the last day of our lives, and until we take our last breath, because He wants to bring all of us to Heaven in His loving presence.

LUKE 11:11-13

If a son shall ask bread of any of you that is a father, will he give
him a stone? or if he ask a fish, will he for a fish give him a serpent?
Or if he shall ask an egg, will he offer him a scorpion?
If ye then, being evil, know how to give good gifts
unto your children; how much more shall your heavenly
Father give the Holy Spirit to them that ask him?

Leviticus 26, verses 14 to 17, helps us to understand the outcome of man's rebellion towards his Father in Heaven. Practically, without His protection and presence, an enemy can destroy the human race completely. Truthfully, the devil knows the strength, power, and wisdom of the Heavenly Father. The Lord's absence from our midst will welcome the terror, wasting disease and fever, sorrow of heart, poverty, and defeat from the enemies. The fatherless children will be under complete chaos because they kicked their father out of their home only to enjoy the desires of their flesh.

Now we will go back to my dream about the terrorist's plans for Israel and their supporters. *Enemies of the people of God have been around from the beginning of creation and will stay around till the End of the Age. The problem is not their existence, the real issue is when they can accomplish their deadly motives. No one can hurt God's people; so far, their confidence is within the Lord their God.* We will look closely to see why people are under the threat of terrorists all over the world. The Lord revealed in my dream that terrorists have installed a deadly machine within the United States borders. We will learn about the roots of this country to reason with—why this prosperous and stable country is shaking, and why its enemies have found the room to hurt them.

Prosperity is diminishing from these nations, and now they are debtors rather than lenders, and a tail rather than the head.

Do you know that this country was originated as one nation under God?

"America was founded by people who believe[d] that God was their rock of safety. I recognize we must be cautious in claiming that God is on our side, but I think it's all right to keep asking if we're on His side."
— Ronald Reagan

The reason for America's success and riches around the world was not its intelligence and hard work. The country was richly blessed due to its faithfulness toward the will of God.

The prosperity of all the nations of the world will plunge due to their indulgence of unfaithfulness toward God, and declining God's counsel. Americans are doing everything opposite by breaking the covenant that was made between God and the people who grew the roots of the United States of America. Diseases, slavery, fear, and terror of heart is a fruit we reap when we sow the seed of sin. We are entering deeper and deeper in these judgments of God as we persevere and carry on with our sinful choices that conflict with God's Will.

The Word of God says in Leviticus 26:18, *"And after all this, if you do not obey Me, then I will punish you seven times more for your sins."* America, as well as all the nations of the world, has already faced the level of judgments described in Leviticus 26:19-33. We also read in Leviticus 26:26, *". . . And you shall eat and not be satisfied."* It is very much evident that God's people had enjoyed the season of abundance and prosperity, but dissatisfaction and greed took over their hearts and minds as they proceeded in their walk against God's teachings and will. Their unsatisfactory greed has helped them to live above their means and brought them to a self-made pit of poverty and destitution. This will exceed even this and grow seven times worse if we refuse to repent from our sinful choices. We will enter into the severity of God's discipline.

The Lord's revelation through a dream of September 8, 2010 is the manifestation of Leviticus 26:36-38. Mankind will be terrorized to such an extreme that *"even a sound of a shaken leaf will scare the nation."* We will be cowered when we encounter our enemies.

God is warning us to help us get out of this dark pit of sin and slavery. If nations seek Him today, He will not turn them away. The Lord will forgive them, heal their diseases, restore their prosperity, and remove their enemies from hurting and harassing them. The Lord God Almighty is the only way out for humanity. Read His promises in Leviticus 26:40 and 26:44 that establish this truth.

Continuation of **LEVITICUS 26**
LEVITICUS 26:40, 44
"But if they confess their iniquity and the iniquity of their
fathers, with their unfaithfulness in which they were unfaithful
to Me, and that they also have walked contrary to Me . . .
Yet for all that, when they are in the land of their enemies,
I will not cast them away, nor shall I abhor them, to
utterly destroy them and break My covenant with them;
for I am the LORD their God."

What is the Reason of Hatred for Israel and her Supporting Nations?

It is hard to comprehend why there is such a hatred for Israel and everyone who is a friend to that nation.

Please read this passage from the Bible. It will help us understand the reason of this inexorable conflict.

JUDGES 2:1-4
Then the Angel of the LORD came up from Gilgal to
Bochim, and said: "I led you up from Egypt and brought
you to the land of which I swore to your fathers; and I
said, "I will never break My covenant with you.
And you shall make no covenant with the inhabitants
of this land; you shall tear down their alters. 'But you
have not obeyed My voice. Why have you done this?'
Therefore I also said, 'I will not drive them out
before you; but they shall be thorns in your side,
and their gods shall be a snare to you.'

> *So it was, when the Angel of the LORD spoke these words to all the children of Israel, that the people lifted up their voices and wept.*

Israel is a covenant nation that was established under oath with the Lord. Similarly, the United States was also established under oath with God. Breach and violation of this virtuous covenant is unacceptable with Yahweh (the Lord), because the Lord said, *"I will never break My covenant with you."* This covenant with the Lord is also nontransferable to someone else because the Lord said in Judges 2:2, *"And you shall make no covenant with the inhabitants of this land."* Therefore, when any individual or a nation tries to alter or break the pious covenant between the Lord and themselves, God removes his favors from them, which provides an opportunity for their enemies to overcome their fences. The biggest mistake that the Israelis made was to make a covenant with the nations that God forbade them to associate with; the Israelis still made this covenant, keeping in mind the materialistic benefit and gain.

Israel was God's chosen nation as to establish His Kingdom on earth by doing what He said: *"You shall tear down their altars."* For this very purpose God prohibited this association, because friendship with idol-worshipping nations will not stop, but will expand, the satanic dominion among His people by converting their souls to idolatry and evil works of the flesh. God also knows that these nations will never keep their promises. Their intentions are always evil with His covenant people.

It would be ignorant to think that peace can be restored by a union of nations of the world. God would have done it already if it was possible. The only truth is that mankind is in a spiritual warfare on this earth, one which will end at the second coming of the Messiah of this universe. Only His kingdom on earth will establish the peace after eradicating all the evil darkness and its followers. We learn a great secret in Judges 2:3, where the Lord God Almighty said, *"I will **not** drive them out before you . . . "* This verse opens our minds to the truth that only a covenant with the Lord keeps us safe, because He Himself drives out our enemies before us. His separation due to the breach of a covenant relationship with Him gives His enemies unsecured boundaries to run over. Therefore it is foolish to think that mankind has any power to bring peace with their strength and wisdom.

Therefore, God judges righteously. God declared in Judges 2:3: *"I will not drive them out before you, but they shall be thorns in your side, and their gods shall be a snare to you."* The whole nation of Israel wept after hearing of this message from an Angel of the Lord, in Judges 2:4, " . . . *that the people lifted up their voices and wept."*

Would we cry and humble ourselves before the Lord?

If you believe, repent, humble, and cry before the Lord, there is still a hope from our everlasting, loving Heavenly Father, who is a perfect Father to discipline as well as forgive us.

Continuation of LEVITICUS 26

LEVITICUS 26:40-42

*"But if they confess their iniquity and the iniquity of
their fathers, with their unfaithfulness in which they were
unfaithful to Me, and that they also have walked contrary to Me,
and that I also have walked contrary to them and have brought
them into the land of their enemies; if their uncircumcised
hearts are humbled, and they accept their guilt
then I will remember My covenant with Jacob,
and My covenant with Isaac and My covenant with
Abraham I will remember; I will remember the land."*

JUDGES 3:9

*When the children of Israel cried out to the LORD, and
The LORD raised up a deliverer for the children of Israel, who
delivered them: Othniel the son of Kenaz, Caleb's younger brother.*

What an awesome hope we have in our Lord God Almighty, who prevails forever. No powerful nations, kings, and kingdoms can stand before Him because He sustains everything. He is the King of kings and the Lord of lords who rules over all, forever. He knows the end from the beginning. He knows the plans of enemies against His people. Only He can defeat all treacherous strategies, including those which have not yet been initiated. What an awesome and powerful God we worship!

On October 1, 2010, God showed me a vision that I have already shared with you. The Holy Spirit revealed that "**God's hand is on him** (Israel and their supporters)." As we read in Judges 3:9: "*When the children of Israel cried out to the LORD, and LORD raised up a deliverer for the children of Israel . . . .*" Similarly, when we as a nation will cry out to the Lord, a miraculous transformation will occur with His strategy, power, and wisdom which no man on earth can imagine and work out to deliver our earth from the threat of terrorists.

Why Such a Conflict Over Jerusalem?

We will explore in depth the reason of a small city, Jerusalem, being a threat to the whole world due to the hatred of satan against it and the love of the Lord for it. This hatred and this love story is not current news; it's been around from the Beginning of the Age and will remain till the End of the Age.

Let's take a dive into this mystical ocean and explore this mind-blowing revelation.

Jerusalem Is a Heart of God

Jerusalem is God's resting place, and He dwells among His people. The Lord chose this place out of the whole earth, where His name is embossed with His majestic throne, and His feet rest on this ground.

PSALM 132:13, 14
For the LORD has chosen Zion;
He has desired it for His dwelling place:
"This is My resting place forever;
Here I will dwell, for I have desired it."

2 CHRONICLES 6:6
Yet I have chosen Jerusalem, that My name may be there,
and I have chosen David to be over My people Israel.

EZEKIEL 43:7
And He said to me, "Son of man, this is the place of My
throne and the place of the soles of My feet, where I will

dwell in the midst of the children of Israel forever . . . "

Why Is Jerusalem God's Dwelling Place?

Jerusalem is a covenant ground zero for the Lord God Almighty. The father of faith, Abraham, obeyed when God called him to take his only son Isaac to be sacrificed at the hill of Moriah in Jerusalem, which is also known as the Temple Mount.

This was the place where Abraham experienced the root of salvation of mankind.

GENESIS 22:2

Then He said, "Take now your son, your only son Isaac, whom you love, and go to the land of Moriah, and offer him there as a burnt offering on one of the mountains of which I shall tell you."

Abraham, a man of faith, obedience, charity, and love, went to the mountain which God directed to sacrifice his only son as a burnt offering; he was still trusting God's promise that all the nations of the world would be blessed through the same child. Abraham had a faith in His Lord beyond our imagination; therefore, he took Isaac, and without a doubt that builds the foundation of righteousness for all of mankind. His trust and faith in the Lord overcame the power of the flesh's uncertainties. The Lord provided a ram at the spot to be sacrificed, and this portrays the salvation plan of God for all of humanity, both Jews and Gentiles.

GENESIS 22:12, 13

And He said, "Do not lay your hand on the lad, or do anything to him; for now I know that you fear God, since you have not withheld your son, your only son, from Me."
Then Abraham lifted his eyes and looked, and there behind him was a ram caught in a thicket by its horns. So Abraham went and took the ram, and offered it up for a burnt offering instead of his son.

And the Lord promised Abraham that his generation would be like the sand of the sea, and it was through his seed that salvation would be provided. At the same time, Abraham saw the day of the Lamb of the Lord, who would be sacrificed for all of humanity, at the very same site of Jerusalem.

GENESIS 22:14
And Abraham called the name of the place, The-LORD-Will-Provide; as it is said to this day, "In the Mount of the LORD it shall be provided."

JOHN 8:56
"Your father Abraham rejoiced to see My day, and he saw it and was glad."

Interestingly, centuries later, the house of the Lord was built at the same exact location where Abraham received the glimpse of God's plan for the salvation of mankind. On the same ground, the Lord appeared to King David.

2 CHRONICLES 3:1
Now Solomon began to build the house of the LORD at Jerusalem on Mount Moriah, where the LORD had appeared to his father David, at the place that David had prepared on the threshing floor of Ornan the Jebusite.

The time of the fulfillment of Abraham's vision about the Lord's salvation plan for the whole of humanity had arrived. The Lord Jesus Christ went up to the same mountain and met with Moses and Elijah.

LUKE 9:28-31
Now it came to pass, about eight days after these sayings, that He took Peter, John, and James and went up on the mountain to pray. As He prayed, the appearance of His face was altered, and His robe became white and glistening. And behold, two men talked with Him, who were Moses and Elijah,

who appeared in glory and spoke of His decease
which He was about to accomplish at Jerusalem.

At the very same hill, Moriah in Jerusalem, Abraham took his son Isaac to sacrifice. It was in Jerusalem where the precious blood of Jesus was shed to procure our redemption. Jerusalem is the source of our salvation in the Lord, where satan's evil against mankind is crushed under the feet of our Lord Jesus Christ. Finally, after being a victor of all things, the Lord Jesus Christ ascended to Heaven from Jerusalem.

ACTS 1:9-11
Jesus Ascends to Heaven
Now when He had spoken these things, while they watched, He
was taken up, and a cloud received Him out of their sight.
And while they looked steadfastly toward heaven as He went up,
behold, two men stood by them in white apparel, who also said,
"Men of Galilee, why do you stand gazing up into heaven? This
same Jesus, who was taken up from you into heaven, will
so come in like manner as you saw Him go into heaven."

The first church of God began its ministry from Jerusalem to reach the ends of the earth with the gospel of salvation. Praise the Lord for His perfection for His people, which is beyond our comprehension.

ACTS 1:4
The Holy Spirit Promised
And being assembled together with them, He commanded them
not to depart from Jerusalem, but to wait for the Promise of
the Father, "which," He said, "you have heard from Me;"

* * *

Rejoice! The Lord of lords and the King of kings is also returning back to Jerusalem.

Behold all the nations of the earth, your Savior—your Messiah—your Lord Jesus Christ, is coming back very soon to shield you from all the pains and sufferings of the earth. All nations will give their praises to the highest for the second coming of the Lord Jesus Christ at the anointed ground of Jerusalem, when He will restore all the things as He had designed from the beginning of the creation. He will bring an end to this curse of sin and evil. Works of the Spirit will overcome the works of the flesh. Evil will be removed forever. Oh yes, uplift your arms and cry with tears of joy for such a marvelous work of the Lord God Almighty. He truly is worthy to be praised and worshipped forever for eternity.

REVELATION 22:20
I Am Coming Quickly
He who testifies to these things says,
"Surely I am coming quickly."
Amen. Even so, come, Lord Jesus!

ZECHARIAH 14:4, 5
And in that day His feet will stand on the Mount of Olives,
Which faces Jerusalem on the east.
And the Mount of Olives shall be split in two,
From east to west,
Making a very large valley;
Half of the mountain shall move toward the north
And half of it toward the south.
Then you shall flee through My mountain valley,
For the mountain valley shall reach to Azal.
Yes, you shall flee
As you fled from the earthquake
In the days of Uzziah king of Judah.
Thus the LORD my God will come,
And all the saints with You.

Zachariah 14:4, 5 describes the mighty day when the feet of the Lord Jesus Christ will touch the Mount of Olives, which will split in two with a giant quake that will shake the whole earth simultaneously. He will come in Jerusalem along with all the saints born from the Beginning of the Age to the End of the Age.

Jerusalem is the heart of the Lord. The Lord Jesus Christ cried when He prophesied for Jerusalem that at the End Times, His people would brutally suffer at the hands of their enemies.

LUKE 19:41-44
Jesus Weeps Over Jerusalem
Now as He drew near, He saw the city and wept over it,
saying, "If you had known, even you, especially in this your day,
the things that make for your peace!
But now they are hidden from your eyes.
For days will come upon you when your enemies
will build an embankment around you,
surround you and close you in on every side,
and level you, and your children within
you, to the ground; and they will not leave in you one stone upon
another, because you did not know the time of your visitation."

The devil will not let any opportunity leave his hands to hurt Lord's people due to their failure to recognize the time of the visitation of their promised Messiah, and failure to welcome Him with open arms. As the Lord Jesus Christ said, *"Because you did not know the time of your visitation."* Instead they rejected their only Savior promised from the beginning of the age. Alas, the devil will do as the Lord said: *"For days will come upon you when your enemies will build an embankment around you, surround you and close you in on every side."* History has proven the multiple suffering from the hands of people. The final days of the earth will bring the last hatred against Jerusalem with full force. We are witnessing the happening of this prophecy that the enemies are beginning to surround Jerusalem politically, physically, and emotionally with terrorism strategies and hatred against them.

Finally, I will ask all the readers to pray for the peace of Jerusalem. This spiritual war of satan against the Lord will bring bloodshed not only in Jerusalem, but also to the whole world. <u>The peace of Jerusalem is the only key to the harmony of everyone.</u> *We are powerless for the things that occur in the spiritual realm, and the people who are under its influence are more powerless.* Prayers are the only weapons that will break the control of evil spiritual powers that are at work with full force to destroy Jerusalem, which is an anointed ground zero for the Lord God Almighty. History proved it and today we are all witnessing it. Your own observation will authenticate this commentary. <u>Do you see this hatred against Jerusalem today? If your answer is yes, then the Bible is the true and the living Word of God. The only way we can have peace on earth is through prayers for the peace of Jerusalem.</u>

Jerusalem is a small piece of land, but its significance is greater than the whole earth, because the salvation of the human race births from there, and reaches to the ends of the earth.

PSALM 122:6
Pray for the peace of Jerusalem:
"May they prosper who love you."

CHAPTER 11

Who ... Why ... and When Does God Judge?

We have heard many times that God judges all wrongdoings. People judge differently from God, and they have a saying to support their brand of judgment. They say things like "what goes around comes around." Some people say, "God will judge the injustice against them and prove their innocence." God does judge at a personal, as well as at a global, level. This is truly a commentary we hear on a daily basis. Many do not understand exactly who God judges, what is the reasoning of His judgments, and when does He judge.

Past stories from the Bible are indications of the forthcoming judgments of God in our lifetime. We will learn and understand the justification of God's judgments by studying past events, such as the Great Flood, where mankind was completely consumed from the surface of the earth; and in specified geographic locations, such as at Sodom and Gomorrah. We need this clarity, as the Lord is getting ready to judge the whole world again, and for the very same reasons, and with the same thoroughness.

First, let us examine the experience of Noah and the people of his era when the only survivors left on the face of this earth then were the patriarch and his family. Do you want to know why? Let's read this story together to comprehend the vital message for present mankind that is embedded in this account.

GENESIS 6:5-8, 13
Then the LORD saw that the wickedness of man
was great in the earth, and that every intent of the
thoughts of his heart was only evil continually.
And the LORD was sorry that He had made man
on the earth, and He was grieved in His heart.
So the LORD said, "I will destroy man whom I have
created from the face of the earth, both man and beast, creeping
thing and birds of the air, for I am sorry that I have made them."
But Noah found grace in the eyes of the LORD.
And God said to Noah, "The end of all flesh has come
before Me, for the earth is filled with violence through
them; and behold, I will destroy them with the earth.

At the time of Noah, the sins of mankind were soaring continuously, and unrestrained. There was no wickedness that these people did not contemplate and put into practice. They all refused to listen to Noah's testimony, a man whom God appointed because he was the only righteous man left on the face of the earth. God chose him to prophesy of His upcoming judgment to every living soul at that time. Alas, no one listened to Noah, but they treated him as a joke as if he had lost his senses because of his obedience to God's instruction to build the Ark on the land, where there was no sign of any body of water like ocean, river, or lake nearby. It seemed ludicrous and impracticable in the minds of the people because sinners don't understand that nothing is impossible with God.

So the Great Flood came just as Noah had predicted, and everyone got destroyed! Practically, who got saved? Of course, Noah and his family were saved. After forty days of continuous rain, the whole earth and all forms of life on it drowned. Mankind was practically wiped from the face of the earth! But God let life continue from the obedience of Noah, through the members of Noah's family, who were the only survivors.

After the Great Flood, God promised that He would never completely destroy this earth with water again. Though this world has seen terrible floods in different parts of the earth, there has never been a match for the deluge that happened at the Great Flood. The rainbow is the symbol of that promise between man and God.

Mankind of today's age is also operating at the same level of extravagance of sins, which will bring God's judgments in a same manner as of Noah's time, when *"the LORD was sorry that He had made man on the earth, and He was grieved in His heart."* Yes my dear friends, we need to ask this question honestly and respond with fairness. Is our earth moving ahead toward an unbearable level of violence and sin, where the Lord will be sorry once again that He had made man on earth, and be grieved in His heart? Why are we hurting our Father in Heaven so grievously? Why couldn't we love Him just as He loves us all? Why are we so blinded by willful denial of the truth of God's existence and His will, which is only placed there for our care and protection? Again, our earth will face the judgment of God as the people at the time of Noah did, because the Lord Jesus Christ said in Luke 17:26, 27: *"And as it was in the days of Noah, so it will be also in the days of the Son of Man: They ate, they drank, they married wives, they were given in marriage, until the day that Noah entered the ark, and the flood came and destroyed them all."*

* * *

We will continue to go deeper into the biblical facts and read another Bible story, this one of the destruction of Sodom and Gomorrah, one that helps us understand who, why, and when mankind is judged by the Lord. We will examine this story more deeply than even Noah's. People often say that the cities were destroyed because of homosexuality, but that wasn't the only reason. Homosexuality was and is abominable to God, but His reason for destroying the city was for the level of wickedness found there. He could not find even ten righteous people in that city, not even within the family of Lot, Abraham's nephew. Please read carefully, because the generation today will become exact replication of the people of Sodom and Gomorrah, and will also see destruction in a similar fashion if their behavior is not checked.

GENESIS 18:20, 21

*And the LORD said, "Because the outcry against Sodom
and Gomorrah is great, and because their sin is very grave,
I will go down now and see whether they have
done altogether according to the outcry against it
that has come to Me; and if not, I will know."*

Verses 20 and 21 prove the justification of the Lord's decision. The outcry of the evil of mankind ascended from the earth to Heaven before the throne of the Lord. The Lord came down Himself to validate the witnesses' account, to establish whether the incident reports of an outcry against mankind's outrageous sins were indeed factual. God is a fair judge; He will not announce the judgment until a crime is proven and established in His court of law. Advocates have a chance to mitigate any adverse judgment against those being judged. Abraham was the advocate who went to counsel in favor of mercy toward the people of Sodom and Gomorrah. Read the next verses to learn how Abraham spoke with the Lord God Almighty on behalf of the people of those sinful cities.

Continuation of **GENESIS 18: 22-33**

*Then the men turned away from there and went toward
Sodom, but Abraham still stood before the LORD.
And Abraham came near and said, "Would You
also destroy the righteous with the wicked?
Suppose there were fifty righteous within the city; would You also
destroy the place and not spare it
for the fifty righteous that were in it?
Far be it from You to do such a thing as this, to slay the righteous
with the wicked, so that the righteous should be as the wicked; far be
it from You! Shall not the Judge of all the earth do right?"
So the LORD said, "If I find in Sodom fifty righteous
within the city, then I will spare all the place for their sakes."
Then Abraham answered and said, "Indeed now, I who am but
dust and ashes have taken it upon myself to speak to the Lord:*

Suppose there were five less than the fifty righteous;
would You destroy all of the city for lack for five?" So He
said, "If I find there forty - five, I will not destroy it."
And he spoke to Him yet again and said,
"Suppose there should be forty found there?"
So He said, "I will not do it for the sake of forty."
Then he said, "Let not the Lord be angry, and I
will speak: Suppose thirty should be found there?"
So He said, "I will not do it if I find thirty there."
And he said, "Indeed now, I have taken it upon myself to
speak to the Lord: Suppose twenty should be found there?"
So He said, "I will not destroy it for the sake of twenty,"
Then he said, "Let not the Lord be angry, and I will
speak but once more: Suppose ten should be found there?"
And He said, "I will not destroy it for the sake of ten."
So the LORD went His way as soon as He had finished
speaking with Abraham; and Abraham returned to his place.

In verses 22-33 Abraham is constantly debating with the Lord, just like an attorney, trying to resolve the case in favor of his client. Abraham had a long discussion to make a way to justify the verdict of total annihilation of the land due to criminal charges for the evil acts of the people of Sodom and Gomorrah. Abraham, who is the father of faith and righteousness for all of humanity, kept begging the Lord for His mercies because of his personal experience of a loving and caring relationship with his Creator. Abraham asked God, *"Shall not the Judge of all the earth do right?"*, because Abraham knew well the perfection of God's decisions. Very humbly, Abraham asked the Lord if He would spare the whole city for the sake of fifty righteous people. The fair Judge of this earth agreed and said yes, but unfortunately there were not even fifty good people there. Abraham, being a good advocate, kept the case going by asking if God would hold back his judgment for lesser and lesser people—until he came down to number ten. Just imagine . . . there were not even ten righteous people in the cities of Sodom and Gomorrah. Amazing, isn't it? See what happened at the end of this court hearing? "So the LORD went His way as soon as He had finished speaking with Abraham; and Abraham returned to his place." Earnestly, God went His way to proclaim a fair judgment, and Abraham went back to his house with the knowledge of a decisive action of the Lord.

God spoke with Abraham just like He had spoken with Noah, because God always reveals His intentions to His servants before executing His judgments. We will continue to read this story to see what happened when God sent His angels to Sodom and Gomorrah to find the authenticity of these sins and crimes, for which an outcry reached Heaven before His holy throne.

God is a fair, impartial, righteous, and honorable judge. We see this when God went to Adam and Eve in the Garden of Eden to check on the validity of their sin with a fair chance of repentance before a finality of His judgment. *Today* is our chance to repent.

God, being a fair judge, will do the same again at the End of the Age. The Messiah of this universe, the Lord Jesus Christ, will judge the outcry over the sins of our world, which are continuously ascending to His holy throne. Eventually, His judgment will fall on all sinners, but He will rescue His righteous children as He did in Noah's era, as well as at the hour of the destruction of Sodom and Gomorrah.

We will go further in this story to understand the revelation of the final days of our earth in relation to the conclusive fate of Sodom and Gomorrah. Let's read together about their depravity.

GENESIS 19:1-3
Sodom's Depravity
Now the two angels came to Sodom in the evening, and Lot was sitting in the gate of Sodom. When Lot saw them, he rose to meet them, and he bowed himself with his face toward the ground. And he said, "Here now, my lords, please turn in to your servant's house and spend the night, and wash your feet; then you may rise early and go on your way." But he insisted strongly; so they turned in to him and entered his house. Then he made them a feast, and baked unleavened bread, and they ate.

The two angels came to Sodom to testify the source of the out-cry against the sins of this city. Lot, who was the only righteous and God-fearing man living in the city, asked the angels to visit his house. The angels accepted Lot's invitation and entered his house. Thus, all those who ask Jesus to be a part of their lives shall be saved, just like Lot received redemption. Lot made a feast for the angels, with unleavened bread; the Lord desires our communion of unleavened purity of heart with a desire to love Him deeply. We will go further with our story to grasp the deeper understanding of what our future holds, because this generation will replicate like the people of Sodom and Gomorrah; then the end will come.

Continuation of GENESIS 19
GENESIS 19:4-9
Now before they lay down, the men of the city, the
men of Sodom, both old and young, all the people
from every quarter, surrounded the house.
And they called to Lot and said to him, "Where
are the men who came to you tonight? Bring them
out to us that we may know them carnally."
So Lot went out to them through the
doorway, shut the door behind him,
and said, "Please, my brethren, do not do so wickedly!
See now, I have two daughters who have not known a
man; please, let me bring them out to you, and you may do
to them as you wish; only do nothing to these men, since this
is the reason they have come under the shadow of my roof."
And they said, "Stand back!" Then they said, "This one
came in to stay here, and he keeps acting as a judge: now we
will deal worse with you than with them." So they pressed hard
against the man Lot, and came near to break down the door.

Verses 4 to 9 are greatly important because these verses talk about our world today, which is full of the exact same kind of sins as the city of the Sodom and Gomorrah. Men of those cities desired to know men carnally over even young virgin girls. Can you imagine Lot's emotional stress when he had to offer his virgin daughters to get abused by these cruel men, just to save God's angels? The people of Sodom and Gomorrah reached the ultimate and unbearable level of sins. They were very cruel, with no consciousness of right from wrong; they were bullies, unethical and immorally corrupt. One can agree that mankind can achieve this sinful nature only when his heart is hardened into reprobation from corruption of the heart, mind, body, and soul. Amazingly, the righteous people of the Lord who have invited Jesus as their Lord and Savior of their lives will also do what Lot did. They will stand before the evil generation of this world to forbid them from demoralizing and taking the Lord's name in vain. His servants will not hesitate to offer their pure and virgin offering of righteousness and good works in order to be His witnesses. Many will be martyrs for His name's sake.

In verse 4 we learn that *"the men of the city, the men of Sodom, both old and young, all the people from every quarter, surrounded the house."* It is a sound indicator that the last generation of this earth, both old and young, will practice the same sexual desires and lifestyle similar to the people of Sodom and Gomorrah. They will surround the Church of God as those people surrounded the house of Lot with the intent to hurt and destroy the people of the Lord. Don't you witness this today in our society, with child molestation and other deviant sexual practices on the increase? *Unnatural sexual practices are now the norm as the society and government legalize such practices, and misleadingly so. It mirrors the description of Sodom and Gomorrah, where both old and young men demanded to abuse the angels of the Lord, and also Lot, over his virgin daughters.* Their appetite was for abnormal relations. Today, society calls those relations "normal" because they think humankind has a "right" to practice any type of lifestyle it pleases. Just imagine how close we are heading to the total destruction of our earth, because the outcry of the evildoings of mankind of the present age are also reaching the throne of the most pious and perfect Lord, just as with Sodom and Gomorrah.

Let's continue to read further to know what happened next.

Continuation of **GENESIS 19**
GENESIS 19:10, 11
But the men reached out their hands and pulled
Lot into the house with them, and shut the door.
And they struck the men who were at the doorway
of the house with blindness, both small and great, so
that they became weary trying to find the door.

Verses 10 and 11 are a prophecy of hope and rescue for the children of God because the angels pulled Lot inside the house and shut the door; God did the same with Noah's Ark: He allowed His servants to enter and then shut the door, offering them sanctuary. The Lord God Almighty will not allow His people to be annihilated.

These verses are bad news for the sinners of this earth, because God will shut the door to grace on His Day. The door is the Lord Jesus Christ, as we read in John 10:9: *"I am the door: by me if any man enter in, he shall be saved, and shall go in and out, and find pasture."* Mankind refuses to enter through the door of salvation due to the stubbornness of his own heart, as we read in Ephesians 4:18: *"having their understanding darkened, being alienated from the life of God, because of the ignorance that is in them, because of the blindness of their heart."* The blindness of man's sinful heart drowns him in his own self-righteousness.

We are also very close to the end of time as we know it. We will definitely face the consequences of being left out from under God's protection if we are not behind the door, like Lot, at the time when sinfully blinded men tried to break through the door, and fire and brimstone destroyed them all. Similar to this, Noah was inside the ark when sinners surrounded it, but the rainwater drowned them all. Praise the Lord for His loving care for His people when he protects them like a hen guarding her chicks from the ravening wolves.

Continuation of **GENESIS 19**
GENESIS 19:12
Sodom and Gomorrah Destroyed
Then the men said to Lot, "Have you anyone else here?
Son-in-law, your sons, your daughters, and whomever

you have in the city - take them out of this place.

In verse 12, the angels of the Lord offered Lot to go to his family and invite them into the place of shelter away from immediate destruction. Similarly, just before the annihilation of our earth, the Lord has sent His servants into the world to summon the family of God to get out of this place of death and destruction and into His Kingdom, through the washing of their sins in Christ. A total separation from the works of the earth is required for the people of the Lord to get saved; otherwise, they will also be destroyed with sinners.

It is important to understand that at every occurrence of the earth's destruction, a family of the righteous got saved. For example: In Noah's days, Noah and his family got saved. In Sodom and Gomorrah, Lot and his family got saved. Now, who will be saved at the End of Age except the church of God? The church of God is the family of the Lord Jesus Christ. The Lord is calling His family inside the protection of His Kingdom. Do you want to become a part of His family?

Continuation of GENESIS 19
GENESIS 19:13
For we will destroy this place, because the outcry
against them has grown great before the face of the
LORD, and the LORD has sent us to destroy it."

In verse 13, the angels announced the Lord's final verdict, that the cities of Sodom and Gomorrah would be destroyed after the proper validation of the true witnesses in the Court of His law, by the angels and Lot; because the outcry against them had grown great before the face of the Lord. Currently, our earth is heading in the same direction by growing in the same enormity of sins. God never passes judgment without witness, and that's who His present day servants are, as were Lot and Noah, as it is said in Revelation 12:11: *"And they overcame him by the blood of the Lamb, and by the word of their testimony; and they loved not their lives unto the death."* Therefore, God's verdict will be the same again for the whole of humanity.

Continuation of **GENESIS 19**
GENESIS 19:14
So Lot went out and spoke to his sons-in-law, who
had married his daughters, and said, "Get up, get out
of this place; for the LORD will destroy this city!"
But to his sons-in-law he seemed to be joking.

In verse 14, Lot reached his sons-in-law to share the good news for an opportunity to escape the wrath of God by telling them, *"Get up, get out of this place; for the LORD will destroy this city!"* But they rejected this offer of salvation due to their unbelief in the Lord and His Word—because God is not a serious business for the lovers of this world. All unperceived warnings were a mere joke for them, as it is said, *"But to his sons-in-law he seemed to be joking."* . . . And so it is true now. God's servants are blowing trumpets to warn and save many with a shout to *"repent for the Kingdom of God has come."* Unfortunately, many will react exactly like Lot's sons-in-law, by taking the warning as a joke in these Last Days.

Continuation of **GENESIS 19**
GENESIS 19:15, 16
When the morning dawned,
the angels urged Lot to hurry, saying,
"Arise, take your wife and your two daughters who are here,
lest you be consumed in the punishment of the city."
And while he lingered, the men took hold of his hand, his wife's
hand, and the hands of his two daughters, the LORD being merciful
to him, and they brought him out and set him outside the city.

Verses 15 and 16 are a wonderful hope for all believers. The Day of the Lord will be like a morning dawning for all the faithful children of God when they will be removed by His angels. Being a human, we like to procrastinate and yield to the temptations of this earth; especially, perhaps, leaving our loved ones behind may be among our worst trials. Fortunately, the Lord's mercy will lead us out just like Lot, when the angels of the Lord took hold of Lot and his family's hands to set them outside the place of destruction. We read: *"And while he lingered, the men took hold of his hand, his wife's hand, and the hands of his two daughters."*

Help your loved ones to seek shelter away from upcoming judgment. Now is an hour to bring them out of this dying earth, and direct them to the path that leads to the new earth where the Kingdom of God will prevail. The angel told Lot to *"Arise, take your wife and your two daughters who are here, lest you be consumed in the punishment of the city."* How wonderful it would be when the Lord will tell us to *"arise, take your spouse, child, parent, friend, and neighbor who are here, lest you be consumed in the punishment of this earth"*.

Just like Noah's and Lot's families were saved, the family of the Lord Jesus Christ will be saved in the Last Days. We read: *"the LORD being merciful to him, and they brought him out and set him outside the city."*

Continuation of GENESIS 19

GENESIS 19:17-23

So it came to pass, when they had
brought them outside, that he said,
"Escape for your life! Do not look behind you nor stay anywhere
in the plain. Escape to the mountains, lest you be destroyed."
Then Lot said to them, "Please, no, my lords!
Indeed now, your servant has found favor in your sight, and you have
increased your mercy which you have shown me by saving my life;
but I cannot escape to the mountains,
lest some evil overtake me and I die.
See now, this city is near enough to flee to, and it is a little one;
please let me escape there (is it not a little one?)
and my soul shall live."
And he said to him, "See, I have favored
you concerning this thing also, in that I will not
overthrow this city for which you have spoken.
Hurry, escape there. For I cannot do
anything until you arrive there."
Therefore the name of the city was called Zoar.
The sun had risen upon the earth when Lot entered Zoar.

Verses 17 to 23 relate to the salvation of believers. They will receive the mercy of the Lord to move from the plain grounds of weakness toward the mountains of strength, where no harm will come near them and death will not abide them; just like when the angel told Lot to *"Escape for your life! Do not look behind you nor stay anywhere in the plain. Escape to the mountains, lest you be destroyed."* We also learn in Isaiah 2:2:

Now it shall come to pass in the latter days
That the mountain of the LORD's house
Shall be established on the top of the mountains,
And shall be exalted above the hills;
And all nations shall flow to it.

Dear saints of God, your complete trust in your Lord will not overthrow you since your confidence, faithfulness, and obedience is in Him only.

Continuation of GENESIS 19
GENESIS 19:24, 25
Then the LORD rained brimstone and fire on Sodom
and Gomorrah, from the LORD out of the heavens.
So He overthrew those cities, all the plain, all the
inhabitants of the cities, and what grew on the ground.

Verses 24 and 25 are a final verdict of the case in the Court of law of the Judge of this universe; after a fair hearing given to an attorney (Abraham), and witnesses (Lot and his family), and with a proper search and investigation of the criminal charges by His angels. The people of Sodom and Gomorrah were proven guilty of their crimes of which the outcry reached the throne of the Lord: *"The LORD rained brimstone and fire on Sodom and Gomorrah, from the LORD out of the heavens."* Everyone and everything in that land was totally corrupted before the Lord, *"So He overthrew those cities, all the plain, all the inhabitants of the cities, and what grew on the ground."*
Currently, the sins and violence of the people of our earth are ac-

celerating at the same speed, pattern, and direction as the people of Sodom and Gomorrah were at the hour of their annihilation. The Lord will not completely destroy us with another Flood, nor He will not destroy us with brimstone either, but there is a Lake of Fire and torment for all eternity, as we read in Revelation 20:15: *"Anyone whose name was not found written in the book of life was thrown into the lake of fire."* The Lord will judge our earth today as fairly as He judged Sodom and Gomorrah.

Let's continue to read this story because the next part is an example of the losers of God's salvation.

Continuation of **GENESIS 19**
GENESIS 19:26
But, his wife looked back behind him,
and she became a piller of salt.

This part of the story is a lesson for those who are confused and cannot put their heart, trust, and desires completely in the Lord God Almighty. These types of people are like a man standing at the edge of a cliff with an obstinate mind, not knowing which way to head. Uncertainties at that point can cost him his life, when his foot can slip down the cliff toward death and damnation. Deadly accidents can occur because his confidence was not in the Lord, who gives the ability to see life as full of peace and joy on the other side of the cliff.

In verse 26 we read that Lot's wife disobeyed the instruction of the angels: "not to look behind," and turned into a pillar of salt. Lot's wife symbolizes those people who have not given up all for the love of God. Such people do not seek the Lord with complete commitment and sincerity. They seek pleasure in the things of the world and a desire to be with the Lord also. We don't recognize that our possessions and loved ones hinder our intimate relationship with the Lord when we don't learn to balance the spiritual and physical priorities. Lot's wife was tempted to look back because her heart was rooted in this city of death. Her home, worldly possessions, and loved ones, like her married daughters' husbands, were left behind, for they made a conscious decision to stay in the city of sin. Sadly, many "God-seekers" are the same as Lot's wife.

They want to run away from the snares of death set up by the devil against them, but they also lose the earnest sincerity and purity (the flavor of their salt) due to their half-hearted attitude toward the Lord God Almighty. God is pure and He desires purity of heart from the people who choose to follow the path of life, light, and peaceful joy in the presence of the LORD.

MATTHEW 5:13, 14
"You are the salt of the earth; but if the salt loses its
flavor, how shall it be seasoned? It is then good for nothing
but to be thrown out and trampled underfoot by men.
You are the light of the world. A city
that is set on a hill cannot be hidden."

Lot and his two daughters did not look back because they trusted the word of God through His angels, and also because they had the fear of God in their hearts; this is the beginning of wisdom. Secondly, they had the desire to obey the word due to their commitment to move ahead toward life and to escape death. They had their confidence and trust in the Lord God Almighty; more than the carnal wisdom of this sinful earth and its evil works. This is what God desires from every person who decides to seek life in the Lord God Almighty.

Do you want to be like Lot or like his wife?

Continuation of GENESIS 19
GENESIS 19:27-29
And Abraham went early in the morning to the
place where he had stood before the LORD.
Then he looked toward Sodom and Gomorrah, and toward
all the land of the plain; and he saw, and behold, the smoke of
the land which went up like the smoke of the furnace.
And it came to pass, when God destroyed the cities of the plain,
that God remembered Abraham, and sent Lot out of the midst of the
overthrow, when He overthrew the cities in which Lot had dwelt.

Verse 27 symbolizes that all the children of God own a place before

His throne, where they are standing now. They will witness the fairness and perfection of the Lord, who has fairly rescued all the righteous of this earth, who were hurt and abused by sinners, like child molesters, immoral sex addicts, drug traffickers, terrorists, gamblers, drinkers, liars, cheaters, cruel, the hard-hearted . . . you can name it, the list will be very long. Abraham witnessed *"the smoke of the land which went up like the smoke of the furnace."* The servants of the Lord will also witness His just and righteous judgments coming to pass in these Last Days.

Praise the Lord for His salvation that He has given, for the forgiveness of all sins through the blood of the Lord Jesus Christ, the blood that grants a chance for everyone to be removed from the list of sinners, when they call His name and repent from their sins wholeheartedly. *God has promised that He will never leave you and never forsake you. Even though God is so pure that He cannot tolerate the evil works, still His love for us is so marvelous that He gave us a hope through His blood, which sweeps away our sins and places them at the foot of the rugged Cross, where He died for us. Who else can love us like Him? Who would die for us like Him? Who would give us eternal life just like Him?*

The story of Sodom and Gomorrah gives us these choices.
Which one will you pick?
- Do you want to stand beside Abraham at the place of righteousness in the Lord and see His judgment done?
- Do you want to be in the land of death and damnations because you did not listen to the warning of destruction like Lot's sons-in-law?
- Will you be conflicted and your faith ambiguous, like Lot's wife, who was half in the world and half with the Lord?
- Or will you be a winner like Lot, who escaped to life because of his confidence in the LORD?

The story of the cities of Sodom and Gomorrah can serve as a reminder for today's generation in understanding who, why, and when God will judge.

CHAPTER 12

Emotions of God

Around April 2008 the Lord God Almighty moved my spirit to write about the "Emotions of God". God desires us to understand His love, compassion, sorrows, hurt, pains, care, and sympathy for all of mankind. This subject will become a seed to breed and nurture the fruit of an intimate relationship with our Creator—our Heavenly Father—our God.

God's Word is bursting with verses that convey His emotions for mankind. The love of the Lord is so intensely deep for us that he created us in His own image. God did not form anything else among all of His creation in His image, not even "the angels."

GENESIS 1:26
Then God said, "Let Us make man in Our image, according to Our likeness; let them have dominion over the fish of the sea, over the birds of the air, and over the cattle, over all the earth and over every creeping thing that creeps on the earth."

His passion is pouring out in these verses:

1 JOHN 4:19
We love Him because He first loved us.

ISAIAH 49:15
"Can a woman forget her nursing child,
And not have compassion on the son of her womb?
Surely they may forget,
Yet I will not forget you.

God loves you more than your own mother. These Scriptures resonate with this. This should be a reason to rejoice!

The Lord's love for you is unchangeable, indescribably forgiving, caring, and protective. When you wander off, He searches for you like a shepherd goes after a lost sheep. It is the intensity of God's love shown for you and me that He sends His servants to mankind: because He desires to save His lost sheep from the evil motives of the wolf (satan) who will kill His sheep without mercy. In Matthew 18:11-14 we read this expression of love of your Heavenly Father.

MATTHEW 18:11-14
For the Son of Man has come to save that which was lost.
"What do you think? If a man has a hundred sheep,
and one of them goes astray, does he not leave the ninety-nine
and go to the mountains to seek the one that is straying?
And if he should find it, assuredly,
I say to you, he rejoices more over that sheep than over
the ninety-nine that did not go astray.
Even so it is not the will of your Father
who is in heaven that one of these little ones should perish.

Every soul on the face of this earth needs to know:
• What is the love of God?
• How can we love God?
• Why does God want to have a relationship with us?
• Does this relationship benefit God or us?
• How does the love of God make us holy?

The answers for all these questions are found in the Bible.

JEREMIAH 31:3
The LORD appeared to us in the past, saying: "I have loved you
with an everlasting love; I have drawn you with loving-kindness"

God has definite plans made out of *His emotions of "loving-kindness"* for the human race. *We will learn God's plan and purpose for mankind in three phases from the day of creation to the end of the age.* After you finish reading this chapter you will be able to comprehend God's rescue plan for us, when God will bring us into His Kingdom while the whole world will be turned upside down by the removal of the dominion of satan.

The First Phase of Human History

We will commence from the beginning of the creation. God created Adam and Eve for a perfect relationship. These verses detail all the blessings that God bestowed upon mankind.

GENESIS 1:27-30
So God created man in His own image; in the image of God
He created him; male and female He created them.
Then God blessed them, and God said to them,
"Be fruitful and multiply;
fill the earth and subdue it; have dominion
over the fish of the sea, over the
birds of the air, and over every living thing that moves on the earth."
And God said, "See, I have given you every herb that yields seed
which is on the face of all the earth, and every tree whose fruit yields
seed; to you it shall be for food.
Also, to every beast of the earth, to every bird of the air,
and to everything that creeps on the earth, in which there is life,
I have given every green herb for food"; and it was so.

We pass our inheritance to someone whom we love most. What do you think God did for us at the time of creation? God created mankind in His own image out of all of His creations with a breath of life. God blessed them with all the riches of earth: food, peace, health, beauty, wisdom of heart, and a perfect love relationship with Him. Man received eternal life in a perfect place called Eden. God was Adam and Eve's friend. God used to visit them in Eden. The first man on earth used to see, talk, and walk with God. The verses above inscribe the intensity of His love from the day of creation. God gifted all His creations to man to rule over.

PSALM 36:7

*How priceless is your unfailing love! Both high and low
among men find refuge in the shadow of your wings.*

We will continue to read about God's outpouring affection on the first man and woman on earth.

GENESIS 2:15-17

*Then the LORD God took the man and put him in the garden
of Eden to tend and keep it. And the LORD God commanded
the man, saying, "Of every tree of the garden you may freely
eat; but of the tree of the knowledge of good and evil you shall
not eat, for in the day that you eat of it you shall surely die."*

In verse 15 we learn that God put man in the Garden of Eden to dress it, to take care of it, and to keep it. The Garden of Eden signifies delight and pleasure. It was adorned with every tree pleasant to the sight, and it was enriched to yield fruit grateful to the taste and good for food. God, as a tender Father, desired not only Adam's gain, but also his pleasure. The Lord gifted mankind with everything he needed—except for a single tree of good and evil, for which, if they ate of it, they would die. Some of you might be thinking: there would be no trouble started if this tree of good and evil was not placed in the Garden of Eden. Yes, you are right. But God does not want robots with a chip installed inside to obey and worship Him. Don't you admire the children of your house who honor, respect, and love you from the depth of his or her heart? A child who knows your needs and desires without asking— his heart touches your heart like no one else. God desires the same relationship of love, one with a free will, for His people. Love is not love without a choice. We always choose our lover. Without a choice to choose a lover . . . love does not exist. This intimate love relationship with God rewards us with the title of a "child of God." Angels were also given the same choice, as lucifer and his follower-angels did not have the will to follow God, through which they are cursed to this day, as satan was, with the powers of evil and darkness. The rest of the angels and all principalities and powers made a free choice to obey and follow the Creator of this universe and, until this day, they love God with a free will. The same principals exist for mankind in all ages.

In the third chapter of Genesis, we discover the change of man's destiny, from prosperity and fulfillment in the Lord his God to turmoil and punishment due to his failure to trust the Lord.

GENESIS 3:1-5
The Temptation and Fall of Man
*Now the serpent was more cunning than any beast of the field which
the LORD God had made. And he said to the woman, "Has God
indeed said, 'You shall not eat of every tree of the garden'?"
And the woman said to the serpent,
"We may eat the fruit of the trees of the garden;
but of the fruit of the tree which is in the midst of the garden,
God has said, 'You shall not eat it, nor shall
you touch it, lest you die.'"
Then the serpent said to the woman, "You will not surely die.
For God knows that in the day you eat of it your eyes will be
opened, and you will be like God, knowing good and evil."*

In verses 1 through 5 we read the trickery of the devil in the shape and likeness of a serpent. Adam and Eve transgress the divine command and fall into sin and misery. Once I was hearing a sermon from Pastor Steve Foss, entitled, "Satan's Dirty Little Secret." Pastor Foss taught "how satan rules over mankind with a spirit of inferiority and insecurity." Satan, who was the first in all of God's creation to disobey and reject God, knew that man's relationship with God would end his dominion on earth, therefore satan's best strategy was to interfere between God and mankind. Satan questioned the counsel of the Lord in order to sow the seed of doubt. This is how satan began, with an inquiry: *"Has God indeed said, 'You shall not eat of every tree of the garden?'"* This question poured into the spirit of inferiority in Eve. Satan still rules over mankind with the same spirit of inferiority which takes away faith, trust, and confidence in the Lord. The spirit of inferiority removes the ground of our stability with an invisible force that throws us into the snare of disobedience to the Lord in every area of life by rejecting His teachings and commandments. Have you ever observed that the people with inferior attitudes towards themselves are more involved in drugs, alcohol, gambling, sex, and all other addictive sins?

In verses 2 and 3 Eve informed satan that she and Adam could eat the fruit of all the trees, except for the one in the midst of the garden, as God has said: *"You shall not eat it, nor shall you touch it, lest you die."* At that, satan told Eve, *"You will not surely die,"* hiding the fact that the Lord spoke about a spiritual death. I think satan is the smartest psychologist. Satan breathes a spirit of insecurity into a woman's heart at an opportunity when she is alone and misguides her against God with mistrust. Satan planted a seed of mistrust in Eve's mind with a contradicting comment of what God had said, and impoverishing her trust by giving her the impression that God lied to them by saying, *"You will not surely die."* Poor women get trapped in satan's lie against God. He twisted God's statement and breath in the spirit of inferiority and insecurity with a false revelation that God is not sharing—knowledge that is false knowledge, by saying that, *"For God knows that in the day you eat of it your eyes will be opened, and you will be like God, knowing good and evil."* This statement made Eve feel inferior before the eyes of the Lord and she completely got trapped in the snare of disobedience to God's command. Mankind does walk away from God on a daily basis, because the same spirit of inferiority hinders him from knowing the Creator with an open heart and mind. People do acknowledge how great and mighty is the God of all creation, but fail to understand how important our intimate love relationship with Him is. The day we acknowledge the truth that God made us in His image for a serious relationship and partnership for a single purpose, to establish His Kingdom on earth,

and with it eradicate satan, we will be complete without pains and sufferings. Satan destroyed this relationship between man and God and
builds a wall of separation between them through mistrust for his own
benefit.

Continuation of Genesis Chapter 3
Chapter 3:6
So when the woman saw that the tree was good for
food, that it was pleasant to the eyes, and a tree desirable
to make one wise, she took of its fruit and ate. She
also gave to her husband with her, and he ate.

In this verse Eve implicated the qualities of the forbidden fruit under the falsehood of devil that: *"it is good for food, pleasant to the eyes,
and desirable to makes one wise."* She did not only fall into this betrayal
against God's counsel herself, but added a partner in crime by handing
over the fruit to her husband. Adam silently listened and followed his
wife. He did not even think about God's will, for a split-second. An important thing to note is that mankind is living off this forbidden fruit
since that day, and thinks that it is good for food by gaining a daily
nourishment to help grow in sin, and undecidedly moving away from
the Lord. This fruit of sin is pleasant to the eyes, also because sin is always more entertaining than boring good works of the Lord for fallen
humanity only. *This forbidden fruit of evil has opened man's eyes to the
knowledge of good and evil as the Lord declared in verse 4.* Just as good
parents like to share only good with a child and separate evil from them,
the Lord did the same, but satan gave a sense of negative comparison in
man's heart, which compelled them to look at that fruit differently than
its real image. Alas, mankind is still doing the same by seeing the fruit
of sin pleasant to the eyes. The last thing that the Eve observed was *"a
tree desirable to make one wise."* Today we are loaded with this wisdom
to defy God and worship our destructive, yet intelligent, minds, which
are destroying us and our earth in every aspect. Don't you think we re-
affirm Adam and Eve every day? Like Eve we share the fruits of evil with
our friends and family—especially our children. The innocent children
learn malevolence because we are transferring them this good, pleasant,

and desirable fruit under the influence of a spirit of inferiority and insecurity. How can we become so cruel to mislead our children toward eternal death and hell?

Continuation of **CHAPTER 3**

CHAPTER 3:7

Then the eyes of both of them were opened, and
they knew that they were naked; and they sewed fig
leaves together and made themselves coverings.

We observe the spiritual and physical transformation after eating of the forbidden fruit.

- *The eyes of both Adam and Eve were opened.* Their eyes were blind to the evil but lighted in righteousness from the time of their creation. But satan deluded them to move from light to the darkness.
- *They found themselves naked.* The robe of righteousness that shined through them and covered them from the eyes of evil was removed immediately after the disobedience to the Lord's will, because darkness took hold of them and they became aware that they were naked and vulnerable.

After this terrible experience *they sewed fig leaves together and made themselves coverings.* Mankind still stitches the fig leaves together, which are the excuses of every fleshly sin and weakness in order to hide their nudity of corruption. Truly our sin nature develops many forms of hiding corners from the truth to indulge in our fleshly weaknesses. We continuously let our conscious press down under the desires of sinful satisfactions. How long will we take to recognize the reality of our nudity in fallen sin and remove this burden with repentance before the Lord?

Continuation of **GENESIS CHAPTER 3**

GENESIS 3:8-10

And they heard the sound of the LORD God walking in the garden
in the cool of the day, and Adam and his wife hid themselves from
the presence of the LORD God among the trees of the garden.

*Then the LORD God called to Adam and
said to him, "Where are you?"
So he said, "I heard Your voice in the garden, and I
was afraid because I was naked; and I hid myself."*

In verse 8 Adam and his wife hid themselves from the presence of the Lord because of their shameful betrayal of His goodness for them. The Lord God already knew their mistake but still called them to be saved and not to be judged. With His loving-kindness the Lord said, *"Where are you?"* Adam responded to his best friend and companion that he was afraid of his vulnerability of imperfection in sin, which births from a denial of the Lord's teachings. Therefore they hid themselves—due to the embarrassment of guilt—from His pious presence. From that day onward, mankind is hiding from the Lord for the very same reasons as Adam and Eve. Today, the Lord is searching His sheep like a good shepherd with the cry: *"Where are you?"*

Unfortunately, mankind will hide from the LORD in a similar manner at the second coming of the Lord Jesus Christ because he has rejected His voice and rejected the chance to repent and get saved. God has prophesied the same behavior of mankind on the Day of Judgment, when humanity will be hiding from His presence once again because they know the guilt of their sins.

REVELATION 6
REVELATION 6:15-17

*And the kings of the earth, the great men, the rich men,
the commanders, the mighty men, every slave and every free
man, hid themselves in the caves and in the rocks of the
mountains, and said to the mountains and rocks, "Fall
on us and hide us from the face of Him who sits on the
throne and from the wrath of the Lamb! For the great
day of His wrath has come, and who is able to stand?"*

Continuation of GENESIS CHAPTER 3
GENESIS CHAPTER 3:11-13

And He said, "Who told you that you were naked? Have you

> *eaten from the tree of which I*
> *commanded you that you should not eat?"*
> *Then the man said, "The woman whom You gave to*
> *be with me, she gave me of the tree, and I ate."*
> *And the LORD God said to the woman,*
> *"What is this you have done?"*
> *The woman said, "The serpent deceived me, and I ate."*

Nothing can be hidden from the Lord God, but still He came to Adam and Eve to offer them the opportunity to accept the mistake and repent, but man put the blame on the woman by saying, *"The woman whom You gave to be with me, she gave me of the tree, and I ate."* And the woman blamed the serpent by saying, *"The serpent deceived me, and I ate."* Humanity does the same every day by not taking the responsibilities of their mistakes but rather blaming anything that comes around handy, including family, friends, and circumstances of life. It's never too late to accept the guilt and weaknesses, because such an act will open the path of hope, future, and prosperity that the Lord has designed for us.

> *For I know the plans I have for you," declares the LORD,*
> *"plans to prosper you and not to harm you, plans to give*
> *you hope and a future"*
> **(JEREMIAH 29:11).**

Sadly, Adam and Eve disregarded God's marvelous plans of prosperity and hope. God did not reject them instead of knowing that they had been disobedient to His command. God, out of His precious love, walked to them, hoping for them to say the simple words "sorry" and "forgive us." But they decided to stand before God in complete denial. Humanity has continued to live with the exact pattern until today. Why is it so hard to accept the guilt, repent, and remove from sins, and hold the hands of the Lord God Almighty and walk hand in hand with Him toward the journey of salvation, where awaits a future full of prosperity and hope?

Let's read the result of man's denial of the guilt, and a rejection of a call of repentance.

Continuation of **GENESIS CHAPTER 3**
GENESIS 3:14-19

So the LORD God said to the serpent: "Because you have done this,
You are cursed more than all cattle,
And more than every beast of the field;
On your belly you shall go, And you shall eat dust
All the days of your life.
And I will put enmity Between you and the woman,
And between your seed and her seed; He shall bruise your head,
And you shall bruise His heel."
To the woman He said: "I will greatly multiply
your sorrow and your conception;
In pain you shall bring forth children;
Your desire shall be for your husband,
And he shall rule over you."
Then to Adam He said, "Because you have heeded the
voice of your wife, and have eaten from the tree of which
I commanded you, saying, 'You shall not eat of it':
"Cursed is the ground for your sake;
In toil you shall eat of it. All the days of your life.
Both thorns and thistles it shall bring forth for you,
And you shall eat the herb of the field.
In the sweat of your face you shall eat bread
Till you return to the ground, For out of it you were taken;
For dust you are, And to dust you shall return."

Now the Lord God, who is the fair and righteous Judge, announced the punishment to all three involved after giving them their rightful chance of a fair hearing.

- The first judgment was announced to serpent because he was the root of evil, mischief, and sin in mankind. The serpent is satan's image, dominion, and obedience, and will be the first one to receive the first rightful judgment which the Lord said: *"Because you have done this, You are cursed more than all cattle, And more than every beast of the field; On your belly you shall go, And you shall eat dust All the days of your life."* The hatred and enmity between him and women continue in such a manner that man will crush the serpent's head because it is a root of satan's brainwave of inspiration that deceived Eve; and serpent will bruise the heels of the seed of the woman, because it was her footsteps that fell into his clever trap of disobedience toward God. As the Lord declared, *"I will put enmity between you and the woman, and between your seed and her Seed; He shall bruise your head, and you shall bruise His heel."* This hatred between the seed of serpent and the seed of women exists till this day because what Lord God put in place no one can change.

- The second judgment stood just and fair for Eve, when the Lord said, *"I will greatly multiply your sorrow and your conception; in pain you shall bring forth children; your desire shall be for your husband, and he shall rule over you."* From that day on, women gave birth with excruciating pains because she was responsible for the birth of sins for humanity. God gave women a desire of her husband's favor, who would rule over her sentiments because woman ruled over man's emotions in disobeying God's command. A woman was justly punished for this because her failure encouraged man to fall into the trap of sin and defiance towards his best friend, God.

- The third judgment was announced for Adam. God created Adam as most precious and favorable being and bestowed love, companionship, and spiritual intimacy with him, but he did not fathom the outcome of his choice in negligence to God's will over his physical and emotional involvement with Eve, when he only heard the woman's opinion. He then blindly tasted the forbidden fruit that God commanded not to eat. As we read, the Lord said to Adam, *"Because you have heeded the voice of your wife."* Thus, man was rightly judged when God said, *"Cursed is the ground for your sake; in toil you shall eat of it All the days of your life."* Man will face emotional and physical hardships because he was emotionally and physically weak toward his free choice toward God's command. The worst punishment that he has to face is to lose his right of eternity. He will return back to the ground from which he was created. Dust will return back to its origin. It is very important to understand that we are worthless as dust without God. God is life. Therefore, if you want to live forever away from Hell— Seek God.

Continuation of **GENESIS CHAPTER 3**
GENESIS 3:20, 21
And Adam called his wife's name Eve, because
she was the mother of all living.
Also for Adam and his wife the LORD God
made tunics of skin, and clothed them.

The beginning of a new phase for mankind began. Adam called his wife Eve as she would be the mother of humanity. Man covered his nudity with fig leaves, but God provided for them the leather tunics, because He was still concerned for man's physical needs against the perils of earth; similarly, He also provides His salvation to protect against the coarse spiritual situations of physical and emotional pains and sufferings. Amazingly, this is a story of every man and woman on earth. We often hide our weaknesses with the fig leaves like self-righteousness, which is not reliable against the coarse situations of life, because no matter how much mankind tries to hide inside his self-made shell, his vulnerability will still be exposed when tempted by the forces of darkness. The Lord God Almighty has provided for us the permanent tunics of skin in the flesh of His Son, the Lord Jesus Christ, who died for our sins at the cross. His flesh is torn down to redefine our fleshly infirmities caused by the snare of sin. Our weaknesses have surrounded us in a wind-swirl of the forces of evil that tear away the fig leaves of our efforts, but the tunic of skin of our Lord Jesus Christ is the only protective defense that hides our nudity, because the love of the Lord took it all for us and became a shame Himself to earn honor and respect for all those who will accept His love. What a marvelous loving God man has!

Continuation of **GENESIS CHAPTER 3**
GENESIS 3:22-24
Then the LORD God said, "Behold, the man has become like

191

one of Us, to know good and evil. And now, lest he put out his
hand and take also of the tree of life, and eat, and live forever"—
therefore the LORD God sent him out of the garden of
Eden to till the ground from which he was taken.
So He drove out the man; and He placed cherubim at the east of
the garden of Eden, and a flaming sword which turned
every way, to guard the way to the tree of life.

Now the human race has gained the knowledge of good and evil, which worried the Lord. Out of His passionate love as a Father in Heaven, He will do everything in His power to keep His children away from any source of separation from His presence permanently, as we read, when God said, *"Behold, the man has become like one of Us, to know good and evil. And now, lest he put out his hand and take also of the tree of life, and eat, and live forever."* The only reason for the Lord's concern was being that mankind would live in sin for eternity if they got to the tree of life and ate this fruit in their current state of infirmity of sin. God eradicated the chance of eternal damnation with an act of kindness toward the human race by doing what verse 24 says: *"So He drove out the man; and He placed cherubim at the east of the Garden of Eden, and a flaming sword which turned every way, to guard the way to the tree of life."* The Lord blocked the way to the tree of life in the Garden of Eden, because His love will not tolerate the human race to live forever in sin without hope. Finally, God put man back to the ground from which he was created, as in verse 23, God decided, *"Therefore the LORD God sent him out of the garden of Eden to till the ground from which he was taken."* Man started his new beginning under the penalty of sin, which is death, that he sowed with his own choice and will live outside of the Garden of Eden, which is a symbol of life and the eternal Kingdom of God. God then protected the tree of life with a flaming sword until it will be the right time for man to receive the gift of life—in God's perfect time. Now we will go further and learn more about God's salvation plan for all mankind. God did not leave man as orphans, but set up a marvelous plan to shield him from the permanent trap of satan, due to His unconditional love.

The Second Phase of Human History

Hundreds of generations have passed since Adam and Eve left the Garden of Eden, and man is now living a life of his choice. Earth is covered with a human race of many ethnicities, cultures, civilizations, and religion. The Word of God, the Bible, leads us further into history, evidencing God's unbroken association with humanity. Great prophets came from time to time to guide and lead God's people. God will continue to send His servants to save His children till the end of the age.

We will begin with the great prophet of God, Abraham. God made him the father of many nations.

GENESIS 17:5

No longer shall your name be called Abram, but your name shall be Abraham; for I have made you a father of many nations.

What was so special in Abraham among all the people living at that time that God only choose him for this perfect plan for humanity? We find the reason in these verses.

HEBREWS 11:8

By faith Abraham obeyed when he was called to go out to the place which he would receive as an inheritance. And he went out, not knowing where he was going.

ROMANS 4:3

For what does the Scripture say? "Abraham believed God and it was accounted to him for righteousness."

Mistrust in the Lord by Adam and Eve resulted in their death and a separation from Him, but the ***trust*** of Abraham resulted in a hope of life for all mankind. His people walk after the example of Abraham's faith; he believed the voice of the Lord without doubting the reasons of His purposes and plans, unlike satan, who challenged God's supremacy. Abraham was the only man on earth whose heart was faithful to understand what trust is. Thus Abraham is a spiritual father of all believers whose belief, trust, faith, and obedience blessed humanity with a hope of salvation that God made possible through him.

ROMANS 4:11
And he received the sign of circumcision, a seal of the righteousness of the faith which he had while still uncircumcised, that he might be the father of all those who believe, though they are uncircumcised, that righteousness might be imputed to them also.

ROMANS 4:13
The Promise Granted Through Faith
For the promise that he would be the heir of the world was not to Abraham or to his seed through the law, but through the righteousness of faith.

Abraham received the sign of circumcision to seal the covenant between man and God, which resulted in the marvelous restoration of souls for entrance into the Kingdom of God. Therefore, the righteousness of Abraham's faith built a covenant relationship with which he reinstated the position that Adam lost. Abraham was chosen when he was an uncircumcised gentile to convert into a promised nation of God that we call the Jews, to bring forth the Messiah from the seed of King David, who fulfilled and accomplished the Salvation Plan of God, by which all the nations of the world got saved, including Jews and gentiles, transforming them into one new man (Ephesians 2:15).

Mankind can claim this right of a covenant relationship with the Lord of the universe only with a circumcised heart that builds a seal of the righteousness of a covenant relationship with the faith like Abraham: that will give him the right he lost due to Adam's disobedience, and allow him to come to a circumcised relationship with his God through the righteousness of faith in the Messiah, in whom the law of God is reinstated and satisfied to its initial state of creation.

Let's learn this awesome work of the Lord in detail so that we can comprehend His perfect ways to bring His people back to the Garden of Eden to the tree of life, with an intimate love-relationship with Him. We will take a journey in the Scriptures of the Bible to understand how the law of God is the only way to the restoration of mankind.

The Love of God Revealed in His Laws

It is very important to understand that God created this whole universe on laws and principles—for physical as well as spiritual existence. In our scientific vocabulary, we have named the physical laws as:

- Law of universal gravitation
- Laws of planetary motion
- Laws of thermodynamics
- Laws of light
- Laws of heat
- Laws of motion
- . . . and many more laws.

The sole Creator of these laws of nature is the Lord God Almighty, who formatted them with perfection by His Word—that is a picture of alpha and omega, without an end.

JOHN 1:1-3
The Eternal Word
*In the beginning was the Word, and the Word was with
God, and the Word was God.
He was in the beginning with God.
All things were made through Him, and
without Him nothing was made that was made.*

God's perfection is proven in His creations in such a manner that a minor alteration to the laws of nature will bring failure and chaos. For example, the whole universe would collapse if any planet moves away from its orbit by varying the Law of Gravitation. *Similarly, the Word of God given in the form of His commandments, teachings, and counsel is a spiritual law and the breaking of any spiritual law will bring failure and chaos to His creation from life until death. Therefore the eternal life ended with the violation of the Word of God in the Garden of Eden with a disobedience to His will. This breach of a covenant relationship between man and God serve the human race with a chaos of death, pains, and sufferings.*

It is only out of His love that God restored His relationship with mankind, one that can only be reinstated by fixing the broken pieces of the spiritual law. Initially, Adam and Eve broke the law of eternal life, in which they had the privilege to live in the presence of the Lord, but they broke it, resulting in death. Therefore, in order to restore this life back to the human race, God made a way to fix the broken law. We will learn this work of the Lord right from His Word. The Word of God teaches in the Scriptures that blood is life. Thus, the Law of God can only be satisfied with a filling in of the deficit of life with life, and of blood with blood.

GENESIS 9:4
But you shall not eat flesh with its life, that is, its blood.

LEVITICUS 17:11, 14
*For the life of the flesh is in the blood, and I have given it
to you upon the altar to make atonement for your souls; for
it is the blood that makes atonement for the soul.'
. . . . for it is the life of all flesh. Its blood sustains its life. Therefore I
said to the children of Israel, 'You shall not eat the blood of any flesh,
for the life of all flesh is its blood. Whoever eats it shall be cut off.'*

Now we clearly understand that blood is the main source of physical life among all living. Man is forbidden to eat blood and it was solely used for the atonement of souls by the animal sacrifices that were given for the forgiveness of sins. Next, we will learn why the blood of the sacrifices was installed, and why it was the only way to save the human race from a total separation with the Lord.

The Law of God Satisfied to Restore Life

The peace that was lost between God and man can only be restored through the Peace Offerings because the Spiritual Law is satisfied with a filling in only of that which was lost; for example, if a magnetic force between planets is disturbed, then it can only be reinstated with filling in the exact portion of that which was lost. We discussed earlier that the blood is life among all living; therefore, the life can be restored only by giving a life with shedding of blood through ritual sacrifices. Let's read how perfectly the LORD continued the relation with mankind, even though he did not deserve it due to the evil of his heart.

LEVITICUS 3:1-2, 17
The Peace Offering
'When his offering is a sacrifice of a peace offering, if
he offers it of the herd, whether male or female,
he shall offer it without blemish before the LORD.
And he shall lay his hand on the head of his offering,
and kill it at the door of the tabernacle of meeting;
and Aaron's sons, the priests,
shall sprinkle the blood all around on the altar.
'This shall be a perpetual statute throughout your generations
in all your dwellings: you shall eat neither fat nor blood.'''

The Peace Sacrifice was instituted to restore peace. God instructed the Israelites to carry out the Peace Sacrifices by each member of the congregation—with an offer of a herd or lamb. They would lay their hands on the head of the offering and kill it before the door of the tabernacle of meeting. Lastly, were to sprinkle the blood of sacrifice around on the altar in order to mend the relationship lost by unintentional sins from the beginning of creation through all generations by the peace offerings. *Ultimately this Peace Sacrifice was replaced with an everlasting sacrifice of our Lord Jesus Christ at the cross; he reinstated a peace that was lost between man and God. The Lord Jesus Christ became a perfect peace offering for the human race and befitting as an unblemished Lamb on whose head our darkest sins were laid down, symbolized by laying hands over the head of offerings in traditional sacrifices. The Lord Jesus Christ was killed right at the door of the tabernacle of meeting, where anyone believing in Him would be able to enter into a pure relationship with the Lord due to the blood of our Messiah that was shed and sprinkled on the altar to bring forth an eternal life back to mankind.* We read about the fulfillment of the covenant of God with mankind through Christ in Hebrews 9.

HEBREWS 9:11-15, 22
The Heavenly Sanctuary

But Christ came as High Priest of the good things
to come, with the greater and more perfect tabernacle not
made with hands, that is, not of this creation.
Not with the blood of the goats and calves, but
with His own blood He entered the Most Holy Place
once for all, having obtained eternal redemption.
For if the blood of bulls and goats and the ashes of the heifer,
sprinkling the unclean, sanctifies for the purifying of the flesh,
how much more shall the blood of Christ, who through
the eternal Spirit offered Himself without spot to God, cleanse
your conscience from dead works to serve the living God?
And for this reason He is the Mediator of the new
covenant, by means of death, for the redemption of the
transgressions under the first covenant, that those who are
called may receive the promise of the eternal inheritance. . . .
And according to the law almost all things are purified with
blood, and without shedding of blood there is no remission.

Christ as the Prince of Peace who made peace between man and God with His blood on the cross. Even though mankind did not cease to live in sin, God on the other hand did not cease to plan a way of forgiveness and salvation for His beloved human race. God's unconditional love never ended for us. The first solution was the sacrifices of flocks to reconnect with God for the forgiveness of sins, but this could not permanently remove the barrier between the man and God due to the stains of ongoing sins. Therefore in order to remove this wall of sin between man and God, a permanent sanctified sacrifice was offered, per Hebrews 10:9: "*He takes away the first that He may establish the second.*" As it is said in verse 15: "*And for this reason He is the Mediator of the new covenant, by means of death, for the redemption of the transgressions under the first covenant, that those who are called may receive the promise of the eternal inheritance.*" Before I continue further, I have a question for you. If your child is facing death and that child's life can only be restored back with your own—Would you die at your child's place? We may not do it, but God did this act for His children.

What do you think God did for us? He never stopped thinking about us, even for a split-second, from the day of creation. God, who created us in His own image, poured His spirit in us that we became his heart and soul, and He came down to earth as a man to take away the first, that He may establish the second, by dying once for all to sanctify us before the Lord, as it is said in Hebrews 10:14: *"For by one offering He has perfected forever those who are being sanctified."* God sent His only begotten son to die at the cross, shed His blood (life) and suffered for us to give us an eternal life as a free gift for all those who believe in faith like Abraham. This was the perfect way to save the human race per the Law of God. The sanctuary of the Lord created here on Earth is put in place back to its original by the fulfillment of a just Law of God that does not favor anyone because of His purity and perfection. Therefore, His own Son abided by the Law of His Father, with death to earn life for us, and shed His blood to wash our sins and inequities. This act reinstates the permanent peace between man and God that was lost at the beginning of the creation due to the seed of sin and disobedience. The Messiah, the Lord Jesus Christ, came from the seed to Abraham that became a path to the salvation for all mankind due to his faith, righteousness, and obedience with the Lord. Therefore, salvation came from Jews to bless and save the whole world. Thus the Lord of the universe put the broken pieces back of spiritual Law that was shattered in the Garden of Eden by Adam and Eve with a restoration of blood with blood, and of life with life. We learn about this marvelous plan of God achieved in the Lord Jesus Christ for us in this Scripture below:

HEBREWS 10:10, 18-22
By that will we have been sanctified through the
offering of the body of Jesus Christ once for all. . . .
Now where there is remission of these,
there is no longer an offering for sin.
Therefore, brethren, having boldness to enter
the Holiest by the blood of Jesus,
by a new and living way which He consecrated
for us, through the veil, that is, His flesh,

and having a High Priest over the house of God,
let us draw near with a true heart in full assurance of faith,
having our hearts sprinkled from
an evil conscience and our bodies washed with pure water.

Our loving Lord God made us worthy enough to enter into His holiest presence. Our sins and iniquities will not be remembered any more before our Heavenly Father because His son, Jesus Christ, removed the veil of impurity with His flesh and become a High priest to lead us to the Holy of Hollies, where a sinful, unworthy, and thankless mankind are gifted with an opportunity to avail themselves of eternal salvation by faith, and can achieve eternity with God.

The Tree of Life Made Available to All

As we discussed earlier when God took Adam and Eve out of the Garden of Eden, God guarded the tree of life from man's reach until the right time. We read in the first phase of this topic how God removed Adam and Eve from the Garden of Eden and did not let them reach to the **Tree of Life,** as it is said in Genesis 3:24: *"So he drove out the man, and he placed at the east of the Garden of Eden cherubims and a flaming sword which turned every way, to keep the way of the tree of life."* God did this not because He did not care, but the reason was that God did not want man to live in a permanent curse like the fallen angels. God took that Tree of Life away in the Garden of Eden only to make a way for eternal peace with an intimate relationship with mankind through a free gift of His only begotten son, the Lord Jesus Christ. He became a perfect sacrifice because life sustains only in Him, as He is a Tree of Life, as Jesus said, ***"I am the way, the truth, and the life and no one comes to the Father except through me"*** (John 14:6). Now, whoever eats of that tree will live forever with blessings, love, and redemption, for it is all accomplished with affirmation of the Lord Jesus Christ on the cross before His last breath, with His last words: ***"It is finished".***

JOHN 19:30
So when Jesus had received the sour wine, He said, "It is finished!" And bowing His head, He gave up His spirit.

Yes my friend, it is finished at the hour when *Christ was offered once to bear sins of many, and now to those who eagerly wait for Him He will appear a second time, apart from sin, for salvation.* Praise the Lord for His second coming, which will be very soon and hopefully in our lifetime.

HEBREWS 9:28
So Christ was offered once to bear the sins of many.
To those who eagerly wait for Him He will appear a
second time, apart from sin, for salvation.

Now after discovering the most important truth of our existence and finding the only way of our salvation and remission, that *"God gave His Son's life to save all of us,"* there remains no other hope for those who still continue to:
- Refuse to learn the fact of God's only salvation plan for all mankind
- Be self-righteous
- Do not repent and continue to live unrighteous lives
- Keep following their own beliefs and reject God's perfection
- Follow the pattern of Adam and Eve, with the blaming of others instead of accepting their own guilt

HEBREWS 10:26-31
For if we sin willfully after we have received the knowledge
of the truth, there no longer remains a sacrifice for sins,
but a certain fearful expectation of judgment, and fiery
indignation which will devour the adversaries.
Anyone who has rejected Moses' law dies without
mercy on the testimony of two or three witnesses.
Of how much worse punishment, do you suppose,
will he be thought worthy who has trampled the
Son of God underfoot, counted the blood of the covenant by which he
was sanctified a common thing, and insulted the Spirit of grace?
For we know Him who said, "Vengeance is Mine, I will repay,"
says the Lord. And again, "The LORD will judge His people."
It is a fearful thing to fall into the hands of the living God.

Today God is giving us a fair chance, exactly like Adam and Eve, when they disobeyed Him before His final verdict of the judgment of their sin. God is pouring out to us the opportunities of hearing His Word from His messengers, who are sent to you for your salvation. Sometimes mankind is judged at personal and global levels only because God is our perfect Father in heaven who will punish his sin, not due to hatred, but out of love to save man from turning into evil and destroying his life. A good father will correct his son's behavior without letting it go. Our heavenly Father who has created you out of love and compassion is doing the same every day of your life. How long you will fail to admit that God wants to protect you from the enemy, satan, who despises you so intensely?

When Adam and Eve did not avail themselves of the opportunity of repentance, they were given the announcement of judgment for their sin because they did not repent but blamed each other. Exactly the same way, if we decide to repeat the same story again with denial of our sins and rebellion against the will of God, and do not accept the Lord Jesus Christ as our Lord and Savior: then we have no hope left. *"For if we sin willfully after we have received the knowledge of the truth, there no longer remains a sacrifice for sins"* (Hebrews 10:26). It is our generations who will face this phase of final tribulations on earth. God has given us a gift of salvation through the sacrifice of His Son, Jesus Christ, to give us redemption and to bring us back to restore the same intimate and loving relationship with our Heavenly Father that was lost in the Garden of Eden. If we reject this offer today, then Hebrews 10:31 is an applicable word for us: "It is a fearful thing to fall into the hands of the living God."

PHILIPPIANS 2:9-11

Therefore God also has highly exalted Him and given Him the name which is above every name, that at the name of Jesus every knee should bow, of those in heaven, and of those on earth, and of those under the earth, and that every tongue should confess that Jesus Christ is Lord, to the glory of God the Father.

It is vital to know that all other theologies followed by mankind will not help except the knowledge of the only truth of whose name is exalted above any other name, and every knee will bow of those in heaven, and of those on earth, and of those under the earth with a confession that "Jesus Christ is the Lord to the glory of God the Father."

* * *

I am sure that you understood God's compassionate love and salvation plan for you. Along with this knowledge, it is also very important to know the reason of God's command for us to love him more than anyone and anything else.

DEUTERONOMY 6:5
You shall love the LORD your God with all your
heart, with all your soul, and with all your strength.

MATTHEW 10:37, 38
He who loves father or mother more than Me is not
worthy of Me. And he who loves son or daughter more
than Me is not worthy of Me. And he who does not take
his cross and follow after Me is not worthy of Me.

The Holy Spirit reveals a very positive reason of why the Lord desires His people to put Him first before anything else. God is the great Lord God Almighty, the creator and the originator of all in all. Why our first priority of Him is so important? We can understand the reason of God's demand with the examples of His great prophets like King David, King Solomon, Samson and Adam and Eve. They were instantly trapped by the enemy satan only when they put someone or something else before the LORD.

- Adam's compassion for Eve was greater than the Lord when he ate the forbidden fruit.
- King David stumbled into a desire of Bathsheba when he ignored his Lord's will. David's negligence got him trapped into a work of evil when he did not obey God's counsel that forbids tempting for a neighbor's wife. He committed the sin of adultery and the murder of her husband.

- King Solomon's passion for women more than a love for the Lord was the trap for his sins and a reason of separation with his God Almighty.
- Samson's weakness and trap was Delilah's love more than His Lord. This act destroyed him completely and resulted into his blindness, imprisonment, and death.

NEHEMIAH 13:26

Did not Solomon king of Israel sin by these things? Yet among many nations was there no king like him, who was BELOVED of his God, and God made him king over all Israel: nevertheless even him did outlandish women cause to sin.

Even though all these beloved prophets of God in our examples stumbled to sin in their life; but God did not let them left out of His protection and presence. They all repented, were forgiven, received restoration and found the refuge in the presence of their LORD: As He is a perfect, loving and caring Heavenly Father of all. If the great prophets of God can fail in their relationship with their beloved Lord and fall into the snare of sin, where do you and I stand in our spiritual walk with the Lord? *God is not thinking about himself when He commanded to love Him more than anything else, but us!* God understands the strength and the strategies of the spiritual powers of darkness more than we ever could; and only His love can protect us against satan's evil motives.

Discovering the Love of God is extremely essential for every soul on earth. Once we understand His compassion for us, we will naturally follow His will and keep Him at the first place in everything. Once we are connected with God in such a way that His Holy Spirit dwells within us to fathom us with His wisdom that helps us to be holy like Him. Then with this spiritual purity we can be righteous enough to learn to reject injustice and cruelty, and become a good, loving, caring, fair, and honest person. In every area of our lives we will experience nothing but peace, joy, love, justice, and a perfection that is a desire of every soul on earth. It is impossible to do what God desires in our own strength, wisdom, and capacity, but the love of God can help us reach the level of righteousness that His word inscribed for all humanity.

MATTHEW 5:44-48

But I say to you, love your enemies, bless those who curse you, do good to those who hate you, and pray for those who spitefully use you and persecute you, that you may be sons of your Father in heaven; for He makes His sun rise on the evil and on the good, and sends rain on the just and on the unjust. For if you love those who love you, what reward have you? Do not even the tax collectors do the same? And if you greet your brethren only, what do you do more than others? Do not even the tax collectors do so? Therefore you shall be perfect, just as your Father in heaven is perfect."

How can a human mind comprehend how to love his enemies and those who are hurting him? Man's humanity and good works are always within his comfort zone. Man's righteousness is an infirmity before God's righteousness, as Jesus said: *"For if you love those who love you, what reward have you? Do not even the tax collectors do the same?"* (Matthew 5:46). God's righteousness is the only way to transform us to His holiness when we learn to: **"love your enemies, bless those who curse you, do good to those who hate you, and pray for those who spitefully use you and persecute you"** Matthew 5:44. We cannot bring peace on earth without loving our enemies. It is impossible to reach this scale of perfection without an intimate love relationship with the LORD first. God does say, *"He who loves father or mother more than Me is not worthy of Me. And he who loves son or daughter more than Me is not worthy of Me."* Matthew 10:37. The reason is that our love ones are as incomplete as we are. To live a life of purity we need to see the face of the Lord rather at our loved ones, because man's ways can never be piously correct. *The influence of our loved ones can lead us to unholy ways. Mankind lives under their traditions, cultures and religions from generations which commonly go against the will of God. How can one repent from a sinful lifestyle of their family, if they love their parents more than God? How can one reject the idols of his or her spouse, if God do not come first in their life? It will be so easy to follow the sinful way of life of our loved ones unknowingly because human love bondage blinds our sight to the goodness of the LORD.* **No one can worship the Lord God Almighty righteously without denying themselves and humble before Him.** It is so correct when the Lord Jesus Christ said, *"And he who does not take his cross and follow after Me is not worthy of Me"*. Matthew 10:38. Honestly every human on earth needs to find out if he or she is worthy of the LORD. It is awesome to know that God is calling all the nations of the world to come and join Him in His Kingdom under His protection, care, love and everlasting life.

Praise our Lord God for His perfect Love, Works & Words.

PSALM 98:2-4
The LORD has made known His salvation;
His righteousness He has revealed in the sight of the nations.
He has remembered His mercy and His
faithfulness to the house of Israel;
All the ends of the earth have seen the salvation of our God.
Shout joyfully to the LORD, all the earth;
Break forth in song, rejoice, and sing praises.

***

The Third Phase of Human History
The Kingdom of God

The Hebrew word for kingdom is *malkut* and its Greek counterpart is *basileia*. Both terms primarily mean **"rule"** or **"reign"**. God began and ended everything with perfection under His rule. God established His Kingdom at creation. He ruled over His people in the Garden of Eden, but satan's deceit brought death, diseases, sufferings and troubles on earth. God intervened continuously to protect His people out of His loving kindness… as we studied in the 'second phase of human history'.

God's plan to crush the head of serpent under man's heal came to pass at the coming of the Lord Jesus Christ. Jesus is the one who reinstated His kingdom on earth as it is in heaven. This victorious work began with the shout of the coming of the kingdom of God -- announced by John the Baptist. He came preparing the way for the King of kings and the Lord of lords – the Lord Jesus Christ, *"and saying, "Repent, for the kingdom of heaven is at hand!"* Matthew 3:2.

The Lord Jesus Christ emerged to the scene revealing Himself as a

King and a Ruler. Jews were waiting for centuries of the coming of the kingdom of God. When they asked Jesus about its coming, *"He declared that His presence is the kingdom of God within them."*

LUKE 17:20-21
The Coming of the Kingdom
Now when He was asked by the Pharisees when the
kingdom of God would come; He answered them and said,
"The kingdom of God does not come with observation;
nor will they say, 'See here!' or 'See there!
"For indeed, the kingdom of God is within you."

The revelation of the Lord's plans is always beyond human comprehension. Jews were confused of the fulfillment of this promise, so is the mankind today. We will learn by the counsel of the Holy Spirit the mysterious redemption of His people in His kingdom.

The kingdom to satan ended, and the kingdom of God came at the first coming of the Lord Jesus Christ.

MATTHEW 4:8-11
Again, the devil took Him up on an exceedingly high mountain, and
showed Him all the kingdoms of the world and their glory. And he
said to Him, "All these things I will give You if You
will fall down and worship me."
Then Jesus said to him, "Away with you, Satan! For it is written, 'You
shall worship the LORD your God, and Him only you shall serve."
Then the devil left Him, and behold,
angels came and ministered to Him.

Man failed against the temptation of satan, but God renovated man's failure with His perfection. Devil tempted Jesus also, the way he tempted Adam and Eve. Satan tempts Jesus by saying, *"All these things I will give You if You will fall down and worship me."* But our redeemer overcame by saying, *"Away with you, Satan! For it is written, 'You shall worship the LORD your God, and Him only you shall serve."*

Mankind now walks victoriously into the kingdom of God. The power of sin is defeated by the power of God's righteousness. After failing to tempt Jesus, devil left Him, and *behold, angels came and ministered to Him.* Now is the rule of the King of the universe on earth, when His angels' minister His obedient servants; because the realm of His kingdom is establish on earth as it is in heaven.

It is only out of unconditional love that God desires to give us this gift, because we are the children of God. Mankind has received this precious gift to come in His Holy presence in His kingdom.

LUKE 13:29
People will come from east and west and north and south, and will take their places at the feast in the kingdom of God.

DANIEL 7:18
But the saints of the Most High will receive the kingdom and will possess it forever—yes, forever and ever.'

Thus, all those who repent from their sins, and believe that the Lord Jesus Christ is the King of the kingdom of God--- receive the freedom from the power of sin in this life on earth. The Lord Jesus Christ is coming again the second time to establish His kingdom bodily on earth. The future manifestation of His kingdom will be overwhelming where His saints will reside under His rule, forever!

Every normal person would desire to get this gift of God, but how? We will explore the hidden path that human mind cannot comprehend, right from the Word of God. I will begin with the verses that will help us understand the seriousness of holiness. God and His kingdom is a matter that every person on earth should be concerned about. Of course, the majority of us don't understand the purity of God, therefore our righteousness that is still uncleanness from the standpoint of God's holiness--- will expel us from His kingdom. Read these verses that confirm the truth of God's firm election.

MATTHEW 7:21
"Not everyone who says to me, 'Lord, Lord,' will enter the kingdom of heaven, but only he who does

the will of my Father who is in heaven.

1 CORINTHIANS 6:9-11
Do you not know that the unrighteous will not inherit the
kingdom of God? Do not be deceived. Neither fornicators, nor
idolaters, nor adulterers, nor homosexuals, nor sodomites,
nor thieves, nor covetous, nor drunkards, nor revilers,
nor extortioners will inherit the kingdom of God.
And such were some of you. But you were washed,
but you were sanctified, but you were justified
in the name of the Lord Jesus and by the Spirit of our God.

To explain this theology of God's unbiased selection, I will begin with Proverbs 9:10, *"The fear of the LORD is the beginning of wisdom, and the knowledge of the Holy One is understanding"*. When we fear God's rightful judgments, we discontinue the same old sins. **God is holy; therefore sinners cannot enter into His kingdom, then, who can?**

God wants us to receive His kingdom like a child. The characteristics that we commonly observe among children are their innocent heart that believes, they are quick to trust and obey, they are void of jealousy, they are not evil minded, full of peace, joy and unconditional loving care, and immorality do not exist near them. Jesus said *"whoever does not receive the kingdom of God as a little child will by no means enter it."*

MARK 10:14-15
But when Jesus saw it, He was greatly displeased and said
to them, "Let the little children come to Me, and do not
forbid them; for of such is the kingdom of God.
Assuredly, I say to you,
whoever does not receive the kingdom of
God as a little child will by no means enter it."

No one can see the Kingdom of God until and unless they are born again.

JOHN 3:3-5
*Jesus answered and said to him, "Most assuredly, I say to you,
unless one is born again, he cannot see the kingdom of God."
Nicodemus said to Him, "How can a man be born when he is old?
Can he enter a second time into his mother's womb and be born?"
Jesus answered, "Most assuredly, I say to you, unless one is born
of water and the Spirit, he cannot enter the kingdom of God.*

We have the same question in mind as Nicodemus had, when he asked Jesus *"How can a man be born when he is old? Can he enter a second time into his mother's womb and be born?"* Jesus answered *"unless one is born of water and the Spirit, he cannot enter the kingdom of God."* Born of water is the baptism of water just like a baby who is completely immersed in water in a mother's womb. It is compulsory to immerse back into a water of baptism to wash away all the previous sins done of the flesh, in the name of the Lord Jesus Christ. Born again in the water is to completely surrender to the Lord's will, and start a brand new life in the righteousness and the purity of the Lord. The second thing that the Lord Jesus said is to be born of the Spirit. No one can enter into the kingdom of God without the Holy Spirit, because the Holy Spirit is the counselor that guide and lead His children in His will on a daily basis.

2 TIMOTHY 4:18
*And the Lord will deliver me from every evil
work and preserve me for His heavenly kingdom.
To Him be glory forever and ever. Amen!*

How painful and agonizing it is to reject this marvelous gift of God? Save your soul, it is very precious to God. God cannot rescue you, without you accepting this universal truth. Draw your hands towards the Creator of this universe with a repentant heart.

LUKE 13:28
*There will be weeping and gnashing of teeth, when you
see Abraham and Isaac and Jacob and all the prophets*

in the kingdom of God, and yourselves thrust out.

Behold, the King of kings and the Lord of lords is returning back to bring His righteous judgment and rule upon all the nations.

PSALM 67:4
Oh, let the nations be glad and sing for joy!
For You shall judge the people righteously,
And govern the nations on earth. Selah

Finally, the kingdom of God will come in its glory and power. This earth will be replaced with new earth and new heaven. Sin will not exist anymore, and the justice and righteousness of the King of kings and the Lord of lords will prevail for eternity. The tabernacle of God will be with men. God will walk and talk with His people, just like He used to be in communion with Adam and Eve in His kingdom at the time of creation. The old universe will be replaced with new. Mankind will never lose the sight of his loving God. There will be no more death. Our lover will wipe every tear from our eyes. Who can measure the extent of the emotions of God for His beloved?

REVELATION 21:1-5
All Things Made New
Now I saw a new heaven and a new earth, for the first heaven and the first earth had passed away. Also there was no more sea. Then I, John, saw the holy city, New Jerusalem, coming down out of heaven from God, prepared as a bride adorned for her husband. And I heard a loud voice from heaven saying, "Behold, the tabernacle of God is with men, and He will dwell with them, and they shall be His people. God Himself will be with them and be their God. And God will wipe away every tear from their eyes; there shall be no more death, nor sorrow, nor crying. There shall be no more pain, for the former things have passed away."
Then He who sat on the throne said, "Behold, I make all things new." And He said to me, "Write, for these words are true and faithful."

The greatest gift that remains forever is a Love of the LORD!

1 Corinthians 13:1-13

*Though I speak with the tongues of men and of angels, but
have not love, I have become sounding brass or a clanging cymbal.
And though I have the gift of prophecy, and understand all
mysteries and all knowledge, and though I have all faith, so that I
could remove mountains, but have not love, I am nothing.
And though I bestow all my goods to feed the poor, and though I give
my body to be burned, but have not love, it profits me nothing.
Love suffers long and is kind; love does not envy;
love does not parade itself, is not puffed up;
does not behave rudely, does not seek its own,
is not provoked, thinks no evil;
does not rejoice in iniquity, but rejoices in the truth;
bears all things, believes all things, hopes all things,
endures all things.
Love never fails. But whether there are prophecies, they
will fail; whether there are tongues, they will cease; whether
there is knowledge, it will vanish away. For we know in part
and we prophesy in part. But when that which is perfect
has come, then that which is in part will be done away.
When I was a child, I spoke as a child, I understood as a child,
I thought as a child; but when I became a man, I put away childish
things. For now we see in a mirror, dimly, but then face to face.
Now I know in part, but then I shall know just as I also am know
And now abide faith, hope, love, these
three; but the greatest of these is love.*

All great achievements of men will come to an end, their mighty possessions will vanish, their riches will stale, their beauty will fade, the mighty man will loosen its greatness in ashes, and all the things will end... but the love of the LORD will remain. Let's come together to embrace His love in our hearts, because it is the greatest gift that gives us a desire to obey His will, and be with Him in His kingdom.

This is our hope of victory over death--- to a life forever!

1 JOHN 4:8
He who does not love does not know God, for God is love.

CHAPTER 13

Why Take God for Granted?

The Lord has put it in my heart to talk about the very common attitude of the human race in terms of how they view Him. From the day of creation until today, mankind has not entirely understood the purity of God, and the reason for His desire to see His people come to Him in complete humility of heart. We will look into the Word of God for the understanding of His justified expectation of our complete obedience to Him, which our human comprehension is so often in complete opposition to. This subject is crucial. For that knowledge, we have to widen our vision and pierce through the invisible reality that the devil desires to keep hidden from us. Before we get to the heart of this subject, we need to clearly understand that God is the same, forever, in every era: from the dawn of creation to today's technologically advanced new world.

HEBREWS 13:8
Jesus Christ is the same yesterday, today, and forever.

MALACHI 3:6
"For I am the LORD, I do not change,
Therefore you are not consumed, O sons of Jacob."

So a study of the Scriptures establishes that the Lord is the same yesterday, today, and forever, without any variation or the shadow of turning. Therefore, His pure counsel with the human race remains the same from the Day of Creation until the End of Time; no matter in what time, or in what culture, or what religion, skin color, or language they belong to.

Most people are familiar with the Ten Commandments, which are given to guide us to live righteously under the direct counsel of the Lord. Let's read some reference verses that express the importance of obedience to those commandments in order to be holy for the Lord.

NUMBERS 15:39, 40
And you shall have the tassel, that you may look upon it and
remember all the commandments of the LORD and do them,
and that you may not follow the harlotry to which your own heart
and your own eyes are inclined, and that you may remember
and do all My commandments, and be holy for your God.

The Lord Jesus Christ affirmed His subjection to the Law of God by His complete obedience to His Father's commandments. The next verses will help us understand the great importance of the knowledge of, and of the obedience to, God's teachings. Missing any of it can bring undesirable consequences to our lives here on earth and can cause our eternal removal from the pure presence of the Lord. This is the reason the Lord Jesus Christ came to fulfill the Law, so that many might be saved. He came to reconcile us from our rebellion against God because of our slavery to our flesh and its appetites. We overcome the powers of darkness by accepting the salvation of Jesus Christ, and through a relationship with His Holy Spirit. Through the enabling of His Holy Spirit, we may walk in the way to the Kingdom of God.

MATTHEW 5:17-20
Christ Fulfills the Law

"Do not think that I came to destroy the Law or the Prophets. I did not come to destroy but to fulfill. For assuredly, I say to you, till heaven and earth pass away, one jot or one tittle will by no means pass from the law till all is fulfilled. Whoever therefore breaks one of the least of these commandments, and teaches men so, shall be called least in the kingdom of heaven; but whoever does and teaches them, he shall be called great in the kingdom of heaven.
For I say to you, that unless your righteousness exceeds the righteousness of the scribes and Pharisees, you will by no means enter the kingdom of heaven."

The Lord Jesus Christ emphasized the importance of the commandments by His obedience to them, even unto His death. For His commandments are vital to such a level that whosoever does and teaches them will be great in the Kingdom of Heaven, but the one who breaks one of the least of these commandments and teaches men so shall be least in His Kingdom. God expects the highest standard of righteousness from His children. He wants it to exceed and continue to exceed the works of great religious leaders such as the scribes, Pharisees, pastors, ministers, prophets, apostles, and elders. There is no other way; *"you will by no means enter the kingdom of heaven."* Matthew 22:37-40 is a revelation of His expectancy for the ultimate level of righteousness.

MATTHEW 22:37-40

Jesus said to him, "You shall love the LORD your God with all your heart, with all your soul, and with all your mind.'
This is the first and great commandment. And the second is like it: 'You shall love your neighbor as yourself.' On these two commandments hang all the Law and the Prophets."

How precious and wonderful is the Lord's teaching! It can fix the life of any individual, every home, and every country: the whole earth. God created everything out of love, and it is our love for Him with our full strength that is the key to a holy relationship with Him. This is the first and the greatest commandment, because all other commandments are impossible to practice and follow without the spirit of love for our personal Savior and Creator. It is the heart full of His love that will desire to know His will and follow it to make our Lover happy. The mind that worships Him with complete understanding will know that there is no better hope than the Lord, and a soul which recognizes its savior will rejoice in the relationship of its first love, which is the Lord God Almighty.

The second commandment that the Lord Jesus Christ insisted on is to love your neighbor as yourself. How can I love my neighbor as myself? This is impossible to practice by anyone without loving God *first*, which opens the door to the knowledge of humanity, and moves the heart to love everyone else like themselves, even the worst enemy. Is it possible to love everyone as yourself? For any natural human mind, it seems an impossible thing to do. But, then how God could expect such an impossible work of righteousness unless it was possible? It's because God knows that all things are possible only in His love, and for this very reason, loving Him is the first commandment. Thus the rest of the commandments will be encompassed—even subconsciously so—when these two commandments given by the Lord Jesus Christ are obeyed. Because who can steal, hurt, kill, envy, and be evil to anyone whom they love like themselves? This is why Jesus said in verse 40: *"On these two commandments hang all the Law and the Prophets."*

The only thing mankind needs to do is to seek a salvation through the Lord Jesus Christ, and obey God with complete humility, as it gives a new birth which transforms us into a new creation that is loving, caring, and understanding with our neighbor as ourselves. This impossible work of righteousness taught by Jesus in Matthew 5:43-48, to love our enemies, to bless those who curse us, to do well to those who hate us, and to pray for those who spitefully use and persecute us, becomes possible—like icing on a cake.

1 JOHN 4:7, 8
Knowing God Through Love
Beloved, let us love one another, for love is of God; and everyone who loves is born of God and knows God.

He who does not love does not know God, for God is love.

Love endures all things of the evil of this earth with a patience that only the love of God can help us walk through. Finally, the Word of God shows us that the beauty of our permanency is in love. The fact is that the righteous will abide in faith, hope, and love, of which LOVE is the greatest, because God is love.

* * *

After your understanding is clear about the will of God for His beloved people, we can move to the main discourse of this chapter: **Why take God for granted?** The Lord has put it in my heart to talk about it because multitudes of nice people don't know the truth of real goodness, which we need to focus on. The consequences are serious if we fail. We are very well focused about earthly things such as work and home. We try our best not to slumber and fail in these areas of life, but when it comes to God we don't apply the same diligence to our obedience to Him. This includes people who are blinded of their own weaknesses and only highlight the good works of their hands, such as a charity-giver will underline this act of giving but will not focus on the infirmities of the flesh. They would be deceived into thinking that they will definitely go to the good place after death due to a good deed like charity. Naturally, mankind is not capable of viewing truthfully many of his weaknesses as clearly as he can single out the few good works he did. This attitude is dangerous and can lead to Hell. There are many more examples of the same form of humanly self-righteous vain satisfaction that has blinded multitudes to comprehend the importance of purity. I will share the examples of great prophets to whom God responded without any favor when they failed to obey His commandment. He is unbiased even to His chosen servants, who touched His Heart due to their goodness, faith, and obedience toward Him. *The examples of God's prophets like King Saul, King David, and King Solomon are presented to help us understand* **the significance of the obedience to His Will, and not to take God for granted.**

* * *

The story of King Saul of Israel is a great example to understand why not to take God for granted. King Saul was chosen by God to rule the nation of Israel; God decreed this through His righteous counsel.

1 SAMUEL 15:1, 2

Samuel also said to Saul, "The LORD sent me to anoint you king over His people, over Israel. Now therefore, heed the voice of the words of the LORD. Thus says the LORD of hosts: 'I will punish Amalek for what he did to Israel, how he ambushed him on the way when he came up from Egypt."

The Israelis had become rebellious and wanted to be governed in much the same way as the people of other nations were. They had kings while Israel had judges and prophets. God decided to give them what they called for, and He sent Samuel the prophet to anoint Saul to be the king of Israel. Saul was then given instructions to go to war with Amalek for the slaughter that king had previously done to Israel. King Saul set out to do what God had instructed him, but he did not obey the command completely. The next part of this story tells what he did wrong.

Continuation of 1 SAMUEL 15
1 SAMUEL 15:9

But Saul and the people spared Agag and the best of the sheep, the oxen, the fatlings, the lambs, and all that was good, and were unwilling to utterly destroy them. But everything despised and worthless, that they utterly destroyed.

Verse 9 clearly gives the reason of King Saul's disobedience: greed. Greed is the root of evil that can pervert the pure heart, which is necessary for complete obedience to the Lord. Mankind's inclination is to never leave his evil ways except upon God's personal intervention. Surely King Saul disobeyed God by sparing King Agag along with the best quality treasures of that land; he only destroyed what was materialistically worthless. This act of disobedience was judged because the Lord God Almighty is a Father of righteousness.

Continuation of **1 SAMUEL 15**

1 SAMUEL 15:10-15

Now the word of the LORD came to Samuel, saying,
"I greatly regret that I have set up Saul as king,
for he has turned back from
following Me, and has not performed My commandments."
Then Samuel went to Saul, and Saul said to him, "Blessed are you
of the LORD! I have performed the commandment of the LORD."
But Samuel said, "What then is this bleating of the sheep
in my ears, and the lowing of the oxen which I hear?"
And Saul said, "They have brought them from the Amalekites; for
the people spared the best of the sheep and the oxen, to sacrifice
to the LORD your God; and the rest we have utterly destroyed."

Oh, how the mind of man is in complete contrast to the heart and mind of the Lord! Just like King Saul, we consider that our lives are spent in complete obedience to the Lord, but in reality we don't understand the will of God because we are so blinded with the greed of the things of this earth. Our own self-satisfaction is the number one enemy keeping us from the obedient and righteous-filled living before the Lord. King Saul is a wonderful metaphor of our daily lifestyle. Look at the contrasting approaches of Saul and of the Lord: In verse 10 *God told Samuel that Saul did not obey His commandment, but Saul contradicted and said in verse 13 that he obeyed God's command.* Why such a contrast? Of course, the reason is the sin of man's heart. God's word confirms it in 1 Timothy 6:10: *"For the love of money is a root of all kinds of evil, for which some have strayed from the faith in their greediness, and pierced themselves through with many sorrows."*

We will go further in this story to understand the seriousness of the Lord's will and why we must not take God for granted.

Continuation of 1 SAMUEL 15
1 SAMUEL 15:16-21
Then Samuel said to Saul, "Be quiet! And I will
tell you what the LORD said to me last night."
And he said to him, "Speak on."
So Samuel said, "When you were little in your own eyes, were
you not head of the tribes of Israel? And did not the LORD anoint
you king over Israel? Now the LORD sent you on a mission,
and said, 'Go, and utterly destroy the sinners, the Amalekites,
and fight against them until they are consumed.' Why then did
you not obey the voice of the LORD ? Why did you swoop
down on the spoil, and do evil in the sight of the LORD ?"
And Saul said to Samuel, "But I have obeyed the voice of
the LORD, and gone on the mission on which the LORD sent me,
and brought back Agag king of Amalek; I have utterly destroyed the
Amalekites. But the people took of the plunder, sheep and
oxen, the best of the things which should have been utterly
destroyed, to sacrifice to the LORD your God in Gilgal."

Verses 17 and 20 hold a great lesson for mankind in any and every generation. God molds and prepares us for His purpose in this life on earth, but we trivialize this mercy of God. King Saul did the same when he could not comprehend the important responsibilities of his position for being anointed "King of Israel." God chose him when he was a man of insignificant stature. We all tend to fail to understand the importance of our existence on earth. We fail to grasp the idea that our purpose is to fulfill the will of God. Obedience qualifies us into a faithful relationship with Him. One day God will ask the same question as the prophet Samuel asked King Saul: *"Why then did you not obey the voice of the LORD? Why did you swoop down on the spoil, and do evil in the sight of the LORD?"* Are we going to respond the same as King Saul by claiming, *"But I have obeyed the voice of the LORD"*? Are we going to falsely believe that the partial obedience to the will of the Lord is right in His eyes? Surely it is not possible to sail on the ocean with one foot on one boat and another foot on another boat. This was the situation of King Saul when he was trying to sail in two boats at once; he was trying to making the people happy as well as the Lord. He held fast to this belief by expressing these words to the prophet Samuel: *"I have utterly destroyed the Amalekites. But the people took of the plunder, sheep and oxen, the best of the things which should have been utterly destroyed, to sacrifice to the LORD your God in Gilgal."*

What a delusion that mankind lives in all the days of his life! God does not desire any twist of hypocrisy in His will for His people. Saul responded hypocritically, and God judged him, fairly, to be removed him from the throne. Are we going to be judged similarly for insincerity with the LORD?

Continuation of 1 SAMUEL 15

1 SAMUEL 15:22, 23

So Samuel said:

"Has the LORD as great delight in burnt offerings and sacrifices,

As in obeying the voice of the LORD ?

Behold, to obey is better than sacrifice,

And to heed than the fat of rams.

For rebellion is as the sin of witchcraft,

And stubbornness is as iniquity and idolatry.

Because you have rejected the word of the LORD,

He also has rejected you from being king."

King Saul did not comprehend that obeying the voice of the Lord was a more desirable work of righteousness than the offerings and sacrifices of earthly treasures. The Prophet Samuel showed King Saul the facts about the true will of God, that will which helps us grow in relationship with Him. Hardness of man's heart that pushed him to the rebellion and stubbornness to God's voice is equal to the sin of witchcraft and idolatry. God truly desires us to heed him and know Him well: To have a true desire to do His will. Such obedience out of love for Him will lead us to obey His instructions in our lives, and then all the good works in obedience to His commandments will be acceptable before the throne of the LORD. At the end of verse 23, the Prophet Samuel announced God's verdict for King Saul that, *"Because you have rejected the word of the LORD, He also has rejected you from being king."* Dear friends,

I wonder if this is what we will hear: "God has rejected us because we have rejected His voice all the days of our lives. "

Continuation of 1 SAMUEL 15
1 SAMUEL 15:24-26

Then Saul said to Samuel, "I have sinned, for I have transgressed the commandment of the LORD and your words, because I feared the people and obeyed their voice. Now therefore, please pardon my sin, and return with me, that I may worship the LORD." But Samuel said to Saul, "I will not return with you, for you have rejected the word of the LORD, and the LORD has rejected you from being king over Israel."

Verse 24 may be our voice on the Day of Judgment when we will tell God that, "I have sinned because I was afraid of the people more than God, and I cared to make people happy more than God. I worried to impress the people around me to get their attention for satisfying the thirst of self-importance, and obeying their voice because I feared them more than an invisible Lord God Almighty." King Saul repented in verse 25 for his sin and asked the prophet Samuel to return and worship the Lord with him; but the prophet refused. He knew that God's word was a finality of His judgment in His will and power against the hypocrite heart of this man. Think of this example: a man sleeps with prostitutes secretly from his wife for many years, and one day his wife finds out about this act of betrayal against her. The husband may cry for forgiveness and may want to restore the relationship with his wife again. Would it be possible for the wife to trust him again? Not until he is found pious in their marital relationship. It may take many years until his wife can vouch for his fidelity. Another result of such a violation of the marital relationship could be a divorce. It all depends on the sincerity and morality—or lack of them—of the heart of a sinner. Do you think that God will forgive sinners on the last Day of Judgment for their crying? Not if they're repenting insincerely! Not if they're doing it because there is no other way out! Their repentance is not borne of the humility of the heart that must happen now! This is why Samuel said to Saul: *"I will not return with you, for you have rejected the word of the LORD, and the LORD has rejected you from being king over Isra-el.*" Therefore, do not take God for granted. People need to understand that if God would judge His chosen servants unfavorably in truth and righteousness, then where do we stand? *Wake up before it is too late to repent. Seek a love relationship with the Lord God Almighty. He is a God of love and mercy for all those who seek Him in humility.*

* * *

We will learn another lesson for understanding *why we should not take God for granted*; this comes from an example of a **man after God's own heart: King David.** He was an anointed king of Israel who replaced King Saul after he was removed from the throne. King David was a man after God's heart as the prophet Samuel delivered a message to King Saul, found in 1 Samuel 13:14: *"But now your kingdom shall not continue. The LORD has sought for Himself a man after His own heart, and the LORD has commanded him to be commander over His people, because you have not kept what the LORD commanded you."* King David was a man who obeyed the voice of His Lord with a love that clearly portrays in the book of Psalms. His whole life is an example for mankind by which we learn how to stand strong in faith, in passion, in obedience, and in wholehearted humility before the Lord God Almighty. God blessed him in abundance with power, prosperity, wealth, peace of heart, satisfaction of mind, and thirst-driven desire to love and obey his Lord. But one sin served him a fair and righteous judgment of his beloved God. Let's read the story to understand God's righteous justice for His people.

2 SAMUEL 11:1-5

*It happened in the spring of the year, at the time when kings go out to battle, that David sent Joab and his servants with him, and all Israel; and they destroyed the people of Ammon and besieged Rabbah. But David remained at Jerusalem.
Then it happened one evening that David arose from his bed and walked on the roof of the king's house. And from the roof he saw a woman bathing, and the woman was very beautiful to behold.*

So David sent and inquired about the woman. And someone said,
"Is this not Bathsheba, the daughter of Eliam,
the wife of Uriah the Hittite?"
Then David sent messengers, and took her; and
she came to him, and he lay with her, for she was cleansed from her
impurity; and she returned to her house. And the woman conceived;
so she sent and told David, and said, "I am with child."

No matter how good we are, and how hard we try to live in righteousness with the Lord, the enemy finds the ways to test our faithfulness through temptation at the hour of our weakness. Being human, no one can escape this trap. No matter who that person is, a common person or a great prophet of God. The same thing happened to King David when he let idleness keep him from the duty of his title to lead his men at war, but instead he stayed back at the palace. We know that the snare of testing and temptation attacks us all, usually when one is alone. Like Eve in the Garden of Eden: she was tempted when she was alone and away from her husband. Unfortunately, King David fell into the same trap of enticement upon seeing a beautiful woman bathing while he was watching from the roof of his house. He inquired about her and found that she was the wife of Uriah the Hittite, who was one of his own faithful soldiers. King David was overcome with lust and commanded her to sin with him in adultery because, at that point, his temptation to sin was greater than the desire to obey the commandant of God, which preaches that "you shall not commit adultery and tempt for your neighbor's wife." Unfortunately, Bathsheba became pregnant with King David's child, which necessitated him going deeper into the ditch of sin. King David had to remove Bathsheba's husband out of the scene to preserve his own prestige and reputation. Alas, King David committed another more heinous sin to hide the first. Let's read about it.

Continuation of 2 SAMUEL 11
2 SAMUEL 11:14, 15, 24-27

In the morning it happened that David wrote a letter to Joab
and sent it by the hand of Uriah. And he wrote in the letter,
saying, "Set Uriah in the forefront of the hottest battle, and

retreat from him, that he may be struck down and die."
The archers shot from the wall at your servants;
and some of the king's servants are dead,
and your servant Uriah the Hittite is dead also."
When the wife of Uriah heard that Uriah her husband
was dead, she mourned for her husband. And when her
mourning was over, David sent and brought her to his
house, and she became his wife and bore him a son. But
the thing that David had done displeased the LORD.

Praise the Lord our God, who is a fair Judge for all; it doesn't matter if it's a beggar or a king, a woman or a man, a common person or a great prophet. His laws are unchangeable for all. King David, a man of God's own heart, committed another sin to conceal the first sin by putting Uriah to death. David had Uriah placed in a position in the war which would ensure that he would be killed. This was an act which grieved God, as it is said, *"But the thing that David had done displeased the LORD."*

So the Lord sent His servant Nathan to King David to announce His just judgment against the evil done from David's hands. Let's read the climax of this action of the nature of humanity, which happens practically with every individual. But nobody understands the deeper reasoning for unfortunate circumstances that arise due to the failures of by our own hands.

Continuation of 2 SAMUEL 12
2 SAMUEL 12:1-15

Then the LORD sent Nathan to David. And he came to him, and
said to him: "There were two men in one city, one rich and the other
poor. The rich man had exceedingly many flocks and herds. But the
poor man had nothing, except one little ewe lamb which he had
bought and nourished; and it grew up together with
him and with his children.
It ate of his own food and drank from
his own cup and lay in his bosom;
and it was like a daughter to him.

And a traveler came to the rich man,
who refused to take from his own flock and from his own herd to
prepare one for the wayfaring man who had come to him;
but he took the poor man's lamb and prepared it
for the man who had come to him."
So David's anger was greatly aroused against the man, and
he said to Nathan, "As the LORD lives, the man who has
done this shall surely die! And he shall restore fourfold for the
lamb, because he did this thing and because he had no pity."
Then Nathan said to David, "You are the man! Thus says the
LORD God of Israel: 'I anointed you king over Israel, and I delivered
you from the hand of Saul. I gave you your master's house and your
master's wives into your keeping,
and gave you the house of Israel and Judah.
And if that had been too little, I also would have given you
much more! Why have you despised the commandment of the
LORD, to do evil in His sight? You have killed Uriah the Hittite
with the sword; you have taken his wife to be your wife, and have
killed him with the sword of the people of Ammon. Now therefore,
the sword shall never depart from your house, because you have
despised Me, and have taken the wife of Uriah the Hittite to
be your wife.' Thus says the LORD : 'Behold, I will raise up
adversity against you from your own house; and I will take your
wives before your eyes and give them to your neighbor, and he
shall lie with your wives in the sight of this sun. For you did it
secretly, but I will do this thing before all Israel, before the sun.'"
So David said to Nathan, "I have sinned against the LORD."
And Nathan said to David, "The LORD also has put away your sin;
you shall not die. However, because by this deed you have given great
occasion to the enemies of the LORD to blaspheme, the child also who
is born to you shall surely die." Then Nathan departed to his house.

This example of God's favored, anointed prophet, King David, is a beautiful testimony for every human being. Sometimes we do not recognize the serious implications that can arise from the errors of the small pieces of puzzles that we like to play within our lives. Our lack of understanding can entrap us into the situations that those puzzles lead us into. God's laws are straightforward, and they do not have any room for human thinking. King David's puzzles led him to sin, which caused greater complications in his life. He was trapped like a fly in a spider's web. His slavery to the desire of flesh invisibly sucked him into this web that blinded him to the commandment of his beloved Lord God Almighty. God's anger arose against him like lightning for his unfairness toward an innocent man, Uriah the Hittite. All Uriah had was one beautiful wife, who was snatched away from him, and also got him killed for the same reason.

But . . . Don't criticize King David, because the filth of our hands is much worse than his. Bringing up of this example is for us to know that taking God's name in vain is an abomination, and rejecting His Word, commandments, teachings, and counsel is a complete exhortation against the Lord God Almighty. We fail to recognize the importance of achieving purification through abiding in the Word of the Lord.

The Lord's love for all of His people is pure and kind; He has regard for the highest in office to very lowest. That's why the work of David's hand gave God cause for an inquiry: *"Why have you despised the commandment of the LORD, to do evil in His sight? You have killed Uriah the Hittite with the sword; you have taken his wife to be your wife?"*

Though David was considered a man after God's own Heart, God had to bring correction to the situation. He judged David fairly as the perfect Father would toward his children. *"Now therefore, the sword shall never depart from your house, because you have despised Me, and have taken the wife of Uriah the Hittite to be your wife.' Thus says the LORD: 'Behold, I will raise up adversity against you from your own house; and I will take your wives before your eyes and give them to your neighbor, and he shall lie with your wives in the sight of this sun. For you did it secretly, but I will do this thing before all Israel, before the sun."* No matter who is standing before God's throne, He does not exhibit partiality. King David faced the impartial equality of God's Justice for murder done through the hands of his enemies. The fallout was adversity from within his own house. An unending feud developed among his children. His own son arose against him. The death of Uriah was evenly exchanged through the death of his own child who came through the adultery with Bath-sheba, and later, his wives taken by his neighbor, just as he had taken someone else's wife and lay with her. God's love for Uriah the Hittite was the same as for King David. God is fair in everything He does: such as love for all, defending the innocent, punishing wrongdoings, and rewarding for good works. God did not let King David die because of his sin; He remembered his other good works and spared David. We will read about all the judgments that the LORD declared for King David, that these came to pass in his life.

Continuation of 2 SAMUEL 12

2 SAMUEL 12:15, 16, 22, 23

The Death of David's Son

And the LORD struck the child that Uriah's wife bore to David,
and it became ill. David therefore pleaded with God for the child,
and David fasted and went in and lay all night on the ground.
And he said, "While the child was alive, I fasted and wept; for I
said, 'Who can tell whether the LORD will be gracious to me, that
the child may live?' But now he is dead; why should I fast? Can I
bring him back again? I shall go to him,
but he shall not return to me."

Just as David killed Uriah physically, we too have our ways of committing murder. When we hurt the hearts of our loved ones and also when we kill their spirits—these are forms of murder. A blaspheming tongue pierces the soul just as if someone stabs a body with a sword. Sometimes the evil words uttered from the mouth of a man do not hurt once but remain for life to wound the soul of an innocent person. <u>Don't think that God will not judge us just like He did with King David.</u>

I like Martin Luther's commentary in this area when he said,

"You must not kill" (Exodus 20:13).

Q. What does this mean?

A. We must fear and love God, so that we will neither harm nor hurt our neighbor's body, but help and care for him when he is ill."

The other judgment of God for King David was this: *"Thus says the LORD: 'Behold, I will raise up adversity against you from your own* house"—and it came to pass. David's own son Absalom stood up against him.

2 SAMUEL 15:6, 13,14

In this manner Absalom acted toward all Israel who came to the king for judgment. So Absalom stole the hearts of the men of Israel. Now a messenger came to David, saying, "The hearts of the men of Israel are with Absalom." So David said to all his servants who were with him at Jerusalem, "Arise, and let us flee, or we shall not escape from Absalom. Make haste to depart, lest he overtake us suddenly and bring disaster upon us, and strike the city with the edge of the sword."

2 SAMUEL 16:11, 12

And David said to Abishai and all his servants "See how my son who came from my own body seeks my life. How much more now may this Benjamite? Let him alone, and let him curse; for so the LORD has ordered him. It may be that the LORD will look on my affliction, and that the LORD will repay me with good for his cursing this day."

This part of King David's life is very painful to read about, when he had to run away from his own flesh and blood, who could not be treated like an enemy to fight with. He was a mighty warrior but couldn't fight his own child. King David, a man after God's heart, had to deal with the consequences of his sin. Absalom snatched the throne from his father by conspiracy; this was pretty much the same that David did when he had taken Uriah's life by conspiracy. The judgments pronounced against David did not all happen immediately; some took years, but they all fulfilled, at the right hour, exactly as God had decreed. Hear the broken-hearted words from David's mouth when a Benjamite was cursing him in the wilderness: *"And David said to Abishai and all his servants, 'See how my son who came from my own body seeks my life. How much more now may this Benjamite? Let him alone, and let him curse; for so the LORD has ordered him.'"* A common man would have blamed and blasphemed God's name for the judgment of God for their own sins;

but look at the character of the man David, a man who was always near God's heart. Read verse 12: *"It may be that the LORD will look on my affliction, and that the LORD will repay me with good for his cursing this day."* God's chosen prophets were not naive like us, but they were very knowledgeable. They knew about the love of and the fear of the Lord. King David knew that God loved him. He also knew that His judgments are true and declare the form of love for him as the Lord is the Heavenly Father who will discipline His people like His own children. Let's see how this man near God's heart honors the judgments of the Lord.

PSALM 119:1-7, 20, 39, 62-64
Blessed are the undefiled in the way,
Who walk in the law of the LORD!
Blessed are those who keep His testimonies,
Who seek Him with the whole heart!
They also do no iniquity; they walk in His ways.
You have commanded us to keep Your precepts diligently.
Oh, that my ways were directed to keep Your statutes!
Then I would not be ashamed,
When I look into all Your commandments.
I will praise You with uprightness of heart,
When I learn Your righteous judgments.
My soul breaks with longing for Your judgments at all times.
Turn away my reproach which I dread,
for Your judgments are good. . . .
At midnight I will rise to give thanks to You,
because of Your righteous judgments.
I am a companion of all who fear You,
and of those who keep Your precepts.
The earth, O LORD, is full of Your mercy; teach me Your statutes.

* * *

We will also learn **"why take God for granted?"** from the life of **King Solomon of Israel**, who was chosen and anointed to sit on the throne of his father, King David. The Lord assigned him to build His house for the purpose of bringing His glory and presence among His people, where they would worship Him day and night. This privilege of overseeing the greatest work of history was given to the man who would be the next beloved of the Lord, as we read in the next verses how much God honored Solomon to be His son. The Lord said to his father King David: *"It is your son Solomon who shall build My house and My courts; for I have chosen him to be My son, and I will be his Father."*

1 CHRONICLES 28:5-9

And of all my sons (for the LORD has given me many sons) He has chosen my son Solomon to sit on the throne of the kingdom of the LORD over Israel. Now He said to me, 'It is your son Solomon who shall build My house and My courts; for I have chosen him to be My son, and I will be his Father. Moreover I will establish his kingdom forever, if he is steadfast to observe My commandments and My judgments, as it is this day.' "As for you, my son Solomon, know the God of your father, and serve Him with a loyal heart and with a willing mind; for the LORD searches all hearts and understands all the intent of the thoughts. If you seek Him, He will be found by you; but if you forsake Him, He will cast you off forever.

The Lord searches for people with loyal hearts and willing minds. How can you not seek God the same way? Does He love only His prophets in such manner? No, God loves you the same way, but we don't acknowledge it. The fact is that the instruction that King David gave to his son Solomon is the same life-changing truth for all of us, which is: *"If you seek Him, He will be found by you; but if you forsake Him, He will cast you off forever."*

The Lord God Almighty came to Solomon and gave him the instruction that was designed to give him an everlasting life in His presence.

1 KINGS 6:11-13

Then the word of the LORD came to Solomon, saying: "Concerning this temple which you are building, if you walk in My statutes, execute My judgments, keep all My commandments, and

*walk in them, then I will perform My word with you, which
I spoke to your father David. And I will dwell among the
children of Israel, and will not forsake My people Israel."*

1 KINGS 9:6, 7
*"But if you or your sons at all turn from following Me, and do
not keep My commandments and My statutes which I have set before
you, but go and serve other gods and worship them, then I will cut
off Israel from the land which I have given them; and this house
which I have consecrated for My name I will cast out of My sight.*

The precious people of God will receive no favors if they go astray
and serve other gods of their own making, over their Creator, who has
made them lovingly with His own hands for His purpose. Mankind is
always the most vulnerable of all of God's creations because of his ad-
versary, satan, aligning against them. This is the very reason that God's
teachings and counsel were given to uplift His people for His works.
King Solomon was also a chosen servant of the Lord. He received guidance, which enabled him to live in the righteousness of the God of his
fathers. Praise the Lord for His teachings, which gives us a life full of
pure fulfillment and prosperity.

King Solomon is known as the richest man in human history. He
lived a prosperous life until he sought out God diligently for guidance
to serve and obey His commandments. It was the season when the nation of Israel expounded with the riches of the world—peace was in the
nation when their enemies became their friends . . . the sickness and
disease hid its face from the whole nation. Peace and joy flourished in
the four corners of the nation of Israel in the days of godly reign.

The Lord can do the same for us if we love Him with the same passion as the great prophets did. We have all witnessed the extreme exhil-
aration through Solomon's intimacy with the Lord. They are expressed
in the Bible through the "Songs of Solomon."

But in spite of such a close relationship with the Lord, God did leave
Solomon when he committed an abomination against Him. Let's read
why God would forsake such a great prophet, for whom He said to King
David that, *"I have chosen him to be My son, and I will be his Father.*

Moreover I will establish his kingdom forever, if he is steadfast to observe My commandments and My judgments, as it is this day.'

1 KINGS 11:1-4
Solomon's Heart Turns from the Lord

But King Solomon loved many foreign women, as well as the daughter of Pharaoh: women of the Moabites, Ammonites, Edomites, Sidonians, and Hittites— from the nations of whom the LORD had said to the children of Israel, "You shall not intermarry with them, nor they with you. Surely they will turn away your hearts after their gods." Solomon clung to these in love. And he had seven hundred wives, princesses, and three hundred concubines; and his wives turned away his heart. For it was so, when Solomon was old, that his wives turned his heart after other gods; and his heart was not loyal to the LORD his God, as was the heart of his father David.

The root of all sins is to worship gods other than the Lord God, the Creator of everything. Men trample and dishonor the name of the Holy of Holiest, God underfoot when idols are worshipped and praised. This is the worst, most intolerable sin from the beginning of creation. Idol worship is not only the idols made by hands, but our idols are also everything that we honor before the Lord. The list of these idols is very long and can include our loved ones, hobbies, activities, entertainment, jobs, assets, and many other tempting riches of the earth. Our acts are the same as King Solomon when he *"turned his heart after other gods; and his heart was not loyal to the LORD his God."* What will God do to us when we indulge in idol worshipping?

Let's read the next verses so that we might learn **"not to take God for granted."**

Continuation of 1 KINGS 11
1 KINGS 11:9-11

So the LORD became angry with Solomon, because his heart had turned from the LORD God of Israel, who had appeared to him twice, and had commanded him concerning this thing, that he

*should not go after other gods; but he did not keep what the LORD
had commanded. Therefore the LORD said to Solomon, "Because
you have done this, and have not kept My covenant and My
statutes, which I have commanded you, I will surely tear the
kingdom away from you and give it to your servant.*

The Lord God Almighty separated from Solomon to whom He appeared not once but twice. If great prophets who had seen God cannot be spared for their sins, then where do we stand who are loaded with sin and grounded in the deep darkness in our souls without a love of God? Solomon was one of few humans on planet earth who had experienced the taste of heavenly glory here on earth in the intimacy of the LORD; yet he also got trapped in sin when he rejected the commandment of God that, *"You shall not intermarry with them, nor they with you. Surely they will turn away your hearts after their gods."*

Unfortunately, Solomon did not listen and this happened in his life. He suffered the pain of a separation from His first perfect love of his life—God. For any child of God it is the worst pain when their Lord is not with them anymore. God judged Solomon fairly by removal of his throne, as the Lord told him, saying, *"I will surely tear the kingdom away from you and give it to your servant."* God's servants are His ambassadors to reign in His Kingdom on earth. God gives this privilege to His anointed kings and priests who are to be His obedient and faithful heritage. God removes His chosen servants from this place of honor when they disregard His righteous counsel to follow the works of evil. Idol worship is the worst of all sins because mankind dishonors God's Throne and honors satan at His place. The Lord, the King of kings and Lord of lords, will never tolerate this deal from the hands of a disobedient generation. Truly, He will tear them away from His Kingdom.

* * *

The marvelous stories of our favorite and highly honored prophets of the living God offer us life-learning messages from the Word of life. Now we understand how we can be saved from all tribulations that can wrap us due to our weaknesses. It is precious to know our position before the Lord because the human race does not follow Him when it does not comprehend its value in His eyes.

What Are We in God?

What is the human race for this earth? **The Bible describes us as the salt of the earth.** Salt is a purest flavor and most important ingredient. No matter how many ingredients you put in your dish, without salt it will not be deliciously edible. The human race is a flavor of the earth only with the work of righteousness according to the will of God. In Matthew 5:13 we read Jesus saying, *"You are the salt of the earth; but if the salt loses its flavor, how shall it be seasoned? It is then good for nothing but to be thrown out and trampled underfoot by men."* In this verse we also learn that if salt loses its flavor then it is thrown and trampled underfoot. Those who don't know the love of God sustain no flavorful salt: they have no good works. They will be removed from the presence of the Lord.

Most importantly **we are the temple of the Living God.** This declaration of human identity in the Lord of this universe is not a simple matter. It is a very important position that needs to be dealt with with extreme care, honor, and love. Let's read the verses relating to this privileged position of human race in the Living God.

2 CORINTHIANS 6:14-18
Do not be unequally yoked together with unbelievers. For what fellowship has righteousness with lawlessness? And what communion has light with darkness? And what accord has Christ with Belial? Or what part has a believer with an unbeliever? And what agreement has the temple of God with idols? For you are the temple of the living God. As God has said:
"I will dwell in them And walk among them.
I will be their God, And they shall be My people."
Therefore "Come out from among them
And be separate, says the Lord.
Do not touch what is unclean,
And I will receive you."
"I will be a Father to you,

And you shall be My sons and daughters,
Says the LORD Almighty."

The message in 2 Corinthians 6:14-18 is a very important information for each and every one living on the face of this earth. God is talking to us here face to face, giving us the instructions for His will for our lives. He illustrates how He abides in us after our obedience to His counsel is fulfilled. The first thing is a complete separation from evil, evil works, and evildoers. God's purity cannot be mingled with the filth of evil works. As verses 14 to 16 we read, *"Do not be unequally yoked together with unbelievers. For what fellowship has righteousness with lawlessness? And what communion has light with darkness? And what accord has Christ with Belial? Or what part has a believer with an unbeliever? And what agreement has the temple of God with idols?"* This statement is a finality of God's absolute will. The human race cautiously and continuously ignores it on a daily basis. I wonder if I can come close to separating myself from unbelievers, lawlessness, darkness, belial (idols), and sins of this earth? I sincerely doubt it. God's great prophets in our previous examples fell and the Lord lifted them up by His mighty hand. He restored them to the path of righteousness because they all admitted the mistakes they made, repented, and honored God's rightful judgment. The biggest problem is that the majority of us do not even know that our lack of commitment to the LORD will lead us to our total annihilation and separation from our living God ,who wants us totally to Himself. Our lack of this knowledge leads us to live diplomatically in the ways of the world, which is nothing but filled with uncleanness, lawlessness, idolatry, and evil practices while partially seeking the holiness in the house of the LORD. God always rejects this half-and-half behavior. The majority of mankind falls among the category of such people. Drinking and partying with friends with lust in the eyes of flesh . . . and then to the next day visit at the house of the Lord is not acceptable according to the Word of God, because we read, *"For what fellowship has righteousness with lawlessness? And what communion has light with darkness?"* After we overcome this imperfection of our fleshly weaknesses, we come into the communion of a covenant relationship with the Lord God Almighty, in which He abides in our body with our new birth in Him. A newborn child of God breathes, walks, and talks by the guidance of His Holy Spirit. In verse 16 we read: *"For you are the temple of the living God. As God has said: "I will dwell in them And walk among them. I will be their God, And they shall be My people."* What a marvelous representation of God's relationship with His people. Who would be foolish enough to reject such a profitable offer of letting the Creator of this whole universe abide in them? I wish each and every individual would desire to live in this relationship with their Creator, who said in verses 17 and 18: *"Therefore, 'Come out from among them And be separate, says the Lord Do not touch what is unclean, And I will receive you. I will be a Father to you, And you shall be My sons and daughters, Says the LORD Almighty.'"*

What is a solution of this "impossible" standard of righteousness?

The things impossible for us are possible only with the Lord. The first thing that the children of God need to learn is to depend totally in Him. This war of flesh is won in the flesh of the Lord Jesus Christ. He took over our sins in His flesh and died a death that a sinner deserves. The only Holy One of Israel is the Lord over all creation, including mankind. We might not be sincere to Him, but His endless sincerity abounds in His grace with the shedding of His blood at the cross for our salvation. Therefore, it is crucial to comprehend that God is waiting to receive us upon our acceptance of the salvation imparted to us by His Son's atoning work.

JOHN 14:6
Jesus said to him, "I am the way, the truth, and the life. No one comes to the Father except through Me."

Once we accept salvation, we become **"justified,"** which means **"just as though we never sinned."** *That means when God looks upon us, He only sees the cleansing work of His Son Jesus Christ; but He expects us to live holy because He is Holy.*

1 Peter 1:16-19
. . . because it is written, "Be holy, for I am holy."
And if you call on the Father, who without partiality judges
according to each one's work, conduct yourselves throughout
the time of your stay here in fear; knowing that you were
not redeemed with corruptible things, like silver or gold, from
your aimless conduct received by tradition from your fathers,
but with the precious blood of Christ, as of a lamb without
blemish and without spot.

How Is It Possible for Human Flesh to Never sin?

All things impossible for us are possible with God. It is the power of the Holy Spirit (Spirit of God) that transform us to hate evil and love holiness, and we become a new creation in Christ. This is a beautiful mystery that the human mind cannot comprehend, but when a heart full of the love and fear of the Lord repents to seek the Lord Jesus Christ for his salvation, the saved person experiences this mind-blowing change that separates him or her from the evil desires of the world.

If we ask the Holy Spirit to live inside of us, He enables us to walk upright and holy before God. That's why Jesus sent Holy Spirit to the earth after He ascended to Heaven to His Father. In case you didn't know it, Jesus died for you. He bore all your sins on the Cross so you won't have to die and go to hell. He spent three days in the grave conquering death and sin and He rose early on the third day. He rose by the power of the Holy Spirit, and if we die after we accept His salvation, then one day we will rise as triumphantly from the grave as He did.

What Should We All Do Now?

Repent from sins and accept salvation if you haven't yet done so, and then invite the Holy Spirit to indwell you so you will be guided into living according to God's Holy Word. In the midst of all the trouble we are facing in our lives on the shaking grounds of this earth, we are not stable enough to rely on ourselves for our keeping. We are living in the last phase of human history; only the words from the heart of the Living God can hold our feet stable in any hour of tribulation on earth. Only

Lord can grant our salvation which will remain forever.

MATTHEW 4:17
From that time Jesus began to preach and to say,
"Repent, for the kingdom of heaven is at hand."

Truly, we become the member of God's Kingdom the day we repent and learn to submit to God's righteousness.

For all those who still will not seek repentance from their sins and will not accept the only one way of salvation in Christ Jesus, they will be condemned on the Day of Judgment because they have not recognized the value and place of their Creator.

They have rejected His passionate love for them in the form of the death of His only begotten son: the Lord Jesus Christ.

JOHN 3:18
"He who believes in Him is not condemned; but he who
does not believe is condemned already, because he has not
believed in the name of the only begotten Son of God."

CHAPTER 14

Disparity Between the Godly and the Worldly

Why does God desire to separate His people from the things of the world and build a wall between the holy and the unholy? The human race belongs to this earth; so why is it required to take apart His people from the works of mankind on earth? Scriptures from the Bible will help us to understand why God demands His people to run in the opposite direction of this world. Let's get deep into the Word of God to explore this disparity between the godly and the worldly.

ISAIAH 52:11
Depart! Depart! go out from there,
Touch no unclean thing; go out from the midst of her,
Be clean, you who bear the vessels of the LORD.

2 CORINTHIANS 6:17
Therefore "Come out from among them
And be separate, says the Lord.
Do not touch what is unclean, and I will receive you."

The Word of God is clearly reciting to all those who hear the voice of God to depart and come out completely from unclean works of the world. All those who believe in God are called to be holy, as their God is holy. His people are the light bearers for the sinners of this world because they now know that their God is light that removes the darkness to bring the light of love, hope of salvation, and charity in the world of dark sin. The great mystery is a continuous war between good and evil, spirit and flesh, holiness and ungodliness. The living Word of God familiarizes mankind with the will of God about ethics, morality, and holiness.

Galatians 5:16-24
Walking in the Spirit

I say then: Walk in the Spirit and you shall not fulfill the lust of the flesh. For the flesh lusts against the Spirit, and the Spirit against the flesh; and these are contrary to one another, so that you do not do the things that you wish. But if you are led by the Spirit, you are not under the law. Now the works of the flesh are evident, which are: adultery, fornication, uncleanness, lewdness, idolatry, sorcery, hatred, contentions, jealousies, outbursts of wrath, selfish ambitions, dissensions, heresies, envy, murders, drunkenness, revelries, and the like; of which I tell you beforehand, just as I also told you in time past, that those who practice such things will not inherit the kingdom of God. But the fruit of the Spirit is love, joy, peace, longsuffering, kindness, goodness, faithfulness, gentleness, self-control. Against such there is no law. And those who are Christ's have crucified the flesh with its passions and desires.

Now we can clearly distinguish between the works of the flesh and those of the spirit. All the days of our lives we are in a continuous war between the flesh and the spirit. Though flesh desires to do something contrary to God's will, the spirit fights back in man's consciousness to go against the flesh. Anyone who contradicts this thought denies the precepts of God. Many deliberately reject the counsel of God because of their egotistic wisdom, their belief that their wisdom is over and above God's. Another reason for rejecting the counsel of the Lord God Almighty is for obedience to satan's will in their flesh. To such, Jesus said in John 8:44, *"You are of your father the devil, and the desires of your father you want to do. He was a murderer from the beginning, and does not stand in the truth, because there is no truth in him. When he speaks a lie, he speaks from his own resources, for he is a liar and the father of it."*

In Galatians 5:19-21 we learn about the works of flesh. The great God Almighty has familiarized humanity with the right path of living, but if anyone knowingly does such works of flesh, he will not inherit the Kingdom of God. Unfortunately, their eternity is an everlasting lake of fire in Hell.

It is definitely true that the LORD has made a permanent dividing wall between His children and the followers of satan. Satan can overpower anyone when they submit their flesh to his will. Commonly, people do not recognize the evil done in their flesh, unknowingly, as they do not comprehend the deceitful misconceptions that mankind believes in, as they do not bother to acknowledge the will of God. Satan is a father of deceit, and he is doing a clever work among his followers by leading them into his will through mankind's lack of knowledge of God's will. How truly the Lord said in Isaiah 5:13: *"Therefore my people have gone into captivity, because they have no knowledge . . . "* satan works forcefully to lead mankind astray from the wisdom of the will of God, because the wonderful awareness of God's loving heart for mankind will remove a person from the evil clutches of devil. Multitudes make priorities to watch riot, sexual, unethical, pornographic, and violent shows on television, the Internet, etc.—these viewings separate them from the love of God, as such choices "smut" the heart and mind of viewers. The moral and immoral choices we make on a daily basis turn out to be our spiritual food, which makes us either holy or unholy. Mankind is speedily lusting after the latest, high-paced technology, entertainment, and media that have occupied heart and minds in the things of the world to such a level that the whole world is literally worshipping these idols over and above the Lord God Almighty. (This is not my personal opinion, but God revealed this knowledge in a dream that I shared in chapter 3, "End Times Tribulations.") Do you know that idol worshipping is an abomination before the Lord? Very cleverly, satan has separated mankind from his God with fulfillment of the desire of the flesh in the form of idol worshipping of the things of the world. Who is spared from the evil clutches of the devil at this age of human advancement except those who love and fear the Holy Lord ceaselessly?

Passion for the Riches of the World

Scripture shares an intelligent thought about man's greatest weakness in the lust of the wealth and the riches of the world. A great number of humanity is running after hoarding the treasures of this world. Either rich or poor, the first love of mankind is money—in all ages. Why does God prohibit such behavior of mankind? We will find the reasoning of this precept from the living Word of God.

MATTHEW 6:24
You Cannot Serve God and Riches

"No one can serve two masters; for either he will hate the one and love the other, or else he will be loyal to the one and despise the other. You cannot serve God and mammon."

PHILIPPIANS 3:18, 19

For many walk, of whom I have told you often, and now tell you even weeping, that they are the enemies of the cross of Christ: whose end is destruction, whose god is their belly, and whose glory is in their shame—who set their mind on earthly things.

How beautifully the Word of God counsels us to choose the path of peace and joy in the best way possible. As in Titus 2:12: *"Teaching us that, denying ungodliness and worldly lusts, we should live soberly, righteously, and godly in the present age."*

I would like to share my own testimony in this reference. My personal repentance of sins and acceptance of the counsel of the Lord has miraculously transformed me. I used to have normal fleshly desires to achieve worldly success in the things of the world, things like success at work, financial prosperity, and prestige in society. I had never been greedy, but I had the mind-set of the commonly human needs of life.

My personal struggles of life were filled with unrest, pains, and toils. But since the Lord has taken over my life, my mind-set has completely transformed to obey the will of God. Now all the struggles of life for success in worldly accomplishments are worthless in my eyes. I do not care to impress anyone but only to make my Lord happy. I don't care if I am not wearing fine jewels because they are now worthless in my eyes. Honestly, from the day I stopped worrying about the things of the world, the Lord has blessed me more than I would have gained with my own efforts. God does not want His people to live in poverty, but He desires His people not to lust after the things of the world, because they only give sorrows, depressions, unhappinesses, and sufferings. Honestly, the more money people hoard, the more unsatisfied and miserable they get. Greed of money is just like a drug addiction; the more drugs a person sniffs in, the more he desires to take, until he dies with an overdose. The lust of the things of the world is the root of all evil. Who will deny the fact that our generation is the most unsatisfied generation, one that is running after the varieties of the things of the world, but is still deeply discontented in its very being? Our Lord only wants us to get out of this misery; he leaves us His principle to follow, one in which he calls us to reject the desire of riches of this earth.

I will share the example of a great prophet of man's history, Moses. He was like a son to the king of Egypt, to Pharaoh, loaded with fame and prosperity. He had no worries, but had only to enjoy life to its fullest, like a king, and to rule over the greatest nation of its time, Egypt. Who can imagine leaving all of that for the Lord? Moses did it. But why—and how—could he do this? This is where the role of God comes into play. Only God can open the blinded eyes, open the deaf ears, and change the hearts and minds of His people. His people are new creations in Christ who do not see, hear, and think like the rest of the world. Moses left everything for his Lord, not because he had the greed for more, but because he trusted the Word of his Creator, whose rewards were much greater than the rewards of Pharaoh, which were perishable.

Honestly, a common person would think that this is stupid because they are blind, deaf, and dead in the spirit of God. In reality, all the prophets of God were wiser and smarter because they were not looking to gain the temporary, but instead permanent treasures. Moses did forsake Egypt and did not fear the wrath of Pharaoh, because he visibly saw Him whose invisible powers are much greater than any pharaoh's.

HEBREWS 11:24-27

By faith Moses, when he became of age, refused to be called the son of Pharaoh's daughter, choosing rather to suffer affliction with the people of God than to enjoy the passing pleasures of sin, esteeming the reproach of Christ greater riches than the treasures in Egypt; for he looked to the reward. By faith he forsook Egypt, not fearing the wrath of the king; for he endured as seeing Him who is invisible.

***

We learn a great mystery, and knowledge, from the example of King Solomon of the nation of Israel. With his example we can understand what God is seeking in a human character. One day God appeared in Solomon's dream and searched his heart. Let's read the Scriptures to see what happened.

I KING 3:5, 8-14

At Gibeon the LORD appeared to Solomon in a dream by night; and God said, "Ask! What shall I give you?" . . . " . . . And Your servant is in the midst of Your people whom You have chosen, a great people, too numerous to be numbered or counted. Therefore give to Your servant an understanding heart to judge Your people, that I may discern between good and evil. For who is able to judge this great people of Yours?" The speech pleased the Lord, that Solomon had asked this thing. Then God said to him: "Because you have asked this thing, and have not asked long life for yourself, nor have asked riches for yourself, nor have asked the life of your enemies, but have asked for yourself understanding to discern justice, behold, I have done according to your words; see, I have given you a wise and understanding heart, so that there has not been anyone like you before you, nor shall any like you

arise after you. And I have also given you what you have
not asked: both riches and honor, so that there shall not be
anyone like you among the kings all your days. So if you
walk in My ways, to keep My statutes and My commandments,
as your father David walked, then I will lengthen your days."

Praise the Lord for giving us such a great example to imitate. The first thing that we learn in this example is Solomon's thanksgiving and graciousness for God's favor and blessings over his father, King David. The second characteristic of Solomon was his humility, as he recognized that God made him sit at his father's throne as an act wholly out of His mercy. Solomon did not value himself as a privileged son of King David with his birthright over the throne, but acknowledged that all good gifts come only with God's favor, benevolence, and love. The third beauty of Solomon was the care of the people of Israel in his heart. He did not "over-smart" himself before the Lord but recognized his immaturity to handle the serious judicial affairs among the people of his nation impartially, truthfully, and wisely. The charity of his heart for his nation was so great that he was not concerned about his personal gain and desire. *These are the characteristics that God desires to see in every human being, such as thanksgiving, humility, and charity.* Do we have that heart? I wish the whole earth to be filled with people like Solomon, and then peace and joy would rule our world.

The very important thing to learn is what God does to people with a heart like Solomon. The Lord is our gracious God, one who desires to prosper His people. He is a provider of everything to all those who walk in faith with Him. The whole Bible is filled with His promises for His people that He fulfills, for He is a true God. Now, in the case of King Solomon, he is still known among all nations of the world for his riches, wisdom, and prosperity, because he had a heart filled with care and charity for others. History proves that no one can compare in riches with King Solomon, because His Lord was His provider. Let's read what God's response to Solomon was in 1 King 3:11-13: *"Then God said to him: "Because you have asked this thing, and have not asked long life for yourself, nor have asked riches for yourself, nor have asked the life of your enemies, but have asked for yourself understanding to discern justice, be-*

hold, I have done according to your words; see, I have given you a wise and understanding heart, so that there has not been anyone like you before you, nor shall any like you arise after you. And I have also given you what you have not asked: both riches and honor, so that there shall not be anyone like you among the kings all your days." We get the clear picture of God's heart in this story. *God repels the greed and lust of the riches of the world, but gives the same gifts to those who seek Him first and also seek the welfare of his or her neighbor (mankind).* Naturally, only those who seek God first are filled with the love of humanity to serve others selflessly. God not only gave what Solomon requested, but added riches and honor so great that no one ever became greater than him. We can only praise the Lord God Almighty for His perfection in all things He does.

Fruits of the Love of Money

Furthermore, let's comprehend from the Holy Scriptures the outcome of a life filled with love of money. Love of money is one of the greatest dilemmas of all times. In our current age, this generation has grown "loftier" and greedier due to much looser and undisciplined societies, ones filled with lust after the everyday latest inventions of fun and entertainment. The problem is not the great inventions that are useful for mankind; the issue is losing the contentment and peace of life due to the greed and unsatisfied attitudes in our highly advanced society. People are greatly focused to gain more riches from the world and to enjoy more tempting things introduced in the market every other day. This attitude itself is a deceitful trap for a human race that separates itself from God and makes an easy pathway toward Hell. The spirit of contentment has vanished from this generation under a diversion toward greed and lust for the riches of the world. Jesus said in Matthew 16:26: *"For what profit is it to a man if he gains the whole world, and loses his own soul? Or what will a man give in exchange for his soul?"*

In the midst of all these things we have completely forgotten our perishable physical existence. All the things that mankind runs after will be left here—except for a saved or unsaved soul. We receive a life-changing counsel in 1 Timothy 6:6-10: *"Now godliness with contentment is great gain. For we brought nothing into this world, and it is certain we can carry nothing out. And having food and clothing, with these we shall be content. But those who desire to be rich fall into temptation and a snare, and into many foolish and harmful lusts which drown men in destruction and perdition.* **For the love of money is a root of all kinds of evil, for which some have strayed from the faith in their greediness, and pierced themselves through with many sorrows."**

Unfortunately, all those who have spent all the days of their lives straying from faith in the Lord, and have separated themselves from His holiness due to their greed and love of money, would have oppressed many innocent people in many ways for the sake of their own success. They would not hesitate to avail themselves of theft and fraud during their treasure hunting, because they have become blind, deaf, and selfish. They do not care about those who get crushed under their feet as they hoard after money. Such cruel treasure hunters have become gods in their own eyes. They will not be spared from the Day of Judgment, as we read in James 5:1-6: *"Come now, you rich, weep and howl for your miseries that are coming upon you! Your riches are corrupted, and your garments are moth-eaten. Your gold and silver are corroded, and their corrosion will be a witness against you and will eat your flesh like fire. You have heaped up treasure in the last days. Indeed the wages of the laborers who mowed your fields, which you kept back by fraud, cry out; and the cries of the reapers have reached the ears of the Lord of Sabaoth. You have lived on the earth in pleasure and luxury; you have fattened your hearts as in a day of slaughter. You have condemned, you have murdered the just; he does not resist you."*

God is still counseling all wealth- and treasure-seekers because of His unconditional love for them. People have a chance . . . to accept God's teachings and get saved to change their lifestyles in contentment and holiness in their spirit, till their last breath is left. If you are born rich in the world, use it for the caring of humanity and for good works. Seek God first and be satisfied, for the love of God is more satisfying than the love of money.

1 TIMOTHY 6:17-19
Instructions to the Rich
Command those who are rich in this present age not to be

haughty, nor to trust in uncertain riches but in the living God, who gives us richly all things to enjoy. Let them do good, that they be rich in good works, ready to give, willing to share, storing up for themselves a good foundation for the time to come, that they may lay hold on eternal life.

* * *

Now we know that there is a strict division between the child of God and a child of satan, between the obedience to the Holy One and the obedience to an evil one, between the righteous and the sinner, and between the Christ and the antichrist. Either we agree with this universal truth or not; knowingly or unknowingly, everyone belongs either to Christ or to the antichrist. All those who have accepted the Lord Jesus Christ as their Lord and Savior are of the Christ, and all those who do not bow down at His feet will automatically be cast away from His Kingdom. The greatest deceit and blindness that the devil misleads people in is the identity of the Lord Jesus Christ—and he does this in many forms: such as, a prophet, an angel, or nobody at all. There is an unbreakable wall between the Holy Lord and the evil satan.

The most important decision of every person before their last breath is: to whom do they belong? To Christ or to the antichrist!?

1 Corinthians 10:21

You cannot drink the cup of the Lord and the cup of demons; you cannot partake of the Lord's table and of the table of demons.

With a passionate heart for my fellow mankind, I would humbly ask each and every individual reading this book (which is not by chance, but by the will of God) to diligently seek to belong to Christ and NOT to the antichrist. Every one of us has sinned and deserves the punishment of death, but by the loving grace of our Creator we get the privilege to repent from all the sins done in our lives, and to commit ourselves into His hands, to allow him to mold us into a remarkable piece of art that can be preserved in the Holy of Holies in His Kingdom.

Though mankind does not cease to follow after the flesh, God does not stop calling people to Himself for His love for them. Truly we are saved by His grace, which abounds to us forever. How beautifully the Scripture translates the love of God in Ephesians 2: *"But God, who is rich in mercy, because of His great love with which He loved us, even when we were dead in trespasses, made us alive together with Christ (by grace you have been saved);"*

All those who have accepted the Lord Jesus Christ as their Lord and Savior are not servants, but receive an honor to become His friends. What a great wisdom it is to be His friend. A friend is the closest relation of all, one who shares the deep secrets. God wants His friends to know the deep thoughts of His heart. He wants to share His great works and mysterious plans designed for our growth. Truly, His ways are not our ways, and His thoughts are not our thoughts. His works are perfect and true for His friends.

JOHN 15:15-17

No longer do I call you servants, for a servant does not know what his master is doing; but I have called you friends, for all things that I heard from My Father I have made known to you. You did not choose Me, but I chose you and appointed you that you should go and bear fruit, and that your fruit should remain, that whatever you ask the Father in My name He may give you. These things I command you, that you love one another.

Dear people of God, do you want to join the group of friends of the Lord? All of His friends shall bear the good fruit of good works that remain forever, which is to love one another as He has loved us faithfully. There is a great advantage to be God's friend, because you gain the total blessings of life, such as health, prosperity, peace, joy, harmony, and protection in this life on earth as well as in life after death. *But there is also a disadvantage for being God's friend. You would be wondering how that can be? His enemies become the enemies of His friends also.* The stronger is your relationship with God, the more severe would be the hatred against you by His enemies. His enemies start with the prince of the power of the air, the spirit who now works in the sons of disobedience. Simply put, we know that there is a gigantic division between the sons of God and the sons of satan, between the Godly and the worldly, between the righteous and the unrighteous, and between the holy and unholy. The children of God are not disappointed to be hated by the world, but rejoice in those sufferings that come for the sake of their sincere, loving, and caring friend—Jesus Christ. How beautifully Jesus explained this dilemma.

John 15:18-22
The World's Hatred

"If the world hates you, you know that it hated Me before it hated you. If you were of the world, the world would love its own. Yet because you are not of the world, but I chose you out of the world, therefore the world hates you. Remember the word that I said to you, 'A servant is not greater than his master.' If they persecuted Me, they will also persecute you. If they kept My word, they will keep yours also. But all these things they will do to you for My name's sake, because they do not know Him who sent Me. If I had not come and spoken to them, they would have no sin, but now they have no excuse for their sin.

The children of God rejoice in this disparity of the godly and the worldly, because this division is a reason of the salvation of mankind. This also appoints a fair judgment to all those who did not pay mind to the Lord's spoken words. Be glad, because His name is our seal that will separate us from the lovers of this earth. Rejoice for the faith in the Lord Jesus Christ, whose sacrifice has sanctified us. He has rescued us from the slavery of the sins that were engraved on our flesh. We will praise the Lord God Almighty for this partition between the holy and the unholy of this earth.

CHAPTER 15

Jesus Is Our Only Rescue

A multitude of believers or unbelievers has heard the name of the Lord Jesus Christ. What is so unique about Him that makes Him our only rescue from the curse of sin, death, tribulation, and hell? This chapter is dedicated to the truth of God, without which we are lost, barren, and consumed in an eternal fire.

Introduction of the Lord Jesus Christ

Before we begin I will thank Perry Stone for sharing his scriptural knowledge because it helped me a lot to fathom the precepts of this subject with the reference Scripture from his program, Manna Fest.

Jesus was the only one born on the face of this earth that has fulfilled all the prophecies of the Bible about the Messiah of the world, from the day of His birth to the day of His death. He did not come for Jews and Christians only; He came for all humanity. Anyone who is reading this book needs Him for his or her salvation. Therefore, let's start to learn how your Savior is above anyone else you have ever heard, seen, or believed. To prove this universal fact, we will study the Word of God that talks about Jesus in the Old Testament (before His birth) and in the

New Testament (from His birth).

Prophecies Fulfilled in Jesus
Born of a Virgin:

The first prophecy fulfilled was that the coming Messiah had to be born of a virgin. I believe that many have witnessed His birth, in the sense that it is celebrated all over the world every year on Christmas Day. The Word of God authentically seals the most important event in Bible prophecies centuries before His birth.

ISAIAH 7:14

Therefore the Lord Himself will give you a sign: Behold, the virgin shall conceive and bear a Son, and shall call His name Immanuel.

MATTHEW 1:23

"Behold, the virgin shall be with child, and bear a Son, and they shall call His name Immanuel," which is translated, "God with us."

Born in Bethlehem

According to the prophecies of the Bible, the true Messiah had to be born in Bethlehem. Jesus fulfilled this prophecy with His birth in Bethlehem.

MICAH 5:2
The Coming Messiah
"But you, Bethlehem Ephrathah,
Though you are little among the thousands of Judah,
Yet out of you shall come forth to Me
The One to be Ruler in Israel,
Whose goings forth are from of old,
From everlasting."

MATTHEW 2:1
Wise Men from the East
Now after Jesus was born in Bethlehem of Judea in the days of
Herod the king, behold, wise men from the East came to Jerusalem,

Born of the Tribe of Judah

The prophecies declared that the Messiah will come from the tribe of Judah, which Jesus Christ fulfilled with His birth. The Word of God and history has proven this.

GENESIS 49:10
The scepter shall not depart from Judah,
Nor a lawgiver from between his feet,
Until Shiloh comes;
And to Him shall be the obedience of the people.

MATTHEW 2:5, 6
So they said to him, "In Bethlehem of Judea,
for thus it is written by the prophet:
'But you, Bethlehem, in the land of Judah,
Are not the least among the rulers of Judah;
For out of you shall come a Ruler
Who will shepherd My people Israel.'

Called Out of Egypt

The Messiah of the world had to be called out of Egypt. The Lord Jesus Christ fulfilled this prophecy when He lived in Egypt till King Herod died. The fulfillment of this prophecy also proves that He is the Messiah of all ages.

HOSEA 11:1
"When Israel was a child, I loved him,
And out of Egypt I called My son.

MATTHEW 2
. . . and was there until the death of Herod, that it might be
fulfilled which was spoken by the Lord through the
prophet, saying, "Out of Egypt I called My Son."

Had to Be Raised in Galilee

The coming Messiah had to be raised in Galilee. This prophecy is also fulfilled by the Lord Jesus Christ as proven in Matthew 3:13, when He came from Galilee to be baptized by John the Baptist. Let's read the following verses that prove the fulfillment of prophecy that Jesus is our Messiah.

ISAIAH 9:1, 2
The Government of the Promised Son
Nevertheless the gloom will not be upon her who is distressed,
As when at first He lightly esteemed
The land of Zebulun and the land of Naphtali,
And afterward more heavily oppressed her,
By the way of the sea, beyond the Jordan,
In Galilee of the Gentiles.
The people who walked in darkness
Have seen a great light;
Those who dwelt in the land of the shadow of death,
Upon them a light has shined.

MATTHEW 3:13
Then Jesus came from Galilee to John at
the Jordan to be baptized by him.

The completion of this prophecy is a great hope for not only Jews but also for Gentiles (every nation of the world), because spiritual darkness is eradicated with the Light of the world, who is the Lord Jesus Christ. John 8:12: "*Then Jesus spoke to them again, saying, 'I am the light of the world. He who follows Me shall not walk in darkness, but have the light of life.'*"

Sold for Thirty Pieces of Silver
The Lord Jesus Christ would not be our Messiah if He was not sold for thirty pieces of silver, as prophesied in God's Word centuries before His birth. Please read these verses for your clearer understanding that Jesus is the Lord.

Zechariah 11:12
*Then I said to them, "If it is agreeable to you, give
me my wages; and if not, refrain." So they weighed
out for my wages thirty pieces of silver.*

Matthew 26:15
*. . . and said, "What are you willing to give me if I deliver Him to
you?" And they counted out to him thirty pieces of silver.*

Hands and Feet Pierced
The Lord Jesus Christ is our Messiah because He was the one whose
hands and feet were pierced at the cross as prophesied by King David
in Psalm 22:16. His hands that healed and resurrected many during His
ministry on earth were pierced by the congregation of the wicked. His
precious feet that descended from Heaven to walk us through the valley
of darkness to the light of life and salvation were also pierced.

Psalm 22:16
*For dogs have surrounded Me;
The congregation of the wicked has enclosed Me.
They pierced My hands and My feet.*

John 20:20-29
*When He had said this, He showed them His hands and His
side. Then the disciples were glad when they saw the Lord.
Now Thomas, called the Twin, one of the twelve, was not with
them when Jesus came. The other disciples therefore said to him,
"We have seen the Lord." So he said to them, "Unless I see in His
hands the print of the nails, and put my finger into the print of
the nails, and put my hand into His side, I will not believe."
And after eight days His disciples were again inside, and Thomas
with them. Jesus came, the doors being shut, and stood in the midst,
and said, "Peace to you!" Then He said to Thomas, "Reach your
finger here, and look at My hands; and reach your hand here,
and put it into My side. Do not be unbelieving, but believing."
And Thomas answered and said to Him, "My Lord and my God!"*

Jesus said to him, "Thomas, because you have
seen Me, you have believed. Blessed are those
who have not seen and yet have believed."

In John 20:20-29 we read about Jesus' appearance to His disciples after His death. Jesus showed them the marks of the piercing of nails in His hands and feet. All disciples rejoiced to see His resurrected appearance, except Thomas, as he was not present at the Lord's first encounter with the disciples. Thomas did not believe his brothers, like many who seek for evidences. Jesus appeared the second time and told Thomas to *"Reach your finger here, and look at My hands; and reach your hand here, and put it into My side. Do not be unbelieving, but believing."* The Lord is asking all of us today to believe that He is the only Messiah pierced for our sake. His statement in verse 29 is a hope for a stumbling crowd of disbelieving multitudes falling into the snare of death and damnation that, *"Blessed are those who have not seen and yet have believed."*

Buried in a Rich Man's Grave
This prophecy was fulfilled exactly as God declared through the prophet Isaiah that the Lord Jesus would be buried in a rich man's grave. Matthew 27:57-60 reports the true happening of this incident, when a rich man, named Joseph, took His dead body at Pilate's permission to put Him in his own grave that he prepared for himself. Praise the Lord for His precious love that He has taken away the graves of all those who will believe in Him and replaced them with eternal life. It means that He has taken away death to replenish it with life for all those who believe.

ISAIAH 53:9
And they made His grave with the wicked—
But with the rich at His death,
Because He had done no violence,
Nor was any deceit in His mouth.

MATTHEW 27:57-60
Now when evening had come, there came a rich man from
Arimathea, named Joseph, who himself had also become a disciple

of Jesus. This man went to Pilate and asked for the body of Jesus.
Then Pilate commanded the body to be given to him. When Joseph
had taken the body, he wrapped it in a clean linen cloth, and
laid it in his new tomb which he had hewn out of the rock; and
he rolled a large stone against the door of the tomb, and departed.

He Must Arise from the Dead

The Lord Jesus Christ is the risen Messiah for all humanity. He overcame the sting of death to earn us a life of eternity. No one else can claim to fulfill this prophecy, no one except Jesus. The Bible refers to this life-changing hope for mankind through the resurrection of the Lord Jesus Christ.

PSALM 49:15
But God will redeem my soul from the power of the grave,
For He shall receive me.

MATTHEW 28:5, 6
But the angel answered and said to the women, "Do not be afraid,
for I know that you seek Jesus who was crucified. He is not here; for
He is risen, as He said. Come, see the place where the Lord lay."

Now we have learned the crucial fact that it was only the Lord Jesus Christ in whom all prophecies are fulfilled that proves that He truly is our Messiah. Well, why is it so important to know about Him and why do we need Him? We will expand our exposure to an understanding of *why everything, everyone, and every life existence should revolve only around Him, about Him, within Him, for Him, and by Him.* Read further to understand **what's so special about Jesus.**

JESUS is the Creator Who Sustains Life and Light

The Lord Jesus Christ is our creator. As we read in Genesis 1:26, God said, *"Let Us make man in Our image, according to Our likeness..* It is not a singular but plural command. The Bible clearly indicates that God is ONE, as we read in Deuteronomy 6:4: *"Hear, O Israel: The LORD our God, the LORD is one!"* The only Hebrew word used in Scriptures for one is *echad*, which means composite unity, instead of using the word *yachid*, which stands for absolute unity. In Colossians 2:9 we read about the Lord Jesus Christ: ***"For in Him dwells all the fullness of the Godhead bodily."***

Jonathan Sarfati from Creation Ministries International (www.creation.com/trinity) explained this doctrine theologically in these words: "The doctrine of the Trinity is difficult for some people to understand. But this is what God has revealed in Scripture about His own Being, so we should believe it. The doctrine of the Trinity states that in the unity of the Godhead there are three eternal and co-equal Persons: Father, Son and Holy Spirit, the same in essence but distinct in role—three Persons (or three centers of consciousness) and one Being. The different senses of one-ness and three-ness mean that the doctrine is not self-contradictory. This is similar in principle to saying that the navy, army, and air force are three distinct fighting entities, but are also one armed service. This is not to suggest that the three persons are 'parts' of God. Indeed, each Person has the fullness of the Godhead (see Colossians 2:9). A better analogy is that space contains three dimensions, yet the dimensions are not 'parts'—the concept of 'space' is meaningless without all three dimensions."

- The Father is called God: Ephesians 4:6: "one God and Father of all, who is above all, and through all, and in you all."
- The Son is called God: John 8:58: "Jesus said to them, "Most assuredly, I say to you, before Abraham was, I AM." God named Himself I AM in Exodus 3:14: "And God said to Moses, 'I AM WHO I AM.'" And He said, "Thus you shall say to the children of Israel, 'I AM has sent me to you.'"
- The Holy Spirit is called God: Acts 13:2: "As they ministered to the Lord and fasted, the Holy Spirit said, "Now separate to Me Barnabas and Saul for the work to which I have called them."

The unison of the Father, the Son, and the Holy Spirit is defined with perfection at the baptism of Lord Jesus Christ. I will take words of Jonathan Sarfati, who explained this doctrine logically as: "They are distinct, e.g. at the baptism of Jesus in Matthew 3:16–17 all three were present and distinct. The Son is baptized; the Father speaks from Heaven, and the Holy Spirit, in the form of a dove, flies down and lands on the Son. See the baptismal formula in Matthew 28:19 *'baptizing them in the name of the Father and of the Son and of the Holy Ghost.'* Note that the word name is singular, showing that all three Persons are one Being."

(Footnote: reference article "Jesus Christ our Creator A biblical defense of the Trinity" by Jonathan Sarfati-- Creation Ministries International—www.creation.com/trinity)

1 CORINTHIANS 8:6

. . . yet for us there is one God, the Father, of whom are all things, and we for Him; and one Lord Jesus Christ, through whom are all things, and through whom we live.

EPHESIANS 4

one Lord, one faith, one baptism; one God and Father of all, who is above all, and through all, and in you all.

Thus we come to the knowledge that the **God is one:** He is a *Father of all* and above all, **He is the Son—Jesus Christ** and *all are through Him*; and *the Holy Spirit* is *in all* of His believers.

* * *

Now after the clearer understanding of the Lord, we will learn right from the Scriptures of the Bible that the **Lord Jesus Christ is a Creator.** The whole universe is by Him, with Him, and for Him in His Word, which says, '*. . . Word was with God as the Word was God*'. This clearly explains Colossians 2:9: "*For in Him dwells all the fullness of the Godhead bodily.*" The fullness of Godhead bodily is beautifully portrayed in John 1:1.

JOHN 1:1-3
The Eternal Word

In the beginning was the Word, and the Word was with God, and the Word was God. He was in the

beginning with God. All things were made through Him,
and without Him nothing was made that was made.

This eternal Word came to earth as the only begotten Son of the Heavenly Father, and He dwelled among mankind to give us a rightful position of the children of God to all those who believe His Word, and abide in His Word of life eternal. John 1:14 declares the occurrence of this supernatural work of God for saving His people, because the Lord God Almighty is our Savior.

JOHN 1:14, 17, 18
The Word Becomes Flesh
And the Word became flesh and dwelt among us, and we beheld His
glory, the glory as of the only begotten of the Father,
full of grace and truth.
For the law was given through Moses, but grace and
truth came through Jesus Christ. No one has seen God
at any time. The only begotten Son, who is in the
bosom of the Father, He has declared Him.

Now the same Word that is the reason of all creations became flesh and dwelt among us. That Word in flesh is the Lord Jesus Christ, who is the only begotten of the Father in Heaven. Mankind beheld the Glory of the Lord on earth when Jesus Christ dwelt among them, and He brings all of His followers into this glory of His Kingdom where abide the grace, truth, holiness, righteousness, and eternal life. Though mankind learned the righteousness within the Law of Moses in His Word, but now the same Word became flesh for our salvation. How wonderful is His loving-kindness for His people. We learn from the Scriptures of the Bible about the eternal life that comes in His Name.

JOHN 1:10-13
He was in the world, and the world was made through
Him, and the world did not know Him. He came to His own,
and His own did not receive Him. But as many as received
Him, to them He gave the right to become children of God,

to those who believe in His name: who were born, not of blood,
nor of the will of the flesh, nor of the will of man, but of God.

**Sadly, the world that was made through the Lord Jesus Christ did
not know Him. Mankind still rejects the reception of this free gift
of salvation.** Christ came to His own people who were waiting for the
coming of their promised Messiah; but they were blinded to see the
light of the world because they did not genuinely know the Father in
Heaven. All those who will receive the Messiah will become the children of God in spirit and truth, and proclaim their inheritance in His
Kingdom. This awesome inheritance is made possible in a covenant of
blood that was shed on the cross. Thus the new blood line begins in a
new birth in Christ Jesus. Now this new generation of His children is
born with the *will of God*: to be abided by the Heavenly Father, the Holy
Son, and the Holy Spirit.

The Lord our God Almighty began universe with His light, and
separated darkness from light on the first day of His creation, per our
teachings from Genesis 1:3-5: *"Then God said, "Let there be light"; and
there was light. And God saw the light that it was good; and God divided the light from the darkness. God called the light Day, and the
darkness He called Night. So the evening and the morning were the
first day."* Similarly, a believer of God becomes a new creation under the
same principle of His creation on the first day. The Lord Jesus Christ is
a light who bought in the light in the whole universe at the time of creation, and made a separation between the light and darkness. Likewise,
He came into this world as a light, that whoever accepts Him as their
Lord and Savior will be separated from the darkness forever, as Jesus
proclaimed in John 12:46: *"I have come as a light into the world, that
whoever believes in Me should not abide in darkness."*

Once you step into this light of the world and separate yourself from
darkness, the power of satan diminishes from your being, and you are
transformed into a newborn child of God who burns and shines in His
pure light. Now your inheritance has shifted from the kingdom of satan into the Kingdom of God, from the kingdom of darkness into the
kingdom of light. What a marvelous and perfect work of God we witness in the Lord Jesus Christ, who is the true light for every human on

earth. Anyone who does not walk into this light will be expelled eternally from their rightful inheritance of God's presence, companionship, restoration, relationship, and eternal life. Let's step forward and hold on to the Lord Jesus Christ, of whom Paul said in Acts 26:18 that He came to this world, *"to open their eyes, in order to turn them from darkness to light, and from the power of Satan to God, that they may receive forgiveness of sins and an inheritance among those who are sanctified by faith in Me."*

There is no other in the whole universe that came to remove us from the sting of death and haunted darkness except the promised "Messiah," who is a keeper of life, light, and salvation. *The Lord Jesus Christ is the only one who proclaimed to be our light, and with that He called us to become the sons of light.* Who would want to be the "sons of satan, of darkness, and evil," who is a father of pains and sufferings, sins and evil, sickness and diseases, and eternal death and damnation! It would be foolish to reject such a wonderful gift of life in the Lord Jesus Christ, who gives us a life eternal in His light of good works, peace and joy, health and prosperity, wisdom of righteousness, and a love of God. Jesus tells us in John 12:36, *"While you have the light, believe in the light, that you may become sons of light."* *These things Jesus spoke, and departed, and was hidden from them.*

JOHN 1:4-9
In Him was life, and the life was the light of men. And the light shines in the darkness, and the darkness did not comprehend it.

John's Witness: The True Light
There was a man sent from God, whose name was John. This man came for a witness, to bear witness of the Light, that all through him might believe. He was not that Light, but was sent to bear witness of that Light. That was the true Light which gives light to every man coming into the world.

Under the law and legal systems the truth is proven by witnesses; thus the truth of the Lord is witnessed by a messenger sent before Him who was John the Baptist. He was not the light but came to witness the coming of the light after him to dwell among men, as verse 9 says: *"That was the true Light which gives light to every man coming into the world."* After learning that we are the light-keeper of this world in faith, within the Light of this World that is only the Lord Jesus Christ, let's bow our knees before Him, forever, for such a great mercy on us.

More testimonies from the mouth of His servants are preserved and prove for mankind to know that the Lord Jesus Christ is the promised Messiah for the human race, including Jews and Gentiles.

JOHN 1:29-34

The next day John saw Jesus coming toward him, and said, "Behold! The Lamb of God who takes away the sin of the world! This is He of whom I said, 'After me comes a Man who is preferred before me, for He was before me.' I did not know Him; but that He should be revealed to Israel, therefore I came baptizing with water." And John bore witness, saying, "I saw the Spirit descending from heaven like a dove, and He remained upon Him. I did not know Him, but He who sent me to baptize with water said to me, 'Upon whom you see the Spirit descending, and remaining on Him, this is He who baptizes with the Holy Spirit.' And I have seen and testified that this is the Son of God."

JOHN 1:49

Nathanael answered and said to Him, "Rabbi, You are the Son of God! You are the King of Israel!"

MATTHEW 14:33

Then those who were in the boat came and worshiped Him, saying, "Truly You are the Son of God."

MATTHEW 16:16, 17

Simon Peter answered and said, "You are the Christ, the Son of the living God." Jesus answered and said to him, "Blessed are you, Simon Bar-Jonah, for flesh and blood has not revealed this to you, but My Father who is in heaven."

The Word of God from the book of Genesis to the book of Revelation identifies that the Lord Jesus Christ is a Light and Life of all and all. There is no other name in which salvation is found. The words of Jesus will seal the fact that He is our Lord and Savior.

JOHN 17:5
"And now, O Father, glorify Me together with Yourself, with the glory which I had with You before the world was."

JOHN 6:35
And Jesus said to them, "I am the bread of life. He who comes to Me shall never hunger, and he who believes in Me shall never thirst."

Ordained in Christ

We are all blessed in His mercy to be created into a holy being when we accept the Lord Jesus Christ as our Messiah. His blood that was shed on the cross cleanses us, and His death on the cross gives us the gift of life. The Lord Jesus Christ is the reason for us to receive the privilege to become worthy to come near the Throne of the Father in Heaven.

The most entrenching feeling that mankind ever experiences after being ordained in Christ is to become consecrated like the Most Holy One. The desire of our Lord is for us to be sanctified in His Holiness. As we read in His Words in 1 Peter 1:16: *"because it is written, 'Be holy, for I am holy,'* and in Leviticus 20:26 we read, *"And you shall be holy to Me, for I the LORD am holy, and have separated you from the peoples, that you should be Mine."* King David exemplifies this in asking God to make him a new creature. The desire of every human's heart should be the same as the prophet said in Psalm 51:10: *"Create in me a clean heart, O God, And renew a steadfast spirit within me."*

How proudly the Lord of all creations sanctifies His people for His glory. How awful it would be to reject an opportunity to be His children. In the verses below, we see expression of God for the people who are ordained only by Him, for Him, and in Him.

ISAIAH 43:7
Everyone who is called by My name,
Whom I have created for My glory;
I have formed him, yes, I have made him."

For the very same reason, Jesus came to this earth for mankind to be sanctified to the level where he can be transformed into the holiness of God, because no one can come before the presence of the Lord on their own good works. This is the very reason that no one can ever be saved without the knowledge of the Lord Jesus Christ, who came for lost mankind to ordain them in Him. His faith sanctifies us to come in the glorious presence of the Lord. This is not a theory but a fact without which no one can learn to live a perfect life that begins to hate evil and love righteousness, by the power of the Holy Spirit that sprouts within our spirit like a new birth, where only the love of God resides within our being ceaselessly. A common human mind cannot comprehend the works of the Lord without a faith like Abraham, who is the perfect example of righteousness with faith. Surely, no one can enter the eternal life without faith like Abraham in the Lord Jesus Christ, who gave His life for us on the cross only to help us to find salvation from pains and sufferings, sins and death, and paucity of righteousness.

ROMANS 3:20-26
Therefore by the deeds of the law no flesh will be justified
in His sight, for by the law is the knowledge of sin.

God's Righteousness Through Faith
But now the righteousness of God apart from the law is revealed,
being witnessed by the Law and the Prophets, even the righteousness
of God, through faith in Jesus Christ, to all and on all who
believe. For there is no difference; for all have sinned and
fall short of the glory of God, being justified freely by His
grace through the redemption that is in Christ Jesus, whom
God set forth as a propitiation by His blood, through faith, to
demonstrate His righteousness, because in His forbearance God
had passed over the sins that were previously committed,

to demonstrate at the present time His righteousness, that He
might be just and the justifier of the one who has faith in Jesus.

Now we are ordained in Christ in present life and for eternity. How can we adequately praise the Lord our God for such perfect works of His Hand? By no means can anyone reject such a free gift of God that must be cherished and preserved in our lives. I really don't have words to thank Him enough for everything He has done for us, as prophesied by the Prophet Isaiah.

Isaiah 53:5, 6
But he was wounded for our transgressions, he was
bruised for our iniquities: the chastisement of our peace
was upon him; and with his stripes we are healed.
All we like sheep have gone astray; we have turned everyone to his
own way; and the LORD hath laid on him the iniquity of us all.

The amazing love of God for mankind is beautifully explained in these verses, that the dying for someone comes only out of extreme love. Now the perfect image that He gave to Adam is restored back for all believers who are born again to be created and ordained in Christ Jesus. All believers are transformed into a new creature in Him.

Romans 5:6-8
For when we were still without strength, in due time Christ
died for the ungodly. For scarcely for a righteous man will
one die; yet perhaps for a good man someone would even dare
to die. But God demonstrates His own love toward us,
in that while we were still sinners, Christ died for us.

It was not only His own (the Jews) who received the privilege to embrace the Messiah, but all nations of the world are blessed from it. The separation wall between the Jew and Gentile is torn down with a new beginning through His ordination that introduces us to His love. We learn in Colossians 3:10, 11: *". . . and have put on the new man who is*

renewed in knowledge according to the image of Him who created him,
where there is neither Greek nor Jew, circumcised nor uncircumcised, bar-
barian, Scythian, slave nor free, but Christ is all and in all."

Thus there is no recognition and preference of skin color, ethics, caste, and religion before the Lord. He has no preference of Jew or Gentile. All are new creations in the Lord Jesus Christ without any distinction of any kind, since Christ came to make a new man from the two, that now we are a new creation in His image, holy and acceptable before the throne of the Lord God Almighty. I would like to welcome each person reading this book to come and join the grand feast reserved for you in the Kingdom of God, where all the newborn men and women in Christ will be welcomed in the loving arms of their Shepherd, who has been so faithful to save His sheep that He did not hesitate to die for their protection. Now we have entered into a permanent peace of God where the law of commandment is fulfilled in His flesh.

EPHESIANS 2:15
. . . having abolished in His flesh the enmity, that is, the law
of commandments contained in ordinances, so as to create in
Himself one new man from the two, thus making peace,

Gain in Christ

The vital question that comes to our mind is: what do we gain through our faith in Jesus Christ? There is nothing to lose, and all to gain, in Christ Jesus. We will review the Scriptures to understand, in depth, His grace that He has magnificently bestowed for His people.

We gain security and confidence in Christ

As we read in the words of the Lord Jesus Christ:

JOHN 10:27-29
"My sheep hear My voice, and I know them, and they follow
Me. And I give them eternal life, and they shall never
perish; neither shall anyone snatch them out of My hand.
My Father, who has given them to Me, is greater than all; and
no one is able to snatch them out of My Father's hand."

This statement of Jesus in John 10:27-29 brings the confidence of His followers to be at peace in the protection of their Savior, where fear does not exist, for He said that His followers shall never perish and neither shall anyone snatch them out of His hand. We gain this confidence not only because He said it, we rejoice in His promises, because we know that Jesus is the King of kings and the Lord of lords. Every knee bows before Him, and when we follow the Lord, who can devour us? No one can! The powers of evil in the kingdom of satan are powerless before His name, and we reside in His protection forever. What a security we have in Jesus! He said: *"My Father, who has given them to Me, is greater than all; and no one is able to snatch them out of My Father's hand."* Therefore, now being a member of the family of God with a blood trail of Jesus in our very being, we are given to Jesus by the heavenly Father. We are the claimed heavenly beings who live for God in the newness of life with the Spirit of Christ, who dwells in us to make us sons of God, as we read in Romans 8:9, 14: *"But you are not in the flesh but in the Spirit, if indeed the Spirit of God dwells in you. Now if anyone does not have the Spirit of Christ, he is not His. For as many as are led by the Spirit of God, these are sons of God."*

Saints rejoice because now you are the sons of Lord God Almighty. We all know the rights of a servant, and of a son. A servant is powerless, but a son owns all the rights of his father's house with the love, favors, and importance, because he is an heir in flesh and blood. A servant cannot even imagine having these amazing privileges in his master's house, because he is not family, but only a servant. Our confidence in our Father in Heaven is beautifully inscribed in Romans 8:15-17: *"For you did not receive the spirit of bondage again to fear, but you received the Spirit of adoption by whom we cry out, 'Abba, Father.' The Spirit Himself bears witness with our spirit that we are children of God, and if children, then heirs—heirs of God and joint heirs with Christ, if indeed we suffer with Him, that we may also be glorified together."* Now, who cares about the suffering of this world that evil diverts toward the children of God, as satan has always been against the will of God. Our trust, faith, and confidence are in our Abba-Father, who will glorify us as He glorified His only begotten Son, the Lord Jesus Christ. Therefore, let's walk fearlessly, enthusiastically, and speedily to grab our promised inheritance in

His Kingdom because we are the family of God.

We Gain the Victory of Life over Death in Christ

There is no other in the whole universe who promises eternal life. All living being dies forever—except for those who are baptized into the name of the Father, the Son, and the Holy Spirit, because now His children earn eternity in resurrected bodies as victoriously as Jesus did when He raised from death and ascended to Heaven to His throne. It is from there that He brings all believers to Himself in exactly the same victorious manner as He exemplified in His life on earth.

JOHN 5:19-21, 24, 25

Then Jesus answered and said to them, "Most assuredly, I say to you, the Son can do nothing of Himself, but what He sees the Father do; for whatever He does, the Son also does in like manner. For the Father loves the Son, and shows Him all things that He Himself does; and He will show Him greater works than these, that you may marvel.
For as the Father raises the dead and gives life to them, even so the Son gives life to whom He will.
"Most assuredly, I say to you, he who hears My word and believes in Him who sent Me has everlasting life, and shall not come into judgment, but has passed from death into life. Most assuredly, I say to you, the hour is coming, and now is, when the dead will hear the voice of the Son of God; and those who hear will live.

Acceptance of the Lord Jesus Christ as our Lord and Savior allows us to triumph over death and to rise up to live victoriously. Understanding of an amazing wisdom and works of the Lord is unimaginable without the spirit of humility that thirsts to live in the Lord. His followers know the chain of command that follows from the Heavenly Father to the Son, and from the Son to His believers. As we read in John 5:20, 21: *"For the Father loves the Son, and shows Him all things that He Himself does; and He will show Him greater works than these, that you may marvel. For as the Father raises the dead and gives life to them, even so the Son gives life to whom He will."* Now, knowing that the Son gives life to whom He will, then we as His faithful children will supersede the judgment, as our sins are washed in His blood that was shed at the cross, as He said again in verse 24: *"Most assuredly, I say to you, he who hears My word and believes in Him who sent Me has everlasting life, and shall not come into judgment, but has passed from death into life."* Who can be foolish enough to reject His word and get expelled from a life of eternity?

Now we know that all those who believe that the Heavenly Father has sent His only begotten Son, the Lord Jesus Christ, will not come into judgment, but will enter into everlasting life. This does not mean that all believers in Christ now need to relax with belief that they are saved already. This attitude is a major misconception among believers. The Lord has given a great sacrifice for a major purpose that requires a complete sacrifice from His believers to establish His Kingdom on earth. Unfortunately, some of the believers do not recognize the required seriousness of their sacrificial faithfulness in their walk with the Lord. Our salvation must come with our obedience to righteousness of His will. Our continual daily sacrifices for His Name's sake exemplifies us as His believers, who will shine like a light with His love, and the love of mankind before the whole world. Church of Christ, where is your faithfulness in this manner? Why doesn't the whole world exemplify the good fruits of believers of Christ so that all unbelievers will begin to acknowledge the "Tree of Life," who is the Lord Jesus Christ, who feeds His people with the fruits of righteousness in its due season? Our good fruits in His will are the witness that helps to save many more in His name. Saints must not be content but learn every day from the heart of God and grow in Him till the last breath.

We Gain Eternity in Christ

We praise our Lord for His revelation of righteousness that is incomprehensible for any human intellect. Of course, we know our own restricted human livelihood in the days of our life on earth, days that begin with birth and end with death. Many religions believe in life after death. The question is, what kind of life after death? In Christ every believer gains a life of eternity in the glorious presence of the Lord.

- Would every human ever born get this privilege to be in the Holy of Holies for eternity?

- Does our current existence here on earth reflect what the heart of God desires to see in His children?
- How can we claim our eternity in the presence of God, and not with satan in hell?

Our minds are loaded with many questions about this subject. There are millions who like to deny such religious concepts. Does our rejection change the spiritual facts? Either we believe or do not believe—that is not very important of itself, because if we try to seek, in- depth, where we stand among the enormous creation of God, among majestic galaxies, among great empire of angels and principalities and powers, among many other creations on earth . . . what is the mere human existence, which dies and turns into ashes? Truly we are nothing without the breath of life that exists in our very being. That is, our soul who will never die, and we will live eternally in our resurrected body like Christ. Eternity is guaranteed either in Heaven or in hell. Only in Christ can we receive eternity in Heaven. Heaven is where the throne of God is. No human on earth can ever translate the holiness of God into his weak flesh without the washing of his sins in the blood of the Lamb of God— the Lord Jesus Christ, who is the life of humanity. Truly His death is our life. The moment we receive baptism in Christ, we bury our sins under the water of baptism when we immerse in it in the name of the Father, the Son, and the Holy Spirit. We rise up victoriously out of water at baptism to walk into the newness of life in the continual glory of the Holy Spirit within our new being, just like Christ who was raised from the dead. Our conquest over eternity in Christ is enlightened, magnificently so in His Word.

ROMANS 6:3-8
Or do you not know that as many of us as were baptized into Christ Jesus were baptized into His death? Therefore we were buried with Him through baptism into death, that just as Christ was raised from the dead by the glory of the Father, even so we also should walk in newness of life. For if we have been united together in the likeness of His death, certainly we also shall be in the likeness of His resurrection,

knowing this, that our old man was crucified with Him, that the body of sin might be done away with, that we should no longer be slaves of sin. For he who has died has been freed from sin. Now if we died with Christ, we believe that we shall also live with Him.

Are you willing to say what Peter said?

JOHN 6:68, 69
But Simon Peter answered Him, "Lord, to whom shall we go? You have the words of eternal life. Also we have come to believe and know that You are the Christ, the Son of the living God."

The Lord Jesus Christ Will Judge Us All

Now the same Jesus who came first to save sinners will come again to judge sinners. The Lord of the universe is declaring that He is the Alpha and the Omega, the Beginning and the End, the First and the Last. The Great Lord God Almighty is coming back very soon to reward everyone according to their works.

REVELATION 22:12, 13
Jesus Testifies to the Churches
"And behold, I am coming quickly, and My reward is with Me, to give to every one according to his work. I am the Alpha and the Omega, the Beginning and the End, the First and the Last."

As we know now, the Lord Jesus Christ will give rewards according to our works. Many will pull up the list of the good works of their lifetimes to justify before the Lord. But who can ever be justified before the pure throne of God? How could anyone stand before Him to say, "Hey, I rejected your testimony in my life on earth because I was pressurized by those who thought you are a false god or false prophet, or do not exist?" Or someone else would say, "I do not need any savior like you because my self-righteousness is good enough to justify me before you or any other god." Some will honor their personal doctrine over the truth of their Creator. Honestly, the human mind can come up with many ex-

THE LORD'S VOICE CRIES TO THE CITY . . .

cuses to justify himself before the White Throne of the Lord. But would all those lame pretexts help anyone?

JOHN 5:28, 29

Do not marvel at this; for the hour is coming in which all who are in the graves will hear His voice and come forth—those who have done good, to the resurrection of life, and those who have done evil, to the resurrection of condemnation.

Now you have heard the good news of the Lord Jesus Christ. God has promised the human race that He will come back a second time after His testimony is declared to the ends of the world. All have known the love of God, that He died for them and that He will also judge. His love is everlasting life and His fear of judgment is the beginning of wisdom that brings us to life, as we read in Proverbs 9:10: *"The fear of the LORD is the beginning of wisdom, and the knowledge of the Holy One is understanding."* This love and fear of God is sufficient to save every soul on earth only if they open their eyes, ears, and mind. If they still reject His Word then there is no other who can spare them from "the resurrection of condemnation." I would request you to read this passage to acknowledge the reality of the Great White Throne of Judgment of the Lord.

REVELATION 20:11-15

The Great White Throne of Judgment

*Then I saw a great white throne and Him who sat on it, from whose face the earth and the heaven fled away. And there was found no place for them. And I saw the dead, small and great, standing before God, and books were opened. And another book was opened, which is the Book of Life.
And the dead were judged according to their works, by the things which were written in the books.
The sea gave up the dead who were in it, and Death and Hades delivered up the dead who were in them. And they were judged, each one according to his works. Then Death and Hades were cast into the lake of fire. This is the second death. And anyone not found written in the Book of Life was cast into the lake of fire.*

Either we believe in this truth or not. The Great White Throne of Judgment of the Lord is unambiguous. Small and great, or rich and poor, will all be standing before the King of kings and the Lord of lords—the Lord Jesus Christ. He who once died a brutal death on the cross to give salvation, will now judge. Humanity once born and living a life of its choice on earth will be resurrected to stand before the Lord. As we read in Revelation 20:13: *"The sea gave up the dead who were in it, and Death and Hades delivered up the dead who were in them. And they were judged, each one according to his works."* All these revelations might sound unreal at this time, but the Word of God and the testimonies of His servants will stand as a witness, where only the white as light will find the refuge, but all the evil will serve an eternal death. Now the books of their works on earth are opened up before the LORD to Judge them accordingly. We read in Revelation 20:12: *"And I saw the dead, small and great, standing before God, and books were opened. And another book was opened, which is the Book of Life. And the dead were judged according to their works, by the things which were written in the books."*

There is an exception applied for those whose name is written in the Book of Life, but the rest of the human race will be cast into the Lake of Fire for eternity, as it is written in Revelation 20:15: *"And anyone not found written in the Book of Life was cast into the lake of fire."* (The Book of Life contains the names of those members of the human race who accepted the Lord Jesus Christ as their Lord and Savior, the Savior who died on the cross to pay off their penalty of sins with His death. In fact, Jesus died for every person ever born on earth, but all those who rejected Him will be blotted out of the Book of Life.)

I wish that at least one movie director could make this move to portray the reality of man's sinful choices on the big screen. No one will be spared from this Day of Judgment except for those who made the choice, not by sight but by faith, in their Messiah, the Lord Jesus Christ. Boldly and consciously, the people listed in the Book of Life have lived righteously in their short visit on earth and trusted not their own good works but the righteousness of God. Praise the Lord for His perfection for His children, who can now live with their Father in Heaven. It was the Name of the Lord for which they were tortured and tormented, and now the same Name has become a permanent seal on their forehead, and they shall be clothed in the white garment of righteousness as we read in Revelation 3:5: *"He who overcomes shall be clothed in white garments, and I will not blot out his name from the Book of Life; but I will confess his name before My Father and before His angels."*

God's Judgment is as perfect as His salvation is. He is a righteous and true judge who will shield His sheep eternally in His Kingdom, but all evil of the earth will be separated from His presence into the eternal darkness that they chose to begin with when they rejected the light of God over the dark of sin. How excruciatingly painful it would be to see multitudes falling into the eternal lake of fire due to their disbelief.

The Last Appeal

I have a final appeal to humanity to come forward and accept the Yeshua Ha'Mashiach—the Lord Jesus Christ—as their only Savior, because only He can save mankind from an everlasting lake of fire. It is the ultimate fact that Yeshua is the Lord, the one who is the eternal Word that sustains life. Jesus Christ is the pre-existing Word that became human and lived here on earth among us for our sake. *The Creator took death at our place; then why do we have to die in sin and get cast out eternally in the lake of fire? The Lord God Almighty should be the most important business for each and every individual who ever existed on the face of this earth—not because He needs the recognition from mankind; instead, mankind needs the acknowledgement from Him.* If He will not identify us as His sheep or as His child, a hopeless eternity without His presence will be our destiny, which is nothing but an everlasting fire in an outer darkness.

God has done an extraordinary act to save mankind. If we still reject the free gift of life, we will lose an opportunity to get our name inscribed in the book of life. Satan desires to deceive mankind in many forms; the worst of his deceit is denying the Lord Jesus Christ as the Lord and Savior. Alas, the dying humanity desperately needs its Messiah, Shepherd, Savior, and King. The Lord Jesus Christ is the only rescue in all ages for each individual, either in life on earth before death, or eternal life after death. Nations are worshipping thousands of gods; which one of them claims to give eternal life? None of them can earn them salvation because they are not the Creator, but the creation, of man's own hand.

These gods are created by man only to satisfy their own self-righteousness; that is only a shadow that will fade painfully at the second appearance of the Lord Jesus Christ.

Finally, if we still willfully sin after receiving the knowledge of the truth, then there is no other sacrifice left that can save us. Why would humanity still trample the Son of God underfoot knowingly, just like satan did, when he rebelled against God due to his pride? Why would we ignore the love of our Heavenly Father? He did not have to do what He did at the cross, because He is a Great Lord God Almighty, and we are mere humans—one of His creations—but we still have the effontery to trample His love under foot. How daring the human race is, without humility and full of pride, filled with the lust for sin?

HEBREWS 10:26-30
The Just Live by Faith
For if we sin willfully after we have received the knowledge of the truth, there no longer remains a sacrifice for sins, but a certain fearful expectation of judgment, and fiery indignation which will devour the adversaries. Anyone who has rejected Moses' law dies without mercy on the testimony of two or three witnesses. Of how much worse punishment, do you suppose, will he be thought worthy who has trampled the Son of God underfoot, counted the blood of the covenant by which he was sanctified a common thing, and insulted the Spirit of grace? For we know Him who said, "Vengeance is Mine, I will repay," says the Lord. And again, "The LORD will judge His people."

It is my appeal to all the followers of the Lord Jesus Christ to sound the trumpet of triumph of the good news of salvation with each person they know, as the End of the Age is right around the corner.

MATTHEW 24:14
"And this gospel of the kingdom will be preached in all the world as a witness to all the nations, and then the end will come."

Now the Holy Spirit is speaking to His church to go into the world and preach the gospel to everyone. Mark 16:15 reads: *"And He said to them, 'Go into all the world and preach the gospel to every creature.'"* Unfortunately, many people who are saved do not recognize the importance of the use of their spiritual gifts and rewards given for the sanctification of souls with their service toward their Lord with their witnesses, testimony, and a sacrificial life that shines as the light of God in the darkness of sins of the world. What a privilege we have to save others to bring them to life eternal. The question is: how much does His church bring revival with their service? The Church of God will also be judged for its sincere use of the spiritual gifts given to bring good news to the world.

ACTS 10:42, 43
And He commanded us to preach to the people, and to testify that it is He who was ordained by God to be Judge of the living and the dead. To Him all the prophets witness that, through His name, whoever believes in Him will receive remission of sins."

The Holy Spirit addresses to every person on earth that they have heard the good news for their salvation from the Messiah of the universe, the Lord Jesus Christ. Everyone will make a decision in their lifetime about the final destiny of their eternity, which leads to either saving or condemnation. The choice is predestined according to the Word of God in Mark 16:16: *"He who believes and is baptized will be saved; but he who does not believe will be condemned."*

The love of God is calling the human race to come to Him for protection, salvation, and life eternal.

JOHN 3:16
"For God so loved the world that He gave His only begotten Son, that whoever believes in Him should not perish but have everlasting life."

End Times Ministries
www.gods-messenger.webs.com

Iris Nasreen
Wallingford, PA
Irisnsrn777@gmail.com
Facebook/irisnasreen
Twitter/irisnasreen